MW00800428

THREE STRIKE RUNNER

An impromptu adventure smuggling

"Whitetail"
Inside cover illustration by Pierce Everett

ISBN: 978-1-09831-388-3(print)
ISBN: 978-1-09831-389-0 (eBook)

CONTENTS

THREE STRIKE RUNNER
An impromptu adventure smuggling

WHEN PLAYING BASEBALL, if the ball is dropped a peculiar rule comes into play. Three strikes and you're out is most certainly a fundamental element of baseball, yet there is this odd exception. If the catcher fails to catch the ball after a "third strike" swing or tip, and first base is open, then the batter becomes a runner...A *Three Strike Runner*. He must sprint down the first base line with little chance of making it safe to first base; but he must try for all he's worth; he must try.

I was a **Three Strike Runner**.

The moon was more easily accessible than first base.

WITH MUCH APPRECIATION TO:

Allan Rinzler for his enthusiastic developmental edit,
and vote of confidence.

Robin Howe for her multi-faceted grammatical editing skills.

And to dear friends who, over the years,
patiently read and re-read the novel as it morphed:

Jeannie Vink,
Sandra Feldman,
Heidi Wilensky,
Ann Campbell
and **Carlos Everett**.

For Bebe

"Our doubts are traitors and make us lose the good we oft might win, by fearing to attempt."

—WILLIAM SHAKESPEARE

CHAPTER ONE
Off and Running / Ms. Jawja

THE DEFINABLE PART OF ME, the person I am, the person you see, was deposited here on this planet amidst a herd of post war babies, all carefully ushered into this part of the world at Crawford Long Memorial Hospital in Atlanta, Georgia.

"Baby Boomers" they called us. Our group was to have monstrous impact as the world began to quickly grow smaller. Our norms and mores, our music, our clothes, our drugs, all railed at convention.

We've always moved to the beat of a different drum. Always will.

My dad was proud when he had mustered the courage to pop the question to my mom and she'd said, "Yes."

I was loved by them both and I'm eternally grateful that Marvin and Frances decided to have another baby, thus giving me a shot at this life. I do love life. I've always said, "Whenever the powers decide that Pierce Everett has had his fair share, I hope I can negotiate for just a little more."

I was two years old when sweet Georgia, a mountainous, dark black woman with a perpetual bright white smile, and an aura to match, entered my life. Georgia wore a light blue cambric dress and a white apron: spotless, starched, and ironed to perfection. She was out to help me get off to a good start…and she did. Georgia cooked, cleaned, ironed, read the Bible, and was part of our family. I was her responsibility. And I was loved.

My mom always called Georgia, Miss Georgia. Georgia laughed at her name in this context being akin to the winner of a beauty pageant. She'd always say, "Yea, it wuz when dem baven suits wuz pulled out dat I pulled waaay out front and won dat show. Miz Jawja. Dats me." Her eyes would shine, and her body would shake all over with uncontrollable laughter.

One fateful day, Miz Jawja looked in on me while I played in my soapy bathwater. She stopped in her tracks, turned around, and threw her arms high in the air. Her hands landed on top of her head. Big white eyes stared in total disbelief. "Whaddis dis," then louder, emphatically, "Whaddis dis!" A finger pointed. "Mr. Peers Ebrett, you in big trubba now." Trouble… huh? Bad timing. The evidence, a little missile ended turd bobbing there on a sea of soapy water. This, I'm sure, was my first experience with big trouble. It will find you when you least expect it. I pushed the little freighter while it slid smoothly on the surface of my bath water visiting many soapy islands along the way. I hunkered down at eye level as I spun it around and sent it off in another direction with its payload of suds. Education always has its costs.

Suddenly I was levitated from the bath at high speed and held out at arm's length, leaving a jet trail of suds and bathwater. Georgia turned her face away from me, holding her nose in the air, shaking her head, her big white eyes rolling in total disbelief.

I was confused because Georgia had always picked me up and cuddled me close to her mountainous bosom. This time was different; I had a full 360-degree view as I was held out in front, feet dangling like a smelly wet monkey.

I'd been captured red-handed playing with a turd in my bath water. "You jes wait 'til Miss Frances get home. You in a hoe lossa trouble."

In trouble? Why? My questions didn't linger long unanswered. Mom came home. I was harshly scolded, eyes crossed in front of a wagging finger. Under no circumstances was I ever to poop in the bathtub again.

"Why would you do such a thing?" She asked, shaking her head, disappointed to the core.

Even if I'd been able to speak, I didn't have any answers. Okay then, so what was I to do with these freighters in the future? It was explained to me, from now on they were to go over here into this different ocean. I watched examples as they spun round and round, chasing each other down into a whirlpool, to then disappear right in front of my eyes. I'd point, and look up at Georgia with wonder…where had they gone? In answer to my questioning eyes, Georgia knelt and looked at me kindly as she explained her idea of where they'd gone.

"De gone way off to uva oshuns an lans so fah'way you ain't nebba nebba gon see 'em 'gain chile."

I was pretty sure Georgia didn't know where they'd gone either, but her story was mesmerizing. Other seas…faraway lands…I never should have listened to her. Where do I sign up?

Shortly, a conciliatory yellow plastic duck, sporting the look of a simpleton, appeared in my bath. It just wasn't the same. Everyone had missed the point. What could a yellow duck possibly know about adventures and faraway oceans. So, I decided the duck should go to these faraway lands, and I sent him spinning round and round till he disappeared. Instantly, I was already in trouble again.

The plumber hit my dad with the bill. I know Dad, being the accountant, figured as soon as I was old enough, he'd get that money back with interest and penalties from me, his wannabe adventurer. Little did he know, years down the road the impact from much of my early learning would translate into adventures of a lifetime. An education from experience and a plastic yellow duck.

The idiot yellow duck, none the worse for wear, was given to a neighbor who had tons of kids. Time passed and later I ran over it with the lawnmower. The loud "crack" startled me. I stopped a minute and smiled. It immediately carried me back to times long passed.

CHAPTER TWO
The Country

F ILLED WITH THE DEEP ASSUMPTION that heaven awaits those who "do right," my parents and a host of others did their best to set me off in the "right" direction. They succeeded for the most part. Good and bad, right and wrong were easily defined. But I soon found there was a place where people often visited. Oddly, everyone knew about it, but no one talked much about it. It was called the "gray area." I've always wondered who oversaw defining "good" and "bad," and hence the tickets to heaven or hell leaving my fate a little shaky.

I found this undefinable zone filled with flexibility. I set about learning there were more ways to glean experience from this life rather than toeing a narrow straight line designed to lead to a most predictable destination. Adventures often required the ability to justify impromptu deviations, particularly when ending up in an unexpected dilemma. Bad decisions often make great stories.

My childhood provided everything a young inquisitive mind could digest. To this day, memories of my grandmother's home in middle Georgia still stirs up antidotes to the conundrums of living. "The Country," as we called it, was a scary place. It generated a respectable fear in this young cowboy's life. I learned many lessons during my tenure on that raw red land in that ancient clapboard house. Even now, memories of "the Country" want to frighten me. Ghosts ran the show.

Many practical lessons of survival were hammered home there in "The Country." I learned to fend for myself in weird circumstances and scary places. Not scary like South Atlanta on a Saturday night, but scary in that special undefinable way. You know you're scared but don't want to find out why.

Annie Lou and me after a successful afternoon at the creek

I learned when to run, when to hide, when to talk and when to shut up. I learned to stop running if nothing was chasing me, and to stop sometimes when something was. I remember the quiet; so quiet my ears hurt. I was exiled there. I had to learn to defend myself from the dangers of real solitude.

I learned to lose myself in my imagination that would dance with dreams of oceans and mysterious places in faraway lands. I got good at dreaming during those years. I got good at a lot of things.

Annie Lou was my buddy. She must have been about 17 years old. She didn't know how old she was, nor did anyone else. I was ten. She liked to laugh. I could make her laugh. We'd go fishing together and bring home strings of little bream to clean and fry in that white lard that lived in an old can over the wood burning stove.

She knew the comings and goings of all people and animals in "The Country." She also had a grip on the whole operation, and my grandmother relied on Annie Lou more than she'd like to admit. Annie Lou would pick cotton, husk corn and dig potatoes. She gathered chickens, cats, and dogs and made sure they were all fed, then called the cows into the barn for the night. She'd squirt me with milk from their udders before she churned it into butter. She'd whitewash the fireplaces, haul and chop mountains of cord wood used for cooking and heating. She always insured I was ready and appropriately dressed every other Sunday, so the traveling preacher could give us our bi-monthly dose of fire and brimstone. Inside the little chapel, packed with believers was hotter than the long walk up that red dirt hill, and I guessed it couldn't be any hotter than that in hell. All the ladies fanned themselves with little cardboard fans stapled to popsicle stick handles. They had bucolic scenes of cows in a field and lines from the scriptures printed on the back. They were powerless against the intolerable heat.

* * *

"The Country" was a way of life now lost. Looking back, I appreciate the hard lessons endured. I feel I am one of a fortunate few to have experienced those adventures. Many years later, I struck out on the adventure I'm about to share. I have constantly employed what I learned during my childhood. I do to this day. I trust my abilities; I stick my neck out. Hey, if you can't lose, what's the point?

"Will it bite?" I wasn't told if it would or wouldn't, I found out when it did. Born from conquering my own personal fears came competence, confidence, independence, and great stories. My mom and dad trusted me, and I worked at that. I moved on from my childhood, understanding there wasn't much I couldn't do. In fact, I thought I was invincible. I was destined to find out the hard way that this just wasn't true. For me, the greatest advantage remained, no one ever told me.

CHAPTER THREE
The 50's & 60's / Leave Them Kids Alone

In the 50's our world was simple. I changed from three years old to thirteen. Formative years. Be home by five or you're in a world of trouble. Simple. I don't think my parents ever considered that I could be kidnapped and hauled away. Nor did I. Hence, not being fed a recipe with fear as an ingredient, my friends and I lived a full and adventurous childhood. Oh, we respected our parents and shared a level of responsibility both to our families as well as to ourselves. There were things that you just didn't do, and things you just did do. We knew them. We, for the most part, acted right. We knew "Yes Sir" and "Yes Mam". We didn't question or argue with the voice of authority, we just worked around it.

I never wore a bicycle helmet or pads, nor did any of my friends. These safety accessories didn't exist. I never knew anyone who was hurt badly while riding a bike. We made our own decisions daily. Those decisions were all based on what was expected of us, both from our parents and from each other. We always were home for dinner at five…without doubt. Our world built individuals who could think for themselves, and somehow, we all survived without computer games, cell phones, iPads, and TV's. Telephone time was limited; most often shared on a line used by at least one other family, a "party line." Everybody knew what everyone else was doing. There were no secrets.

Gina Simmons who I'd gone to school with since the first grade began to look different to me. Hmmm. In my dreams I kissed her. I dreamed about her at night, I touched her. I even told her I loved her. I was floundering.

Emotions lost to the specter of innocence. And then…"Wow, talk about something I'll never forget." Control was removed from my dictionary. Everything began to spin. I turned 16, got my driver's license, and launched into a whole new world. The back seat took on new duties.

Things began to happen fast. A nocturnal exchange enabled me to swap my accordion for an electric guitar. I dreaded the day my mom would notice. Mom always had visions of me being the new Lawrence Welk, not the new Chuck Berry. I was painfully learning to play Santa Lucia on the squeeze box. Mom would say, "Pierce, when are you going to learn to play like that" while she pointed at the black and white screen where Myron Florin was just tearing up the Beer Barrel Polka. Elvis had caught my attention. I found a drummer, a good lead guitar player, and a pretty good singer who could sling the microphone around like a pro. I played bass guitar. We made music. We'd rent venues in empty buildings in the neighborhood and sell tickets to Saturday Night Dances. The plan worked over and over. We played at all the school dances and had a good reputation for fun gatherings. Money began to flow. Lots of money. In 1963 I was sixteen, free on the face of the earth and mobile with a pocket full of money. Life was magical.

In 1966 I turned 19, graduated from high school and moved out of my family's house to North Atlanta, where two friends and I put enough money and fake ID's together to rent a penthouse.

Musicians have always been the testing ground for altering one's state, and we were no exception. Experimental drinking went with the territory. But as the sixties matured, an interesting little green plant was experiencing a rebirth. We would twist the leaves into a cigarette that resembled my long-lost little turd, then take a long puff and hang on for the ride.

Good god. What a nice thing…oh yeah, what a really nice thing. Marijuana quickly became the altered state of choice. It made the music sound better, and everything was much more fun. We laughed at each other while we played. We still do.

CHAPTER FOUR
Alethia / Reefer

In 1970, after a stint in the U. S. Army where discontent flourished, I finally got an honorable discharge. The Army and I shared a mutual disrespect for each other. Luck prevailed, and I missed going to Viet Nam having spent my time at Fort Bragg and Fort Jackson in the motor pools.

While in high school, I had fallen head over heels in love with Alethia. She was Greek, beautiful, and I was in love like never before. In 1971, as soon as I was freed from my military obligation we married.

I also cultivated, so to speak, a lucrative little side business. I'd become intrigued with marijuana. Playing rock and roll always seemed to conjure up this little plant. When I had some good seeds, I'd plant a little patch in a discreet spot. There was always enough to sell a few ounces. A few pounds.

Over the years, my interest in sailing began to take hold.

Alethia's dad had a nice 36' Morgan sloop down in the Florida Keys. She shared my enthusiasm, and soon we bought a sailboat up on Lake Lanier, a big lake, just north of Atlanta. Things could hardly be better. She and I began dreaming of a bigger boat with the plan of spending a couple of years sailing the oceans.

We found our boat up on Nantucket, an island off the Massachusetts coast. As with most wooden boats, she needed a lot of work. I planned to get her ready to go before the winter set in. I wanted to move her to warmer waters to finish the rebuild. I left Atlanta headed for Nantucket to begin working on our new boat.

Sadly, Alethia stayed in Atlanta making other plans. Unbeknownst to me, none of her plans included me or coming to Nantucket. Simply put, she wanted babies and a family, and I wanted boats and adventure. She "ran off," as they say, with her boss, leaving me all alone in the winter, on that cold Atlantic island, with a broken boat and a shattered heart.

Her change of heart precipitated a divorce, something I never thought I'd have to do. Where'd I gone wrong? Nevertheless, I had no choice. Alethia and I unceremoniously split the house, the boat, the cars, the cat, etc. I stood in our driveway and said goodbye with a halfhearted wave, as she backed out and away in her new baby blue convertible. I admired how beautiful she was. I hurt bad…really, bad. I had a hard time breathing as I turned to walk back down the driveway, back into the empty house, my heart hollow, never to see Alethia again.

CHAPTER FIVE
Diana / Whitetail

A MUTUAL FRIEND saw the possibilities and introduced us. In 1978, I was 31 years old and she was 26. I was instantly in love. She was beautiful, smart, erotic, and exotic. Neurosis did not miss a chance with Diana, and we often paid a high price for her radical swings. Everything combined to create one tempestuous woman. One mean woman. A passionate woman. A woman you want to keep on your side... so I thought.

We immediately began a famously volatile relationship and married in 1980, I was 33 years old. We celebrated on the island of Eleuthera in the Bahamas, where my sailboat lay moored. We paid a cocaine cowboy to fly us over and the celebration began in full force. For reasons unclear, Diana fell prey to her to her testy side, and in a rage, she ripped my favorite shirt right off my back and threw her new wedding band far out to sea. Despite this outrageous beginning, we somehow worked together, shoulder to shoulder to ensure our "whole" remained intact.

And it did...for 16 years.

Many explosions and battles, much love and serenity, many dreams fulfilled, many dreams lost.

Diana worked as a model, while she wrote three novels that, like so many, never caught any traction in the publishing world. Then she developed an environmental awareness program. Her idea was to gather children's artwork from around the world, giving them a chance to air their concerns regarding the environment in their countries. She'd then brand the images for use on calendars, clothes, and anything else that would interest an international buyer's market. She did well with her efforts, garnering interest, and support from several well-known clothing manufacturers.

❊ ❊ ❊

I carried on in the construction, design and build business as I had for the past five years. I also opened a wood working machinery business. I'd buy out whole defunct shops, rebuild the machinery, and then resell it. Everything was working, and the machinery business served to funnel justify proceeds from a relatively small but none the less lucrative reefer business. Yep you heard it, marijuana was everywhere, and I knew suppliers and growers. I quickly and easily became the person to call on the sly, if you wanted an ounce or a pound…or even two pounds. The process was all very innocent, and I, like so many others preferred a puff rather than a sip. Much healthier, plus the buzz went hand in hand with making music, an ingredient as important as the lyrics and chords.

Using these accumulating moneys, I put together an investment idea with a few friends. We began riding on the booming real estate market and started buying houses in exclusive North Atlanta neighborhoods, fixing them up and reselling them. After a year of carefully budgeting our income, Diana and I began to see financial liquidity. Then, the following year, I began looking for investments of my own.

I followed the same plan that had been working so well. I sought out houses in high end areas of Atlanta that needed work. I'd rearrange them, inside and out, then put them back on volatile market for sale. I had the golden touch. Everything I did was wildly successful. I could do no wrong. I loaded up with four more houses in the North Atlanta area known as Buckhead, with the presumption that this lucrative time was going to last forever unchallenged. I didn't realize that nothing ever lasts unchanged. I know now. Boy do I ever know, and oh so well. Always factor a variable for change into your plans. Always, but not always the way you'd like to see it happen.

December 1986 arrived; I was 39 years old. I took advantage of the circumstances in this time of affluence to put in several months studying at The Atlanta School of Art. I've painted all my life and I wanted to brush up on some techniques with valued input on portraiture. I still paint with some small amount of success. I'm always working on the next painting, or the next book.

Painting, making music, writing and boats are, and always have been, passions of mine.

Diana instantly shared my enthusiasm for sailing. We decided to search for a boat that could take us to places we'd only dreamed of. We planned to afford the funds and time it was going to take to make our dreams a reality.

In April of 1986 we bought a beautiful sloop, *Whitetail.* She was an F&C 40, a Sparkman and Stephens design, designed and built by Herman Frers, a famous designer by his own right, who made fame and fortune while he was employed by S&S and Nautor Swan. Diana and I found her on the north coast of the island of Mallorca 100 miles east of Barcelona, Spain.

Whitetail was built at his yard, "Frers & Cybils just north of Buenos Aires in the small town of El Tigre. The myriad of rivers that converge and flow through the area have given it the name, "The Venice of Argentina." I once went there when I was in the area on another project. I spent a month in Buenos Aires working with a well-known documentary film maker, negotiating the use of a reconfigured Ultra-Light airplane, designed to help film the migration of the Right whales through the Peninsula Valdes at Puerto Madryn. While in Argentina, I visited *Whitetail's* birthplace.

She was rigged as a famously strong fast center cockpit sloop. Her lines would take your breath away. While at anchor, other boaters would row out to compliment *Whitetail's* lines and ask questions. I installed a removable forestay, on which I clipped a small staysail to use when the wind kicked up her heels. This turned out to be most valuable in years to come, with the task I eventually set about to pursue with her.

Before long, we were planning departure times and calculating methods of continuing business in Atlanta, while spending chunks of time in Mallorca, Ibiza, and Menorca. I was particularly excited, in that these islands are considered possibly the best in the world for light and colors for artists. Fortune worked its magic and once we were settled in, I immediately met several artists who kindly extended an invitation for me to join them for a weekly round of *plein aire* painting. We became fast friends and spent many years studying together for years in the Balearics.

By June 1986 Diana and I left the house sales to our trusted agent and spent a year in the Balearic Islands, reveling in a "pinch me to be sure it's real" life. I carried on studying painting and drawing with local artists on the islands of Menorca, Mallorca and Ibiza. The international monetary exchange rate was in our favor, and nothing was too much…nothing at all. In fact, everything was half price. We lived in a "dream land".

During this year, while living on *Whitetail*, Diana carried on with her business. She took advantage of being close to the European market and made use of this proximity to travel and garner interest from a number of schools located in several different nearby countries.

In early May of 1987 Diane and I came home to work out a complicated contract on one of the three properties we had for sale. The sale helped with our finances and gave us a much needed assurance regarding our plans, but, unfortunately, it also sparked unrealistic expectations regarding our projected finances. We stayed in Atlanta for about two months while we made improvements to the remaining two houses in hopes of facilitating quicker sales.

In July of 1987 we returned to Mallorca, excited to get back to *Whitetail* and our dream-life. We'd hoped to spend the better part of another year there, but our trip home had left us more apprehensive regarding our finances.

Wiser fools may have made any number of smart moves, but we refused to let impending disaster or better judgment affect our dream.

CHAPTER SIX
The Party's Over / Black Monday

OUR WORLD BEGAN TO CRUMBLE...QUICKLY. We were in Ibiza aboard *Whitetail.* We had plans to move further eastward to Yugoslavia, then Italy, all the while looking for a place that we might eventually call home. A place to set up a studio for my painting and Diana's passion for writing.

In late September of 1987, we got word from our trusted realtor that things in Atlanta were changing fast, and we should get back as quickly as possible. We had hoped that this agent would be able to work miracles, against all odds, but buyers for our last two properties remained nonexistent. We needed to make some major adjustments to sell our last properties while the possibility still existed. That scary word, "recession" began to pop up.

We left *Whitetail* tied safely in her slip at Puerto Pollensa, while we flew home to assess our situation and what could be done.

* * *

We arrived in Atlanta mid October 1987 just in time for "Black Monday" which occurred on Oct 19th, 1987. The Market lost some 22% of its value. Then, incredibly, at the same time, the "Savings and Loan Crisis" began to boil and was coming to a peak. By early 1988 more than 1,000 Savings and Loan banks had failed. Fear ruled the day.

A blanket of apprehension covered everything. We were in trouble and working through the maze of problems that had seized the opportunity to grow in our absence. A daunting challenge was at hand. The properties looked tired. They smelled stagnant when you opened the doors. The grass was knee deep. They seemed to be responding to this pervasive negative financial cloud.

Immediately, we set about doing anything that would help expedite their sale. We repainted both houses in and out and added a wide front porch to the more expensive one. Our efforts seemed to help, but no potential buyers came running up with cash in their hands. Our indebtedness was nauseating. We had bet on a long shot to fuel our time spent in Mallorca and Ibiza. Now we were in the process of losing everything.

"Hey Baby, are you awake?" We began waking up at 3 a.m. both of us worried and considering every possible scenario that might save us. Our loans on the properties as well as their maintenance had quickly put us on a spiraling course towards failure. They had amassed enough expense that there was no way we could sell them at drastically reduced prices, without having to write a check to the bank. We knew we had to change our plans.

Luckily, a house in Ansley Park that belonged to our friend John, was still vacant. He'd had no luck for months trying to rent it.

"Pierce, if you and Diana would like to stay at the Avery house in Ansley Park it's fine with me. I need to have the place lived in, cared for, pool cleaned, and the utilities paid. I'll even leave the utilities turned on and all the furniture."

Despite our overwhelming situation, we still intended to leave again in a year or less, to carry on with our exploration of Yugoslavia. John's offer would allow us to work on our properties and push toward their sale while we took care of his vacant house.

In August of 1990, Iraq's invasion of Kuwait drove the oil prices up from $15 per barrel to $40 per barrel and put the last nail in the coffin for home sales and mortgages. The impact from these untenable catastrophes precipitated the American recession of 1990-1991. Following that, Yugoslavia became a dangerous "no man's land," mired in an ethnically fueled civil war that would continue for the next ten years.

After much thought and consideration, we decided to leave *Whitetail* in dry dock. With a phone call to the boat yard in Mallorca, we explained our plight, and asked that they keep a good eye on her for another year. But even as those words left my mind, I knew this just wasn't true. I knew nothing substantial would change during the next year. So, we decided to auction off the remaining two properties while they were looking better with their new paint and repairs, We dumped the two Albatrosses to the highest bidder. Never had so much pain felt so good. The two dead houses were gone taking with them the monthly overhead that was eating us alive. We were still overboard in debt looking for a way out.

Fortune struck. An old friend purchased a huge house in North Atlanta that needed monumental repairs and design changes. He asked if I would help him. He had played his cards smartly and turned the negative financial tone to his advantage. He'd gotten the house for a fraction of its value and could afford to do a proper job on a renovation. Perfect timing! I set about doing drawings for the project. Two more years quickly slipped away. I was totally immersed managing all the changes, all the while dreaming of *Whitetail* and Puerto Pollensa.

This project was a life saver. I could make enough money for us to live in a slightly less than worried state. Diana carried on with her nonprofit organization that was gathering a little notoriety from some high-profile people. Things were changing for the better in our financial turmoil. We were repaying friends for their invaluable financial assistance during our most difficult times.

Diana and I had been in Atlanta well over two years now, working to fix our many predicaments. We were still relentlessly lying to ourselves, projecting our stay in the US to last just another ten months, not wanting to accept a year...or years. Determined, we planned to finish straightening things out, and return to our dream world in Mallorca, with the perpetual idea of possibly staying there forever.

Whitetail awaited our return. At least she was still safe. It was June of 1991.

Soon, darker clouds began to build on the horizon.

CHAPTER SEVEN
Bankruptcy / Three Peachtree Ave.

In the summer of 1991, I was 44 years old and feeling cornered and stymied at every turn, with no way out. The recession had tumbled into a reality. Our credit card balances spiraled to nauseating highs until they began to be rejected. God knows I spent every waking hour trying to invent new ideas for generating income. There was nothing to work with, no cards to play. Bank robbery seemed an option, but there was no money in the banks. Lady Luck seemed to have forgotten Pierce Everett.

I had finished the big construction project months ago and was looking for another. But, like everything related to real estate, there just wasn't a profusion of projects at hand. We'd used just about all our money, and there seemed to be no way to get money coming in. The little bit of reefer business that trickled a miniscule bit of money our way, was barely enough to buy groceries if we were careful. I decided to liquidate what was left of the Machinery Business. A quick auction cleared out the warehouse. The proceeds disappeared like water on a hot griddle.

I found hopeless desperation unique to me, and I wasn't sure how to handle these feelings. I honestly could not dream up a solution. I knew we had gotten ourselves into quite a predicament, and I knew what we had to do. The thought was nauseating.

Bankruptcy was a word akin to divorce in the Everett dictionary. Not an option. Suicide first. Our only remaining asset on the face of this earth was *Whitetail.* Our bankruptcy attorney explained how we had no choices. He must have read my mind when he mentioned, " any effort to keep, hide, run or protect *Whitetail,* would be considered an illegal pursuit, and an obstruction of justice, frowned on heavily by the courts." She must be brought home, included in our bankruptcy, and liquidated to the highest bidder. The court wanted her home within their grasp. No entity in the judicial system was a sailor. The largest body of water they'd ever crossed was likely the puddle at the end of their driveways. Preparation to facilitate this request was massive and expensive. The court persisted.

* * *

Then, in the early Fall of 1991 Lady Luck finally tossed us a bone, and that luck we'd awaited, materialized. Our phone rang, "Pierce, this is Sharon. I've got to sell 3 Peachtree Ave. The house I've purchased in Richmond needs attention and I've got to get there as soon as possible. I've thought up a plan that you may be interested in. When can we get together to discuss possibilities?" We met over a cup of tea. She lamented, "The housing market in Atlanta is so terrible, I am desperate to liquidate my house and gallery in Buckhead." She approached us with an idea that was doable. We were to buy her house under the most reasonable terms. Fifteen hundred down and $1,000 per month with a balloon payment of 10% interest plus the balance due in five years. This would allow her to get on with her move to Richmond and give us a base from which to work our recovery.

We presumed that surely our plight would improve over the next five years, so we purchased Sharon's house from her. A powerful gift that saved us in the nick of time. I've always felt somehow Sharon knew of our predicament and wanted to help. She was that kind of person. Now, sadly gone, forever missed, and forever remembered.

The house was a lovely, old, two story Victorian house on Peachtree Ave., right in the heart of Old Buckhead in North Atlanta. This area was a destination for people coming to Atlanta. Great restaurants were everywhere, and the real estate here was some of the most valuable in Atlanta. Oddly enough, the dead real estate market that had devastated our world was now incredibly played to our advantage. Thank you, Sharon.

There was an eight-foot-tall picket fence around the front yard. When you entered the gate, the yard was landscaped with pea gravel pathways divided by ancient boxwood hedges, all presided over by two large concrete lions lying in wait on either side of the front door. A garage apartment found shade under a huge old flowering Magnolia in the rear.

We set up Diana's business in the lower level of the garage and moved into the tiny garage apartment overhead. We then rented the three-bedroom front house for Buckhead prices. So, for the next five years we had free rent, an income from the front house, and an increasing asset in the hottest part of Atlanta. How 'bout that!

Incredible how life evolves. Overnight our world began looking better. The first evening we spent over the garage, we bought Lady Luck a pricey bottle of wine which Diana and I shared with her. Every sip evoked a fancy toast, and a tear or two. Our relief was so monumental we had to temper experiencing these feelings of success… happy again. Relief.

How not to fear wanting, for fear of losing?

CHAPTER EIGHT
What are you doing? / Heading for the Rif

With this tremendous relief from our doomsday agenda, my mind began running out of control like a fire hydrant without a governor. Ideas began to flow easily. However, we still were having to file bankruptcy and I needed to retrieve *Whitetail.*

One evening I awoke from a sound sleep. The Spirits had planted a seed, and an idea had begun to sprout. I felt inspired. I went to the kitchen and put on a pot of coffee. The stove clock read 3 a.m. I hadn't felt this hopeful in months.

The faded numbers on the keys of the old calculator told me that this looked like a pretty good plan. Certainly, better than some of the others. Let's say comfortably desperate. Diana was to be the acid test. A couple more hours passed slowly by, until the smell of coffee lured Diana. She appeared at the kitchen door, still asleep, leaning against the door jamb, her eyes weren't open. It was 5 a.m.

"Hey Sweetie, what are you doing?"

I had been waiting for her arrival with great anticipation. I pounced: "Sweetheart, I want to pick *Whitetail* up and sail her home at the court's request But, along the way I want to stop by Morocco and load her with as much hashish as she can carry and bring that load home to sell. Finding a buyer should be easy if the quality of the hash is superior. We would make enough money to get us completely out of debt, keep *Whitetail* and pay Sharon for our house." With every word, she was more awake. But when I came to the part about stopping by Morocco and taking on a load of hashish, she fell into a chair beside me at the table, almost missing the seat. I reached to catch her. She straightened herself and was instantly wide awake. Astonished, brow raised, she cast an incredulous look my way, which I translated to say, "Are you outta your mind?".

I held up my hand. "Listen to me… just a minute."

I shared my calculations, and thoughts on how my plan could be done, who would help, the exciting outcome if we won, and the cost of a total loss if we failed. I could see Diana's waking moments with every sip of hot coffee. Her head began to nod slowly in a positive plane as she turned over the possibilities of the plan, while she checked my figures with the calculator.

Should the result be a total failure, we wouldn't be much worse off than we are at this moment. If we won, all our problems would be solved, with enough cash to pay off our debts, rekindle another business, and hang on to *Whitetail.*

"What if you get caught?"

The kitchen was quiet. I had no answer. In my excitement and enthusiasm, I had never even considered that possibility, or any other circumstances that might prove devastating. Being captured with a load of hashish was one of many horrible things we probably should consider. In my slight irritation with the shower on my parade I retaliated, "The boat could sink. An Arab could slit my throat and take the money, an Arab could not slit my throat and take the money. I could fall overboard in the night, or get run down by a fast-moving freighter, or torn to pieces by rabid dogs before this day is over

What if everything went perfectly…what about **that** possibility?" "Let's cross those bridges if they happen." Diana just watched me through my tirade. Knowing me well, she waited for the smoke to settle and said, "Okay, let's make a new plan, I honestly have no other ideas in mind."

When the sun rose that morning, we were caught hopping around to a crazy dance and moon walking around the house in celebration of a new and different plan. A very desperate plan…

"Sweetheart, I'm going to miss you so badly, but I feel it's best for me to travel alone for the obvious financial and practical reasons. Also, I'm not sure it'd be safe for you in the Rif Mountains where I've got to go to meet with the hashish makers in that area of Morocco. I hope to go there and select the quality hashish that will make the whole plan work, then get out of there as quickly as possible. This hash has simply got to be the very best quality imaginable. You, being with me could even prevent the auditions I'm hoping to experience with the growers. The area has historically been less than friendly to Westerners traveling there."

"Pierce," (she rarely called me Pierce), "I know, you must go alone. I miss you already and I'll worry about you. Also, I think we'd be better off if I stayed here to nurse the program, "Visions United," along and I possibly could even land some modeling work."

Diana was still enthusiastically marketing her environmental program. Grants had become now a possibility, and there had been a few substantial retailers interested in working with her and her children's artwork.

I began calling the airlines, chomping at the bit to get out of town headed for Mallorca and *Whitetail*. I had not seen our boat in almost three years. We high fived when the credit card approved my ticket purchase, and the next afternoon, I was sleeping at 30,000 feet headed to Barcelona, then onward to Mallorca. It was the 2nd of September 1991.

CHAPTER NINE
Recon / Philippe and Sea Lion

I HAD TO ASSESS *Whitetail's* condition after her dormant three years. She needed attention prior to mounting such a grand undertaking. I also had to find a contact in Morocco who could help with procurement and loading of the hashish. A timeline and itineraries needed to be confirmed. Costs had to be established, and a search for investors set in motion. This was a recon trip. Once I arrived, I immediately set up shop on the boat. I began working like a madman, prepping her for an extraordinary adventure.

Dove, an old friend, had for years run a successful restaurant on the Caribbean island of St. Barts. He had met every sailor around the Caribbean at one time or another. He knew them all, and they all knew him.

I indirectly sent Dove a message to find out who he might know as a candidate to supply me safely with hashish in Tangier. After about a week, I got a note from Dove at my Post Office Box on Mallorca. The note contained a phone number and a name, Phillipe. This would connect me with a French sailor who smuggled hashish from Morocco to Spain on a regular basis. Phillipe would then introduce me to a connection in Tangier, *Yousef Abboud.*

The note included an ominous warning for me to trust only Phillipe and further warned me not to speak with anyone in Tangier except Yousef Abboud.

"You will most certainly be accosted by numbers of wannabe suppliers" Dove firmly reiterated. "Ignore them all. Do not speak to them."

I called the mysterious number. The woman who answered in a thick French / English accent had expected my call. Plans were already in the works, and I was to meet with Phillipe at a small bar in the port town of Puerto Cristo, on the southeastern coast of Mallorca in seven days, on September 9th, 1991.

The week passed quickly with me working ever harder on *Whitetail.* I needed help. I had hoped that one of two sailing friends would be interested in joining me on this adventure to help me sail a small boat across the North Atlantic Ocean. Both were capable and understood the risks and gains from such an undertaking. Both declined. One had fallen in love, which had, as he happily lamented, "replaced his brain with his heart." The other couldn't get ready with such short notice and asked that I contact him again if I didn't have luck finding a candidate able to work within my time frame.

A dear friend, known as El Capitan,' had heard from Dove about my plans and was interested in knowing if I was looking for investors. Perfect…I most certainly was. I told him I'd let him know as the plan materialized. He also recommended that I call another mutual friend, Finn, for my crew and gave me his contact number.

Finn was German, and had a successful beach concession for years, renting wind surfers to tourists in Greece. I knew of him more than I knew him. I had met Finn years earlier one cold snowy night in New Hampshire. He'd borrowed a truck from our friend, Tango, who Diana, me, and El Capitan' were joining for dinner. He hit a patch of black ice in the road then slid along gaining speed and losing control. He finally rolled the truck over into a ditch and found himself hanging upside down in the cab, held by his seatbelt like a possum. Finn cut himself loose with his pocketknife and walked several miles in the snowy darkness to Tango's home. He came in and joined us for dinner, never mentioning the truck. After the meal and a good brandy, Finn casually mentioned he'd left the truck back up the road a few miles, upside down in a ditch. We all pitched in getting the truck back on the road, then went back to Tango's fire to continue with a grand desert of Crème Brule with berries, Gran Marnier, a strong expresso, and a nice long toke.

Finn was the ultimate adventurer. The perfect character. I left a message with his contact in Greece. I hoped he would be interested in my offer. He was a positive entity on this earth, and nothing was too hard, too hot, too cold, too dirty, or too dangerous for his taste. He was a big guy and wore his hair in a long ponytail. He had an athletic physique, and coordination orchestrated his movements. He struck an image of competence and never walked into a place without making friends with everyone there before he left. His perpetual broad smile radiated his love of life.

When I contacted him, he was in the middle of a project, adding a room to his house in Greece. He jumped at the chance to help with the Atlantic crossing. Normal assistance across the Atlantic would be about $5,000 plus expenses, but after telling him about the added freight I planned to be carrying, his take would be $40,000, Finn adamantly wanted to be included. He needed a break from his house project, and funds for the project were running low. For Finn the timing was perfect.

I told him to be making plans to be in Mallorca in about 4 weeks, sometime around the end of September 1991. I pressed ahead ever more enthusiastic about the plan as components began to come together.

* * *

With Finn on board, one of the most important pieces of the puzzle had been found. His enthusiasm provided the validation I needed. This whole undertaking had been born, and existed, under the sign of the question mark. Every step was all new territory for me, and there was nothing to vouch for my success. Each component had to be found, assembled, lubricated and fired up. Each would be done without an instruction manual to assist. Diana's list of "what-ifs" kept rearing its ominous head. I needed a copy of "Smuggling for Idiots".

On the seventh day, per our plan, I met Phillipe at El Pozo, a bistro beside the bay in Puerto Cristo, Mallorca. It was the 9th of September 1991. That morning, the town was soaked by a hard rain. Streams of water raced down the streets along the sidewalks. Big drops soaked everything they touched. They fell from the trees that lined the walkways and gathered in the streets, rushing along the curbs, carrying everything, spinning and dancing along the way.

I had borrowed a faded old red Renault to make the hour-long drive from Puerto Pollensa where *Whitetail* awaited, to Puerto Cristo where I was to rendezvous with Phillipe. I'd left the little car parked a few streets away as I walked in the rain to find El Pozo. The cool wet air left a clean fragrance in its wake. I was wet. I was nervous. This, right now, was reality -- the very first step. All through the previous night, I'd practiced over and over what I planned to say. How would I handle Phillipe's questions, and how would I address my own?

I knew I was on the right track when I saw Phillipe's big steel cutter, *Sea Lion*, lying just offshore where he'd dropped anchor behind the café. She was a heavy working sailboat not a yacht. Her hull was painted dark blue, almost black. Despite her displacement she sported fifty feet of pretty lines. Her sails and rig were complicated, yet everything was ready to spring into action when needed. His dinghy, with oars folded in their locks, could be seen tied to the big boat's stern. I knew he hadn't rowed to meet me yet, probably waiting for the downpour to subside. I also knew he could see me from his boat. I began to walk with a purpose, standing as tall as I could, sucking my stomach in and holding my shoulders back. As I walked on, I transformed myself into what I thought to be, a force to be reckoned with.

The little café was dimly lit. I shook off the rain, leaving a pool on the floor behind me. It was about 11 a.m. and I was the only customer. The bartender nodded my way. I nodded back and glanced out the window. The dingy had left its nest beside the big boat. I watched as he rowed effortlessly, gliding toward the dock on the mirror smooth water after the rain. Phillipe walked in, and the little café' seemed to brighten. There, I saw the man I was trying to be. A brilliant aura shown about him. His well-worn, stained, yellow foul weather jacket glistened with the rain, and a small bright red towel, tucked in around his neck kept the rain from pouring down his back.

He pulled his hood back, removed the red towel, and began to dry his jacket. The towel danced, picking up pools of rain that had formed in the folds. With his hood pulled back, a striking character emerged.

Bright green eyes looked intensely through me, and a ruddy complexion told tales of his time at the helm of the *Sea Lion*. He nodded at me and pointed with his thumb, eyes doing the talking,

"Yes, I'm Pierce," I ventured, breaking the silence. I pointed to the empty chair at my table, hand open, palm faced up. He hung his jacket on the chair carefully and sat down.

"Phillipe," he said.

We shook hands. Firm and calloused, he exuded capability.

We were the only two customers in the place, and the bartender, mainly from boredom, seemed curious. No doubt, we weren't the usual European touristas. Surely, we were up to something interesting. He lingered near the end of the bar, not far away, pretending not to be listening. What he heard was two men communicating in a blend of broken Spanish, broken English, and broken French with a constant show of sign language, hand gestures and laughter. I don't think anyone could have deciphered our discussion. He also heard me order two Fundador brandy's, and two cortados, larger than normal expressos steamed with a little creme. It was that kind of day. Phillipe and I liked each other instantly. We had another round.

Phillipe knew that I wanted to be introduced to Yousef Abboud, in Tangier, but in the meantime, he also thought he might sell me part of his load that was hidden away on board his boat, *Sea Lion*. He insisted that we row out to his boat to have a look. The rain had let up to a drizzle, so we struck out in his dinghy headed for *Sea Lion*.

We drifted slowly and quietly up to *Sea Lion's* transom. I guessed his boat was about 50' long. Her decks were wide with a low flush cabin, making it easy to move around. Intricate systems of lines and sails were tied perfectly in their respective places, ready to spring instantly to action at their captain's command. Phillipe shipped the dinghy's oars, then instructed that I climb up and aboard, using the maze of the self-steering vane's mount, to access her cockpit. Phillipe knocked hard on the steel hull with a secret rhythm that let all on board know he was back, and everything was OK. A different knock might have sent everyone running. He called in Portuguese to his crew down below. Once onboard, he told me to slide the companionway hatch open and drop down into the main cabin.

As I leaned over to slide the heavy companionway open, I noticed two perfect little round dents in the steel bulkhead on the starboard side of the hatch. It was easy to guess what had made them, but I couldn't tell if it was 9mm or a 38. I put my finger in one of the little dents and smiled back at Phillipe who was climbing up the framework behind me. He didn't respond as I'd expected. Without humor, his lips tightened, he shook his head, then helped me slide the hatch open without further discussion. I was reminded that his was a dangerous business, a serious business, and danger was always waiting for the unprepared or the unsuspecting.

I dropped through the companionway hatch, down to the main cabin below. The warmth of the cabin was a relief. I'd been cool all day, unable to gather my body heat. The wet coolness had enveloped me early on this rainy morning , and the old, borrowed Renault Quattro, amongst other things, had no heater.

On *Sea Lion*, there was a mild fragrance of incense in the warm air. I thought it may possibly be the aroma from the hashish on board. Phillipe's wife, Pele, was in the galley with a pot of water boiling on the stove. She was a lovely Portuguese woman, with kind, inquisitive eyes, full of empathy. She nodded hello as Phillipe introduced me to her in Portuguese, with an abbreviated description of who I was, where I came from, and what I wanted.

Her welcoming smile shined brilliant against her bronze complexion. Then, in Portuguese, she offered me a cup of mint tea.

"Thanks, yes, that would be great."

I looked up when I heard a rustle from the forward cabin. A dog? Through the arched passageway in the bulkhead, the cushions began to move, and a tiny little girl appeared.

"This is my daughter Julietta," Phillipe said.

Her hair full of tangled locks, Julietta climbed out of the pillows, smiled shyly, yawned, and stretched her arms over her head. After she climbed out of her nest, I was her first stop.

She stood beside me on the cushion of my long settee and balanced herself with her hand on my shoulder. Then she took a long look at this visitor. I can't remember ever being so interrogated so thoroughly, so quickly. I seemed to have passed the first inspection as she came to life, bouncing over me to take the cup of tea from her mom, and present it to me with a flare uncommon to a three-year-old.

The main cabin of *Sea Lion* was well appointed with beautiful hardwood panels and old teak and holly flooring. Heavy bronze port lights allowed light to enter making the boat ever more comfortable. I appreciated this impressive sailboat, capable of going anywhere, and handling anything that came her way.

Phillipe was proud of his boat as well as his load of hashish. He was a competent sailor and had removed his engine years ago to use the space to carry as much hashish as he possibly could. He had quite a load on board, 500 kilos, neatly packed in the place where an engine and transmission would normally be. He broke off a piece from one of the pucks and handed it to me with a cigarette to prepare it for smoking. I'd never prepped a clump of hash to be smoked with a cigarette. Most often, when the rare opportunity came, I'd light it up in a small, long stem hash pipe. Again, a copy of "Smuggling for Dummies" would certainly have covered my ineptitude.

Phillipe was closing the door to his engine compartment when he noticed my confusion. He did a double take and instantly threw up the dreaded red flag. It was easy to see the pool of aggression he had at his command. He spun around, his face one inch from mine.

"Who are you?" he roared, in perfect English. He never faltered his interrogation, searching closely, deeply, into my eyes, looking for any clues.

I could smell the coffee and brandy on his breath. The air in the cabin changed instantly to hard, fragile, and tense. I slowly held up both my hands, palms facing him. I hoped to defuse any feeling of confrontation. My heart pounded in my ears. I tried to wipe that look off my face. I chose my words carefully, calmly, hoping to swallow, but my mouth, was conspicuously dry and made talking very difficult.

"I am who you think I am," I croaked. "I've only smoked hashish from a small Moroccan clay pipe, or a Chillum from Pakistan. I've never used a cigarette."

Phillipe backed away, never dropping his visual investigation, he sat down on the opposite side of the cabin. Then without a word, he took the hash from me. He squeezed the tobacco out of the cigarette onto the table and took a small piece of hash and worked it together with the tobacco in the palm of his hand. I noticed the muscles in his hands and forearms danced with every move. He then tore off a piece off the cigarette's filter and carefully filled the empty paper with the tobacco hash blend. He tamped the cigarette tight on the table and handed it to me, still not totally convinced that I could be trusted. Maybe I was working for the DEA or the Guardia Civil, or even worse, an independent agent working as a mole.

Peli and Julietta had vanished somewhere in the confines of the boat. They were out of site and made not a sound. I reached for a wooden, blue tipped match in a box on the table, and fired up the hash cigarette, took a long puff, then leaned over to hand it to him. He reached out, seized the spliff from me and took a long toke.

My inner self began to relax. We shared a few more pulls, and I began to feel mighty stoned. Phillipe's body language, even without conversation, seemed to indicate we were getting back on track again. I felt relieved that I would most likely not be spending the night on the floor of the Mediterranean Sea.

I was so relieved that my eyes uncontrollably began to close. Over and over, I fought to keep them open. Hopelessly, I succumbed and fell into a deep sleep in the warmth of the soft cushions, and the quiet of the rain falling on the cabin top.

I'm not sure how long I slept, maybe half an hour. When I woke, Phillipe was up and sliding the heavy companionway open. A breath of cool wet air rushed in. The day was a darker grey now, later than I'd expected. A light rain had begun to fall again, and Phillipe indicated we'd better get me back to shore before the rain picked up momentum.

I hoped to check his take on our meeting. "Is everything OK?"

He took a long look at me, "Digame (you tell me)"

"Seguro mi amigo (definitely my friend)", I responded.

The dinghy ghosted along toward the rocky beach where I stepped out and turned to hold the bow. Phillipe instructed me to meet him in seven days at 9 a.m. on the 16th of September 1991 in Algeciras at a small cafe, Enrique's, near the Ferry Terminal. He would find me. The plan was for us to take the ferry across the Strait of Gibraltar to Tangier together, where he'd introduce me to Yousef Abboud, the key I needed to progress with my grand adventure. Phillipe had money he needed to deliver to Yousef.

I hopped out onto the wet beach and pushed the dinghy out into water deep enough for Phillipe to row back out to *Sea Lion* and his family. I waved, and he nodded as he slowly slipped away.

"Phillipe, por favor, adios y hasta la vista a Pili y Julietta."

He nodded and called back, "Merci!"

I wished that I didn't have the feeling that something was missing from the afternoon. Whew! I was hungry and overwhelmed with the events of the day. It was a relief to be alone. What had just happened? Walking back to El Pozo I recanted the last several hours. I wished I hadn't fallen asleep. I thought I could have done better, but at least this difficult juncture was done, and the outcome seemed to be successful. There seemed to be no doubt that he and I would be off in a week to meet Yousef Abboud. I appreciated Dove's connection here. I wouldn't have gotten this far without his help.

When I entered El Pozo, there were several men, all with their elbows resting on the bar: glasses of brandy warming between their hands.

A couple sat at a table by a window in the graying afternoon light. Errant drops of rain pecked at the window then trickled down the panes of glass pooling on the sill outside. They held hands and gazed deeply into each other's eyes. They were immersed in conversation; with a language I didn't recognize. A bottle of red wine waited patiently.

I sat at an empty table and ordered a bowl of chicken stew, bread, and a glass of Rioja from the same bartender who was there four hours earlier. He had that same suspicious look. "Sus amigo?" he asked. Ah, si, mi dia es terminado, y yo voy a mi casa en el norte de la isla dispues comida. Pero, ahora yo tango mucho hambre."

I hoped I'd avoided any further interest with my oblique Spanish.

CHAPTER TEN
Tangier / Pint Sized Bandits

WHEN I FINALLY ARRIVED BACK AT *Whitetail,* evening was approaching and there was a huge full moon precariously hanging in the early night sky. It lit my way along the docks, now alive with boatyard cats. I knew them all and we shared leftovers when I had them.

"No fellas, nothing tonight."

A couple of them were brave enough to come on board for an occasional visit. They were a bunch of tough guys.

Time roared by, while summer turned to autumn. I worked around the clock, morning to night, getting *Whitetail* ready to go. Days began to get shorter, and I needed for Finn to come on. I needed him sooner than the end of September, and worried that he might not get to Mallorca before I departed for the next phase of my plan.

The 13th of September 1991 was on us and Phillipe was to be in Algeciras on the 16th. The plan was to take me with him across the Strait of Gibraltar to Tangier where we'd meet with Yousef Abboud. I called Finn one more time to confirm his ETA. The person who answered the communal phone, said Finn had left a message, "He'll be in the airport in Palma de Mallorca on the afternoon of the 30th of September 1991." I was relieved Finn had set a firm date for his arrival. The frustration of Finn's variable arrival time had been working on my patience level, and I'd hoped he would be there in time to help me with the preparation for the voyage.

I pressed ahead and was off to meet Phillipe in Algeciras, where we'd go together to meet Yousef Abboud. Abboud would arrange for my trip up into the Rif Mountains to the small reclusive town of Ketama, famous for its quality hashish. I would personally select my product to ensure the best quality. The price, the timing, and the payment methods had to be determined. This leg needed to be organized as quickly as possible.

Once I returned to Tangier from Ketama, I'd go immediately to Madrid, and onward to New York. Then to New Hampshire where I'd talk about investment possibilities with El Capitan', my old sailing partner, and an experienced investor in these games. From New Hampshire I'd fly to Atlanta for a few days to check on Diana and spend as much time as possible with her going over our plan, again and again. My next leg would take me far from Atlanta, and there was no way I could tell how long I'd be gone. We had not spent much time apart during our relationship and leaving Diana didn't agree with me. I was already sad…missing her. The whole plan depended on so many unknowns.

After this whirlwind trip, I'd head back to Madrid to meet with a constituent and make half payment for the load. From Madrid I would return to Mallorca to finish prepping *Whitetail* for the long dangerous trip. I needed to get Finn, finish the boat prep and head for our first rendezvous on the north African coast to pick up my load.

There was too much to do and too little time. I had to move quickly, no time to rest. Since Finn wasn't going to arrive until the last day of September, I carried on despite not having his help. I had to finish the details prepping *Whitetail*. So, with plans in a mild state of confusion, I launched my crazy loop on September 14, 1991. The itinerary would put me back in Mallorca in 16 days to pick Finn up at the airport in Palma de Mallorca..

The trip from Mallorca to Algeciras where I was to meet Phillipe was a long haul. I confirmed that *Whitetail* was safely tied in her slip with double dock lines and struck out at seven in the morning with Pepe, a taxi driver from Puerto Pollensa. We were heading to the airport in Palma de Mallorca. About 4 p.m. I finally got settled in Algeciras. I booked a cheap room, found "Enrique's", and had a bowl of soup with bread and a glass of red wine from

Rioja, a successful area where vineyards were making good reputations in the world of wine production. Do try "Marques de Caceres". You'll like it.

At 6 a.m. the next morning I was up and rested. I went back to Enrique's and enjoyed a thick cup of coffee and a sweet roll. I watched as the crowds grew with the morning sun.

Phillipe saw me way before I saw him.

"I've two tickets for the ferry," he said, "so we should go on down and get aboard."

Minutes later we were standing on the bow of the big powerful ferry, watching as it rumbled out into the turbulent waters of the Strait of Gibraltar. After several hours banging into choppy seas, we hopped off the ferry in Tangier.

As soon as Phillipe and I passed through the chain link fence where the ferry passengers disembarked and entered Tangier, we were surrounded by what seemed to be hundreds of little kids. They were yelling, pushing, and fighting with one another. Little hands rifling my pack and every pocket. Before I knew it, my belt was slipping off my jeans. I grabbed it in the nick of time to see the little bandit take off into the crowd, empty handed. Phillipe yelled above the crowd in his best English.

"With me. No…no stop. Come, come. Go with me." He waved frantically, "No stop, no stop. No hands in pants. They take all. Careful move, move. No stop!"

A few lazy police officers stood by, talking, and watching, in case anyone got out of hand, but for the most part, our fate was cast to the wind in this sea of pint-sized pirates. Phillipe quickly turned up a narrow street, and walked straight up a hill, where he ducked into a doorway to a small café and flopped down at an empty table.

I'd never seen him smile before, much less laugh, but his contagious smile and hardy belly laugh were impossible to ignore. I followed suit and laughed so hard I couldn't stop until I got the hiccoughs. Phillipe knew the owner. He and Phillipe, shaking their heads, discussed, the problems of the ever-increasing population of street kids. Even though they spoke in Arabic I could surmise what was being said. Still chuckling to himself, Philippe asked for a glass of water to cure my tenacious case of hiccoughs, and two cups of mint tea.

I assessed my losses. I was missing my favorite little pocketknife but nothing else. Phillipe had forewarned me on the ferry ride. I had put money, credit cards, passport, and anything of real value in the bottom of my shoes and laced them up tightly.

Around five in the afternoon I was overwhelmed with exhaustion and hunger. I needed to shower, eat, and sleep. Phillipe walked out to the curb and a taxi came up immediately, presumably called by his friend there at the restaurant. We rode along for about ten minutes while he directed the driver to pull up the next street on the right. The driver wheeled his car around the corner barely missing a camel. The camel driver and the taxi driver yelled epithets and shook their fists with vile contempt for each other. They must have been friends.

Phillipe instructed the taxi driver to pull into The Hotel les Almohades. Using the special language, he and I had created, he explained he would drop me off here and continue on his way to see Yousef Abboud where he had some unfinished business. My mind wandered, remembering the load of hashish on Sea Lion. Phillipe said he would send a driver or a taxi back to pick me up here at the hotel at 8 p.m.

I walked up wide well-worn marble steps to the grand entrance of an elegant old hotel. The doorman looked kindly at me, as if he knew exactly what I was doing in his town. After booking a room, sleep overwhelmed me. I was comatose before hitting the bed, leaving the room door wide open behind me. I woke up around six, confused, not knowing where I was. After a few seconds I remembered who I was and what I was doing. I knew I was hungry and needed a shower. Dirty from travel, I'm sure I weighed a pound less after the water massaged my back and neck for an hour. Then, thinking of sustenance, I walked down to the marble lobby where huge palm trees stood beside tall columns and a funny looking cat, "Marmot" stood guard. I asked for a menu and ordered a meal of lamb, couscous, and a green salad.

My plan was beginning to take shape and move forward. I began to feel less stressed and more optimistic.

CHAPTER ELEVEN
Yousef Abboud / Ever Closer

I HAD JUST FINISHED MY MEAL when I saw someone come into the hotel and ask the doorman a question. They both looked over at me. The doorman nodded and came to where I was sitting,

"Sir your transportation has arrived." I stood, thanked him, and walked over to the driver. He explained in Arabic, presuming I understood, that he'd been sent by Yousef Abboud to collect me and bring me back to his palace. I followed the driver out to his taxi and was surprised to see a young Moroccan boy in the back seat. Fears from memories of my afternoon came back. What did this young boy want? Instinctually, I reached for my pockets. I climbed into the front seat, looked back, and nodded at this young fellow. I figured he must be a relative to the driver just along for the ride. Suddenly, he spoke, clearly in perfect English,

"My name is Henri, Yousef Abboud is my friend." Your name is Pierce, correct?" Astounded, I nodded. "Monsieur Abboud has asked that I work for you while you're here in Tangier. I am here to help you anyway I can." I confirmed, "We are now on our way to visit Yousef Abboud, am I right?" I was startled to hear myself speaking English. "Yes, we are on the way to his palace now." Palace? Now what?

The road twisted as we got higher and moved further back into the city of Tangier.

Finally, it got so narrow that it was difficult to drive the taxi between the high walls. At a prescribed point, Henri told the driver to stop and let us out. He told the driver that Yousef Abboud was covering the expenses tonight.

The driver, quiet till this point, turned and in perfect English said, "Okay, Henri, you be very careful out on this bad town tonight. Get in touch with me if you need anything."

Henri seemed deeply connected in Tangier and handled himself perfectly. He lent me confidence in his abilities. He asked for me to follow him along the ever-narrowing street which finally came to an end in a cul-de-sac. He motioned for me to come and look over a low stone wall. I walked up and was gifted with a site and a scene, neither of which I'll ever forget. Henri welcomed me with a grandiose gesture as if he were a stage manager introducing the next act.

It was now 8 p.m. and evening was upon us. The sun had just touched the ocean far off on the western horizon. Reds, yellows, and oranges lit up a few small clouds, and then began to play with the waves dancing far below. Brilliant colors reflected off the towering stone precipice where I stood. I walked out to the edge and took a deep breath. I was introduced to a most foreign fragrance.

Henri asked if I would like to wait for Yousef here, or in a café. He explained that Yousef had a visitor who'd stayed later than expected and he could meet with me in about an hour. I thought his visitor must be Phillipe.

I didn't want to leave the light show I was watching. The sunset was pulling out all its tricks.

"Just come get me when he's ready Henri. I'll wait here for you. Okay?"

I turned and walked back to the precipice, and for the first time I noticed two young mothers nicely dressed in western garb sitting on a low wall at the edge of the cliff that terminated its fall far below in the Strait of Gibraltar. They were conversing intently in Arabic about things I couldn't understand. What has stayed in my mind from that evening, were these three little kids out on the brink of that cliff playing with a little black scorpion. There were two little girls maybe eight or nine years old. Both wore yellow dresses, pressed to perfection: Maybe a uniform for a private school. A little boy, about six, wore a pair of black shorts and a pressed white short-sleeved shirt. The scorpion was big, black, and totally put out with being pushed around with a stick by these kids.

The women showed no concern for the children. Neither the scorpion nor the precipice suggested danger to them. They presumed the kids knew better than to go too near the edge, or they'd fall to their death, and they also knew not to touch the scorpion, or he'd sting them and make them very sick.

The hour passed quickly. It had gotten darker and cooler after the sun sank below the horizon. The moms and their kids had packed up and gone.

I felt Henri may have been any number of places in the shadows keeping an eye on me. He suddenly appeared out of the darkness.

"Monsieur Abboud is ready to see you."

It must've been about 10 p.m., Henri walked along showing me the way, talking about the sunset. Finally, we came to an ancient arched wooden doorway. Henri knocked with an old iron ring, and the door opened with a time worn creak. Loud sounds of drums, music, and singing boomed from within the palace. We passed through a tall carefully lit room supported by carved marble columns. There must have been a hundred people, mostly women in brightly colored long dresses. Everyone was having a great time, laughing, talking, singing, and dancing. They would spin around while their brightly colored dresses rustled, creating whirling dervishes of dancing color.

I followed Henri through the smiling crowd, then turned up a steep narrow set of old spiral marble steps. They were barely wide enough to pass through without turning sideways.

When we arrived at a little door, he knocked. The door swung open and thick smoke billowed out, bringing with it the distinct smell of burning hashish. I followed Henri through the doorway and there, finally, stood my quest, tall and thin, with a most pleasant smile. He spoke his first word as he pointed back down the steep steps behind us,

"Birthday."

Yousef Abboud looked a bit like my vision of Ichabod Crane. A tall thin, short waisted willowy gentleman, with long legs, dark eyes, and a prominent nose that led the way. He wore a white linen, long sleeved, collarless shirt, top buttons opened, and sleeves rolled to his elbows. His pants were light weight khaki, very baggy, with multiple pleats at the waist. His clothing seemed comfortably draped on him. His movements were graceful and welcoming. Yousef spoke perfect English, French, Spanish, as well as his first language, Arabic. His air instantly established a comfortable trust to his countenance. It was easy to like him.

The little room was small and sparsely furnished. There was a large low table off to one side, and the floor was covered with rugs of all sizes, shapes, and colors. After a meaningful handshake, he motioned for me to sit. Henri had disappeared.

"Has the boy been of assistance?" he asked.

"Yes indeed," I replied, "and I appreciated his help, especially after my experience earlier at the ferry."

Suddenly I heard a low groan, and the rugs close to my feet began to move with a mind of their own. Yousef laughed and pointed into the dark corner.

"I believe you two have met." I squinted to make out Phillipe, who looked like a sleeping lion spread out on the floor. Yousef and I laughed at his intermittent snoring and began to speak in whispers.

Yousef offered me a pipe, but I politely declined. Better not to smoke at this moment. I needed my already taxed mind to remain clear.

At first, we spoke of mutual acquaintances we shared. He knew of Dove. He knew El Capitan.' We talked and laughed about my day with Phillipe. He was curious about sailing and wondered what my plans were when I got the load back to the US. Our conversation flowed easily, and I began to like this character. Meeting Yousef was the culmination of all my efforts to this point. Here he was, sitting with me, answering my needs perfectly. So far, the plan had gone like clockwork. I relaxed a bit. Things were progressing so easily. "Ha!"

As my eyes became more accustomed to the dim light, I noticed the photos that covered the walls all around the room. The photos were of incredibly famous rock stars, poets, writers, actors, royalty, and politicians. Each included a salutation to Yousef, then a signature. He certainly seemed to be well respected in all the correct circles.

He asked, "What can I do for you my friend?"

As I began to discuss my plan with Yousef, I became nervous, working hard to keep my cool. I reminded myself, above all else… be cool.

"Yousef, you have a great reputation, and I've been referred to you to help me procure 600 kilos of quality hashish and to help me get it onboard my sailboat, which I'm taking back to the US." The plan seemed so simple. What could possibly go wrong?

"Yes, I've spoken with Philippe regarding your plans. I will be happy to help you with your project. To begin, do you have any questions that I may answer for you?"

Not really knowing where to begin, I asked the obvious, "When can I see the hash?" "Can I select the product I want?" "How much will 600 kilos cost?" How will I make the payment?" "What's the process for loading my boat?"

We talked for over an hour as the evening wore on. I was beginning to feel quite tired. Phillipe who hadn't budged the entire time continued a low rumble as he breathed heavily in his sleep. The harder I tried to keep my eyes open the more determined they were to close. Phillipe's rhythmic breathing lent no help with my effort. Yousef saw me nodding, and in a moment, Henri appeared at the door. Yousef had him to escort me back to my hotel. I stood, steadied myself on cramped legs, and bade him good night.

"In the morning, look for my cousin Ahmed at 9 a.m. He will collect you at the Hotel."

"What are we going to do?"

"You want to go up into the Riff, to select your product, right?" he answered with a smile.

"Yes, oh yes" I was immediately wide awake and astounded that my plan could be facilitated so easily.

Everything was moving along so effortlessly. I was fooled into thinking this was going to be a simple process.

I could not have been more wrong. Yousef continued.

"You and Ahmed will drive up to Ketama tomorrow morning. The trip will take about five hours. You'll return to Tangier the next day. The trip is interesting, and I think you will enjoy the people and the scenery. While you are there, Ahmed will make appointments for you to meet with the smaller growers, or the younger producers. Their products are consistently exceptionally good, as their competition is fierce. They take great pride, and more care with its production as compared with the growers who produce thousands of kilos. Do exactly as Ahmed instructs. You are safe with him."

"You mentioned wanting 600 kilos. The cost will be $100 US per kilo. You will deal with me on all money issues. Choose from the hashish samples you're offered. Your selections will be tagged Pierce and will belong to you. I will want a deposit of $30k, half payment as soon as possible to hold your hashish in Ketama for three weeks. The balance of $30k will be due to the fishermen when they bring your load out to your boat." Call me if you have problems with this schedule.

Henri had a taxi waiting outside the heavy arched doorway. He insisted on riding with me to insure I would arrive back to les Almohades Hotel and safely in my room.

I was exhausted.

CHAPTER TWELVE

Ketama / Kaboom!

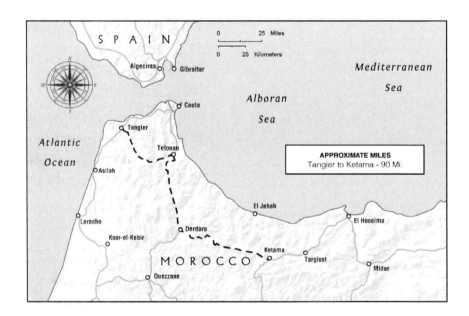

I REVELED IN A LONG COMATOSE SLEEP, and somewhere during the night, tomorrow arrived. I went in search for a cup of coffee in the hotel café. I sat amongst the big palm trees in the hotel's black and white tiled foyer, and enjoyed a sweet roll with a cup of thick black coffee you could stand your spoon in. I played with Marmot, the hotel cat, and waited for Yousef's cousin, Ahmed, to arrive. I was wonderfully rested, refreshed, and excited, ready for the next phase of the journey.

Finally, 9 a.m. came, and punctually to the minute, an old rusty car pulled up at the bottom of the steps of the hotel's entrance. A clean-cut

Moroccan man of slight build opened the driver's door, stepped out, and walked around the back of the car, all the while looking for me at the top of the steps.

Ahmed must have been about 35 years old and was dressed in a plaid button-down shirt tucked into a pressed pair of khaki pants. He was clean cut, and when he saw me, his radiant smile was enough introduction. His dark eyes beamed as he reached to shake my hand.

"I am Ahmed, Yousef's cousin. I am to escort you to the Rif today. We will spend the night there and return to Tangier tomorrow morning. Is that good with you?"

"Yes of course; I appreciate you taking me there. My name is Pierce."

Off we went.

Ahmed was a satisfied man. He was easy moving in every way. His face seemed to express a deep kindness and disarmed all that crossed his path. I was instantly comfortable as we sorted out our language differences. He was fluent in French, Spanish, and of course Arabic. A little English would work in a pinch. We settled, working around my limitations, with Spanish and a bit of English when needed.

Ahmed was eager to talk. He had an insatiable curiosity for new knowledge. How long had I been in Morocco? Where in the US did I live? How big is my sailboat? Had I ever done this before? Did I have kids? Why not?

Two hours roared by with not an instant of silence. When the conversation took a short break, the noise of the old car took over. We began to increase our elevation and entered a rocky terrain. The narrow road was one quick sharp turn after another as it passed amongst boulders larger than the car.

Suddenly, out of nowhere, as Ahmed slowed for one particularly sharp bend, a tall uniformed police officer stepped out into the narrow road with his hand held high, waving for us to stop. Then another officer stepped out.

I could see their Moto Guzzi's just out of easy sight, around the corner leaning against a large boulder.

Both the police officers were fit, tall and serious. I wondered if they practiced their intimidating appearance. If they did, they certainly had the look mastered to perfection. They wore matching grey uniforms with jodhpurs tucked into tall shiny polished black leather boots. Each officer wore a white half helmet with a short, shiny black bill and leather side straps buckled under their chins.

One walked around to Ahmed's window, which he quickly rolled down.

"Window down." the other calmly instructed me with a spin of his forefinger aimed at my window handle. I obliged, and he leaned into the car, his face inches away, looking closely to see what was in the back seat. I could smell him, a pungent blend of serious body odor, garlic, and cigarette smoke. I was choking for fresh air when I heard Ahmed and his inspector talking and laughing in a surprisingly casual way. I would have breathed a sigh of relief if I could have filtered out the caustic smell attacking me from the officer on my side.

He stood up in the nick of time and backed away, looking at me with unflinching fierce eyes. I was going over a mental list of what I might have done wrong, and what I needed to do to make it right. I looked over at Ahmed for an answer. I saw he was reaching into his pocket, pulling out something he cupped in his hand. Without ceremony, he leaned over and held out his hand, palm down, while the officer accepted the gift with a nod, stepped back and motioned for us to pass by and continue our journey.

My guy was still standing there, hands on his hips, giving me a, "Just wait till next time" look.

So onward we went into the brilliant day, heading up and up into the Rif mountains to Ketama. Ahmed explained our meeting with the Moroccan Royal Gendarmerie was totally normal. Everyone knew the routine. The tariff was to pay these guys to forget they ever saw you. Ahmed smiled and shrugged. The price of doing business. He felt it was fair for everyone.

Another hour passed pleasantly. Ahmed asked if I was hungry. I was. In a mile or two there was a small white stucco building perched on the edge of a precipice. Ahmed stopped. Ahmed knew everyone, and it was obvious they all wanted to know about me. He ordered for both of us, yogurt with nuts, honey, and dried fruit mixed in and a cup of black mint tea. It was just what the doctor ordered. I sat at a table by myself, overlooking the valley below, enjoying every bite, while Ahmed, surrounded at the bar, fielded question after question regarding him, his brothers, his dad, his mom… and me.

They all stared at me; I was a peculiarity in their world. I felt like the new monkey at the zoo. Some would walk into the little café just to have a look at me, then continue inconspicuously with their loop back to the door and outside. There was no doubt what I was doing up there.

An hour or so later Ahmed motioned to me that we should go.

Next stop, Ketama.

A couple of hours later, my ears popped with the increased altitude. The rugged little road began to flatten out and came to an ambiguous end on this flat rocky hilltop. Ahmed opened his door. We were up high in the Rif mountains, and dusk was coming. It had become surprisingly cool.

Ahmed turned off the motor, and neither of us spoke as we rested in the thick silence. After a moment, he asked that I stay in the car while he found his family and told them he was here. He wanted to explain who I was and why I was there with him. The slam of the car door at his departure intensified the silence it left behind. I strained in the coming darkness to define movements that stirred the shadows. I could see nothing.

Then…

KA-BOOM!!

I jumped straight up and out of my seat, hit my head on the windshield, and landed on the floor of the car.

Adrenaline instantly diluted the blood in my veins, and chills covered my body. While my eyes were trying to find their way back into my head, I gulped over and over, my mouth was dry. What the **hell** was that?

I stayed down on the floor. In fact, I tried to get down even lower.

KA- BOOM!! Good-God…I'm outta here! But a quick moment of indecision regarding where to run, yielded no place safer than the car I was in. Anyway, this is where Ahmed had left me, so I guess I'd better just hang on.

KABOOM!!

The driver's door opened just as I had decided to give up and run. Ahmed's face peered in, dimly lit by the interior light of the car. There was another person with him, impatiently pushing from behind, scuffling to see over Ahmed's shoulder to have a better look at me. Ahmed searched the car for a second before he saw me huddled in the dark of the floor. I think he may have bridled a little chuckle.

"Don't worry, it's my father." "Ohh, okay, don't worry you say. Your father?"

KA-BOOM!!!

It was louder and closer now, just outside the car. Ahmed spun around long arms raised, up and out to his side. He firmly addressed his father, no doubt the source of the explosions. Gunpowder scented the air. He spoke in Arabic, with a kind but firm tone, bordering on loving frustration. I suspect the discussion went something like this.

"Father, you don't need to shoot your gun right here next to the car. I told you someone has come with me for a visit and he's here in the car waiting for me. Anyone would be scared with you sneaking up on them and firing your shotgun in the night. Another person may even have shot back at you. Let's stop for a while. okay?"

Ahmed turned and stooped towards me, squinting in the dim light. I was finally sitting upright again in the passenger's seat.

"I'm sorry Pierce, my father is shooting at wild dogs. They're bad around here. They eat his chickens in the night."

Wild dogs eh? I'm not sure sharing that info had the calming effect Ahmed had expected. I've always had a justified fear of dogs based on vast experience, and *wild* dogs seemed even more reason for concern.

"Are there many of these *wild* dogs around here?" I asked, hoping their population was now minus three.

As the last **KA-BOOM** echoed down throughout the mountainous terrain, Ahmed's father, a most extraordinary person, entered the dim little circle of light coming from inside the car. He must have been at least 6'5" tall and wore a rough shapeless old wool robe, a Jellaba. It hung from his broad shoulders and draped all the way down to where it almost dragged the ground. I noticed the hem around the bottom was worn thin from years of hovering along just barely above this rocky terrain.

His head was wrapped with a turban made of the same material. The dark face, dimly lit there in the cool evening, was artwork. Every deep wrinkle told a story. There must have been a thousand of them. His black eyes twinkled, and a mischievous smile kept beaming out from not far beneath the surface. Bright eyed and sharp witted I guessed he was at least 90. He kept his eyes on me as he came my way. I wasn't sure what he wanted, but knew whatever it was, I'd do my best to provide it.

As he reached my side, a sinewy brown hand reached down and grabbed my shoulder firmly. He smiled and in a wonderfully deep unwavering voice said something in Arabic. Ahmed translated.

"Please, welcome to my land, I think I've disturbed you. I am sorry, I meant no harm."

I returned the smile and jumped up, giving them all a start. I looked around wildly, arms waving, and mimicked a loud "Boom". We all laughed, and I followed Ahmed and his dad down the steep hill to a little earthen hut, tucked out of sight, back into the side of the mountain. I'm pretty sure I heard his dad chuckling as he walked ahead with his hard-worn old single shot 12-gauge shotgun, riding comfortably on his shoulder, held in place by his hand on its long barrel.

Ahmed's mother was in the hut with a stew brewing on an old wood stove. The aroma was mouthwatering. The burning smell of wood mixed with the aroma of lamb and carrots in a savory blend reminded me I was hungry. The four of us sat down on the floor at a low table and shared this wonderful meal, soaking up the last of the juices with a piece of gnarly bread. When the meal was finished, Ahmed stood and first spoke to his parents in Arabic, then to me in broken English.

"I'll be gone a few hours to arrange our meeting with five small boutique growers who'll show you their hashish at another location tomorrow midday. Then you will select your preferences which will be labeled with your name, Pierce. We'll return to Tangier the following day to meet with Yousef and work out the details of our business."

I was shown a thick rug and a blanket by the open wood stove, guarded over by a smart and smelly, old goat. From the look he gave me, I got the feeling he was a member of the family, possibly the father of the one we just ate. He watched me closely to ensure I was only looking for sleep, and only intended to count sheep.

Ahmed's father had stepped outside with Ahmed when he'd left. Ahmed wasn't long out of site when the old fellow came in and insisted that I go with him out into the night. There was urgency in his demeanor. I hesitated, my mind racing with all the scenarios that could possibly be on his mind. He tried his best to communicate, but quickly became frustrated with the lack of a common language.

He went back into a small back room in the cabin and brought out his tired wife, pulling her along by her hand. He pointed at me, then at the door, and released a quick round of Arabic, looking at her for translation. She looked at him and shrugged her shoulders. He grew quickly impatient with our ineptitude at conversation. I don't know how he figured she could help. I imagined she had gotten him out of many scrapes during their many years together. I bet that when things needed repairing, it was his wife that was the mediator, the communicator, the level head.

Finally, he gave me the universal body language for "come on, follow me". Then he turned and headed for the door, and never looked back presuming I would follow. I had no option; I followed him into the dark cool night.

I glanced at his wife with a "save me" look. She returned my questioning eyes with an, I don't have any idea look and a shrug. I became slightly more concerned when he picked up that blasted shotgun which was leaning on the wall beside the door. Was he taking me down the hill to blow my head off for some reason? I didn't understand a word of this strange Arabic language. Maybe there so many wild dogs lurking in the night he felt he'd get a shot at one before it made off in the dark with one of his chickens.

I followed him down along a rough narrow path in the cool of the night. I feared what might happen. Should I turn back to the security of his wife. I desperately wished for Ahmed. I realized the impossibility of this whole folly without proper connections. We quietly walked along for about half an hour. The path continued to go steeply downhill. I stumbled and slid along each step of the way in the dark. Suddenly the old fellow turned sharply to the left where we came face-to-face with an ancient dilapidated barn.

He motioned that I stop and wait here for him. A moment later he reappeared and bade me to come along. I stumbled along behind him until he came to a large doorway in the side of the barn. He stepped through and I heard him moving things around as he searched for something in particular. Then through the doorway I saw a few bright yellow sparks leap into action. They landed in a small pile of dry wood shavings. In a few minutes, the flame had grown sufficiently to cast light around the interior of the barn.

A pungent smell greeted me as I entered at his request. Excited, Ahmed's father took me by the arm and pulled me over as he broke off a dry stem with leaves attached. I must say, I'd never seen anything quite like this. There were so many plants in that barn, there was no way to venture a guess at how many kilos were in there. Thousands. The roof was probably 30 feet tall and I guess the old barn measured 50' x 80'. Every inch from floor to ceiling was being used to store these plants. Now, I know marijuana well; and over the years, I've seen, smelled, and smoked enough to easily be able to tell the quality of what I'm looking at. This old barn was full to the top with plants that just barely resembled marijuana and smelled more like dried hay, far from that smell of quality marijuana. As the torch grew brighter, allowing me to see better, I noticed the plants were lacking buds. There were only stems and leaves. It was scraggly reefer carelessly grown and harvested. The entire barn was full, floor to the ceiling with tons of super bad marijuana. Amazing.

But oh, he was so proud. He'd pull me here and there, strong hand on my arm, and point out the plants and leaves. Then he'd step back and look intently at me to weigh my response. I was pretty sure we could have smoked the whole barn and not copped a buzz. I guessed his crop was destined to be pressed into low quality hashish or kief. Most certainly the end result would reflect the same quality I found myself admiring here in this old fellow's barn. If I were to have the misfortune of owning this pile of reefer in the States, my best move would be to bury it in a landfill asap. Maybe this barn full of hay could be used as filler to bulk out the final product thus making the good stuff go further and increasing the bottom line. I worried, oh God, is this possibly typical of the marijuana in this territory. Please, this must be a bad dream…not a bad reality.

I did my best. I'm a terrible liar. I need to work on that. He watched me intently. I smiled, spread my arms wide as if taking in the whole world. I shook my head in disbelief. In response, he smiled a toothless grin, slapped me damn hard on the back, pointed and laughed aloud, "Ahah!" all the while nodding affirmatively as if to say, you needn't look further, what you've come for is right here. I feared that out or ignorance I may make some move or gesture, that would indicate I'd like to buy his crop. With impeccable timing, right about the time I'd run out of gestures and accolades, I heard footsteps outside.

The old fellow's demeanor instantly changed. He had sort of a, "I've been caught" look about him. He watched the doorway, knowing who was there. At the same time, Ahmed's face appeared in the dim light. They almost ran into each other. Ahmed looked in the barn, saw me, and evaluated the situation. He knew exactly what was going on. His father had hoped that he may have a chance to sell me some of his marijuana while I was in town looking for hash. Ahmed nodded at me and excused himself and his father for a minute while they talked.

They turned and stepped out into the dark. After their footsteps wandered up the path a little way, I could hear Ahmed in his perpetually calm voice explaining to his dad why I was there, and why I wouldn't be the one interested in buying his crop. I'm sure he explained someone else would be coming soon for his plants.

It must be midnight. I stuck my head out the door and breathed in the cool clean mountain air. There were stars in the night sky firing across the Milky Way, like I've never seen before and rarely since. They reminded me of the same Milky Way that hypnotized me so many years past in the Country. The best Pink Floyd light show ever.

A few minutes later, Ahmed and his Father returned to the barn where I was waiting.

We doused the torch, closed the door and walked in silence uphill along the path, to the modest home of Ahmed's parents, and an ornery old goat, with whom I'd be sharing the floor this evening. I was almost asleep as I walked.

* * *

The cool morning came bright and sunny. I woke to the sound of Ahmed's mother working in the little kitchen. She always seemed to be washing up or prepping for meals. Me and the goat watched as one of the chickens the wild dogs didn't get, was brought in by the old man for his wife to prepare for a meal later in the day.

Ahmed and I had a cup of thick sweet mint tea with a roll made from a pressed blend of figs and other dried fruits. His father smiled and nodded at me as he sat down by the fire and lit his pipe. Fragrant smoke spiraled up into the cabin. I thanked him for his hospitality and reveled properly at his barn full of terrible pot. Ahmed made communication easy, and we talked about where I was from, sailing, hashish, and his years in the Rif.

Soon, Ahmed stood and motioned that I come along with him.

"We have a long day."

Then he reached over and kissed his mother and hugged his father. "Will I see them again?" I asked.

Ahmed turned to his mother and discussed something in Arabic. She nodded yes. Ahmed said she would prepare chicken stew for our dinner this evening.

"Wonderful," I said.

She smiled a warm smile as we turned to leave.

"I've organized our meetings to take place at one house. I have asked all the growers to meet up at Doc's home," Ahmed said as we drove along a trail barely wide enough to accommodate the car.

A rugged hour passed with Ahmed wrestling the steering wheel as the tires found their own way between deep ruts. Suddenly we slowed and turned hard to the right which put us on a gravel driveway that went steeply uphill and ended on a flat plateau where we could park in the company of several other cars. I noticed they were all big black SUV's with 4-wheel drives, all made in the USA.

A small house was perched on the hillside above the driveway. A large deck overlooked the parking area and downward to the valley far below. The time must have been about 11 a.m.

Ahmed opened his door, stepped out, and motioned for me to follow. As he walked up the steep steps that led to the deck, three animated young men came to the top of the steps and welcomed us warmly in Arabic. When Ahmed reached the deck, there were hugs, back slapping, and laughter.

I followed Ahmed up the steep steps and received a similar welcome, as if I was family. I instantly lost all my awkward anxiety. The extraordinary view swept out far below, with bright green open sunlit fields, spotted with shaded wooded areas. I could see a few people way off in the distance, bent over, hard at work.

The last one of the group that Ahmed introduced me to, nodded and spoke to me in perfect English. "Hello Pierce, welcome to my country and my home. I am called, The Doctor, or just Doc. I studied medicine in London and have a degree from University there. My friends and I are happy that you have come for a visit. My dear uncle sent word yesterday that you would arrive here today."

I couldn't believe my ears, what a relief. The first conversation in English since I'd left Tangier.

We sat around the table and drank sweet mint tea. Conversation ran high. They were intently interested in me, the boat, sailing, Mallorca, and the US. Question after question came with hungry listeners spawning lengthy answers. They were unusually interested in the American Civil War. The fact that I was from the south bode well for me. Doc and Ahmed piloted the conversation when language barriers threatened.

They proudly told how Morocco had been the first country to recognize the US in 1777, when it was first founded.

"Oh yes," I pretended I knew this bit of history…I thought I should have.

The conversation went on enjoyably for an hour. I could easily have spent the afternoon with these gentlemen. Doc stood up, and without a word, disappeared into the back of the house. He returned shortly with two boxes about the size of a shoe box. He placed them on the table and offered that I open them both for inspection. At the same time, another of the fellows excused himself and walked down the long steps to his car in the parking lot, to return a minute later with a third box.

Time had come for business. Everyone here was involved at different levels with the production of this hashish. We all knew what was going on. There was no need for explanation.

I was now, at this moment, where I'd only dreamed of a month ago. I was in the company of the boutique hashish producers of the Rif Mountains. They had all grown up in the hashish business here in Ketama. All their families made good livings from hashish.

Doc resumed his position as narrator. He went on to tell how the younger generation was very involved with the proper treatment of the marijuana plant. He explained how they go to the trouble of producing a very potent strain of the plant. They pick the buds from the plant before it goes to seed. They then grow other plants specifically to produce seeds for the next generation. Some of the buds are kept for smoking and others are marked to produce the incredible hash that I was about to try. These fellows were bordering spiritual regarding their livelihood. Yes…I was nervous.

Suddenly, Doc's demeanor made an odd change. His words turned into a growl, his fist balled up on the tabletop, his face now red, turned into a fearsome look; "It is impossible for us to comprehend these people who bulk out the hash before they make the sale. Weight is added with inferior ingredients, some not even hash at all. They alter our first-hand hash by cutting it with contaminants like henna, animal dung, wax, and other foul ingredients."

To Doc and his crew, this was a sacrilege. Everyone was quiet.

His thoughts took control. He stared up into the bright blue afternoon sky, "Forgive me. This is a sore topic, and I should know better than to bring this into our conversation. From up here in these mountains, there is no way we can have any impact on these scoundrels. In the old days this practice simply wasn't' tolerated."

A thought crossed my mind. This odd interlude may have in part been for my benefit. Maybe a fair warning borne from his knowledgeable concern. A shot across the bow. Doc's plants were the result of a tedious cultivation process not comparable to the plants Ahmed's father had in his barn. This crew produced a smaller volume, and yielded a much more potent, hashish.

The group was sure to let me know that they all had other businesses and aspirations. While they were taking advantage of their parent's legacy, with aspirations to be educated and successful businessmen. One had an automobile importation business, another ran his own successful auto body shop, and two were studying business and accounting at University in Madrid. They were proud and I liked 'em all.

On opening the two boxes, the initial aroma was all I needed to know. I was looking at extraordinary hashish. There were four samples. A small long-stemmed clay pipe appeared. There was no need for a hammer. The hashish was malleable due to the high resin content.

Doc lit the pipe and smiled. Then stifling a cough, he passed the pipe over to me. I took a small toke and instantly I wanted all of this I could find. No doubt, the most wonderful THC I think I've ever experienced; an exotic spice powered with high octane resin. I was off like a rocket, riding a buzz I'll forever remember.

I surprised them all when I stood and spoke, powered by a potent high. "This is incredible hashish. I wish I could share it with everyone I know."

They all smiled and passed the pipe around. Doc almost apologetically tested the waters and said, it would be $100 US per kilo.

"How much of this quality do you have?"

"How much do you want?"

"600 kilos."

I had measured *Whitetail's* interior carefully, and I felt we'd be able to carefully find room to lay 600 kilos in the interior of her hull, then cover it with fiberglass and paint. This would aid our ruse when customs agents came knocking in the Canaries, Antigua, and finally Thunderbolt, Georgia.

Wow, the world was oh so right at that moment. I'd found what I'd come for. Mecca.

CHAPTER THIRTEEN
The Commander / The Saddle

Just as dusk was falling, we left the house and the young growers. Ahmed and I were having a wonderful time and could have stayed for days. These were good people. We were drawn together by our common interest in hashish. With Uncle Ahmed's blessings, I placed my order for 600 kilos. I was instructed to work out the payment and pickup details with Yousef.

Ahmed said we'd head back early in the morning. The car groaned and popped at each rut. The ride up the mountain seemed easier, as compared to our ride down. We arrived back to Ahmed's family hut which welcomed us with a warm fire and the smell of stew that reminded of my hunger. The old goat eyed me,

"Oh my god, not this guy again. He needs to go back to where he came from."

So much had happened. Incredibly, I had arrived here just yesterday evening. We sat down on the floor at the short table. Two other women were there this evening helping Ahmed's mother with the dinner. His father, I was disappointed to see, was not there. I felt sure he was out terrorizing the wild dog population. I'd hoped to spend more time with him, especially with Ahmed there to help with translations. Ahmed said his father would not be joining us this evening. The meal was prepared and served at the table in a different way as if planning for dinner company.

I jumped at the unexpectedly hard knock on the door. Everyone in the hut stopped what they were doing and looked at each other. Their eyes, wide with the silence, made me a bit concerned regarding who was on the other side of the door. I looked at Ahmed, he read my concern and nodded at me with an "it's okay" look. He knew who was there.

Then the door opened…instantly the place turned into a movie set as Ahmed graciously welcomed three men. The first had a presence that immediately commanded respect even before an introduction. He must have been about 6'3" tall. A dark man with coal black eyes, sharp cheekbones, an Arabic nose, and a need for a shave that lent a rugged bottom line to this character. He wore a heavy, long dark, double breasted wool overcoat. His hair fell down his back when he removed the scarf that held it in place, while keeping him warm against the cool night.

Ahmed gave him a hard hug with a pound on his back from an opened hand, then held him back at arm's length, looking intently into his eyes.

"Are you okay?" he asked with a smile.

The star reciprocated with a smile of his own.

The other two men stood just inside the door with their backs against the wall on either side of the doorway. They wore what seemed to be parts of uniforms with dark wool coats that had large collars and epaulets with big thick black buttons. They were a somber pair, never meeting anyone's eye, always looking around the group, and tuned constantly toward any unsuspected sound from the outside. I would not want to be making any sounds outside.

The leader nodded at them, indicating they should stay by the door. They settled into their positions and never opened their coats. I was certain these soldiers concealed weapons, held in capable hands, all under the cover of their coats and capes.

Then the star directed his attention toward me. He looked at me directly in the eye with a most non-committal attitude that I hoped didn't change. Ahmed stood nearby, closely watching. His demeanor certainly didn't help to ease my apprehension. The women began to stir in the kitchen again, preparing the meal. Their movements loosened the tension in the air.

Ahmed came over and put his arm around my shoulder, and in Arabic explained my purpose for being here. He looked at the star and spoke to me in English.

"This is my brother. He is known as "The Commander".

"The Commander" came over to me and reached out with his left arm. I followed suit as he grabbed my left forearm, I grabbed his in a common Moroccan handshake. I think he intentionally pulled me towards him and threw me slightly off balance. Then he spoke in perfect King's English.

"My name is Mohammed; I am Ahmed's brother. People call me "The Commander," a nickname given me when I was in the service of the king. I am pleased to meet you. Ahmed has told me about you and your unusual business," he went on. "He tells me that you are interested in only a small quantity of the very best hashish to take back to America with you on your sailboat. Correct?"

"Yes, this is correct. My name is Pierce, and I am from the South of the United States. I am pleased to make your acquaintance Commander. Ahmed introduced me to a group of young gentlemen, not far from here, who have enough extraordinary hash to suit my purpose perfectly. I am looking for 600 kilos.

Then "The Commander" spun around and motioned to the two women helping his mother in the kitchen. He told them in Arabic to feed his soldiers by the door and prepare our table in a room just off to the side of the main area that belonged to the grumpy old goat. He then motioned for me and Ahmed to join him in the private area for the meal. He was harsh and demeaning to the women helping his mom. They only nodded barely looking at him and did exactly as commanded.

Ketama is a "man's world." We sat on the floor at the table, and "The Commander" apologized for the need to speak to Ahmed briefly in Arabic. I could only guess his concerns. He was possibly looking for a way that he may make money from my visit. Or he may have been checking my credentials to ensure his family was safe from this total stranger. Ahmed was nodding then shaking his head at different intervals. I heard him mention Yousef.

"Merci," the Commander said as he turned back to me. A striking character. "So, you are from the South of the United States. I have never been there but would like to go some time. I am a horseman, and I hear Kentucky has wonderful thoroughbreds, but now it seems Florida may be developing a successful breeding business too." From my brief experience in the horse business, I felt comfortable concurring with his assumption.

We continued with lively conversation. I answered the usual questions and asked the safe ones. Ahmed was an indispensable asset for me this evening. With his savior-faire, he could put out the fires of hell if needed. No one could ever come safely to this corner of the world without proper contacts. The meal was exactly what I needed. It was made from the chicken that didn't get away and an assortment of root vegetables all on a bed of wonderfully seasoned couscous.

When the meal was done, the Commander leaned over to me.

"When you return to the US would you get for me a very high-quality Texas western saddle? Send it back to Ahmed. He will ensure that I get it."

"Of course," I said, "it would be an honor."

I meant that. I would get a western saddle for this hero.

Then "The Commander" was gone as quickly as he'd come, back into the cool night.

His two soldiers ever watchful, by his side.

CHAPTER FOURTEEN
Accelerating the Pace / The Plan

THE SUN ROSE ON AHMED AND ME heading north back to Tangier from our successful visit to Ketama. Now I was to meet with Yousef at his palace to make plans, set timing, arrange for money movement, set pick up points and answer all the pertinent unanswered questions.

As we rode along, I asked Ahmed questions regarding "The Commander."

"He and the King were very close," Ahmed explained. "He was quite an accomplished horseman, and the King wanted him in his service to play polo competitively. Then, however, something happened, and no one knows for sure what. "The Commander" was put at odds with the King, and is now sadly, a wanted man on the run.

We arrived back in Tangier about three in the afternoon, and Ahmed dropped me off at the Hotel les Almohades.

"Meet me right here at the entrance at 7 p.m.," I thanked him and stepped out. "We will go to meet with Yousef. You will make scheduling plans this evening."

I would then know the timing on the delivery of the hash to the north coast. I'd know how I was to pay, as well as the exact location for the pick-up.

Only three days had passed since I'd last spoken with Diana. It seemed like years. I took a short nap, then called her. We talked at length. I really looked forward to seeing her in a few days. She would be standing by to help me as I passed through Atlanta, from New Hampshire, on my way back to

Madrid, then finally back to Mallorca. Everything was falling into place. The faster the better for me…so I thought.

* * *

Ahmed picked me up from the hotel steps at 7 p.m. We rode in the familiar little car up the hill to Yousef's palace. Then up the narrow steps and into his perpetually smoky room. Yousef stood as Ahmed opened the door to let ourselves in. There were three other men in the room, all leaning over a big yellow marine chart spread out on the table. I didn't recognize any of them.

We all shook hands, and I was introduced in Arabic to these new men. Yousef and Ahmed worked together to translate from me to them and from them to me. The process worked well, and I felt confident that I had a grip on what was happening.

Two of the newcomers were about fifty years old and wore a rough, life hardened appearance. The third was young. I think he knew a bit of English, but he opted not to speak, and predominantly watched and listened. A smart young man. Best I could tell, one of the older two was the transporter from Ketama to the coast. He had the appearance of a farmer. He would oversee packaging the product for shipping, then take care of getting it down to the coast. The other would supervise loading from the beach onto my boat. He was no doubt a fisherman and had a small fleet of boats at his disposal. They all agreed that it was likely going to take four boats to facilitate the on-loading process.

The discussion seemed common and easy going as they talked, smoked, laughed, and pointed to different places on the chart. I had the feeling they'd done this many times before.

The quiet young one asked in perfect English, "Are you the captain of the sailboat?"

"I am," I said. Ahmed introduced us. This young fellow was the son of a cousin. He was attending the University in Madrid, studying to be an architect. He was to oversee the money transactions.

We got down to business pleasantly and quickly. The plan looked like this: I would leave Tangier tomorrow headed for Madrid, then NYC, and finally New Hampshire, to see El Capitan'. I planned to pick up the investment capital then carry onward to Atlanta for a few days with Diana. From there I'd fly back to Madrid, where I would meet with this young fellow in the airport, between flights to give him $30k, half of the payment. He'd be off to Tangier and I'd be off to Mallorca to finish preparing *Whitetail.* I had to do more than I could handle. I wished for Finn, but he was to arrive on the 30th of September, another week away.

Back at Yousef Abboud's palace, six of us leaned over a chart in the smoky dimly lit, room. The fisherman pointed with a well-worn finger to a place on the chart, El Jebha on the North Coast of Morocco. It looked as if El Jebha was about 400 miles south of Puerto Ibiza and about seventy miles east of the mouth of the Strait of Gibraltar.

I planned to strike out from Mallorca to Puerto Ibiza on October 11th, 1991, a one day's sail. On October 12th, we'd be poised in the marina there in Ibiza, awaiting word from Yousef to launch to El Jebha to make the pickup. It all seemed so simple at this point.

The sail from Ibiza to El Jebha would take about seventy hours, so we'd need to allow three 24-hour days. Judging from my schedule, I could be poised and waiting in Ibiza on October 12th, checking with Yousef each morning at 10 a.m. When my load struck out for the coast, he'd give us the word to begin the three-day sail from Ibiza to El Jebha. In El Jebha, fishing boats loaded with my hashish would be waiting near the shore for my arrival. Once I arrived, I'd contact the boats via three bright flashes from a powerful flashlight and look for confirmation from the shore with another set of three bright flashes.

Both, the fishermen and I would monitor Channel 14 on a VHF radio. I was to be called Yankee, and the Moroccans were to be called Rebels, names inspired by Ken Burns new epic, "The Civil War." These guys were crazy about that documentary. I made a brief suggestion that I would like to be Rebel, if no one really cared, since I am from the South and all, but realized it would be prudent to drop this train of thought immediately. They really wanted to be "Rebel." I was doomed to be "Yankee." A smart man picks his battles.

September 20, 1991 was here, and I needed to get ready and be waiting in Ibiza on October 12th, for Yousef's OK to launch. There was a three-day window here that would depend on the weather and any other variables. Ultimately, I figured the rendezvous to load up the hashish would likely take place between the 16th and the 18th of October at midnight.

Sounds like a solid plan doesn't it?
But demons were hard at work.
Fiends brewing dark mojo.

Little did I know what lay in store. No one could have known.

CHAPTER FIFTEEN
El Capitan / Two Shoeboxes

THE FLIGHT FROM TANGIER TO MADRID was short and grueling. Every person on the plane looked to be clandestine, shifty, and just plain dirty. I felt as if I stood out so overtly that I must be quite the fool to be aboard with the rest of these operators. I was sure everyone was staring at me and asking themselves (and each other) what is this guy up to? He's gotta be the heat.

I contracted a serious headache as a result of being stuffed on board a stifling over-loaded plane, with people who had a variety of body odors and reeked of cigarettes. When we finally landed, I hit the ground at high speed and went straight to the loo where I rinsed my face with cold water.

I threw open the exit door to the parking lots in hopes of finding a breath of clean air to run through my tainted lungs but was quickly stricken with another round of hacking and coughing.

I put my hands on my knees just to get myself together, when through watery eyes I focused on a pair of black leather boots with a super high shine, not more than a foot in front of me. I knew the man who put those boots on this morning was there patiently waiting for the moment when I would straighten up, so he could address me to determine why I was acting so erratic. To him, my actions stood out and were cause for suspicion.

When I did rise slowly from my crouched position, wiping my eyes with the back of my hands, my vision rested first on an evil looking small black machine gun the big man cradled like a baby. He was for sure, one of the biggest baddest soldiers of the Guardia Civil. He wasn't smiling, he was smirking. His feet were now spread apart, and his head was cocked to one side. He shook his head disdainfully.

"Buenos dias senor." I could only nod. Any effort at talking would most assuredly have led to another coughing breakout.

"Passport por favor" with an outstretched hand. "Ahhh, Morocco. You were in my country for only a few days. What were you doing there?" He was just fucking with me, but I knew it could turn unpleasant with one wrong word.

"Visiting friends in Tangier," I responded, with a look as innocent as I could possibly muster.

"Did you travel south of Tangier to the Rif Mountains?"

"No, I was told by my friends, that I should not go there under any circumstances".

Could I possibly look guiltier? Then quickly,

"What is your friend's name?"

"Ahmed Abboud." I hoped that would work.

"Did you and your friend smoke any hashish while you were there?"

"No, I don't smoke. I was there to go to a concert with him." Oh no, now I'd dug myself deeper, knowing he was going to want to know all about the concert, but he relented. I think he'd gotten bored of messing around with me. His attention had found his next victim. I figured his job was to terrorize any obvious candidate. A real criminal would never have been so nervous.

He flipped my passport closed and smartly, with a click of his boot heels, handed it back to me.

"Have a nice journey Mr. Everett."

He spun away. It took a while for my breathing to return to almost normal. I saw him several more times before I got aboard my flight to New York. I thought he may be watching me. He was nobody's fool.

Once we'd taken off, I slept, oh I slept so well on the long flight to New York. Nothing woke me until I heard a faint announcement.

"We are preparing to land at JFK airport, please put your tray tables up and move your seat backs to their upright position. The weather in New York is clear and fifty-five degrees." The plane pulled into its gateway, and we all filed off and down the accordion shaped tunnel, to disappear into the crowd never to see each other again. I stopped for a moment and had a cup of coffee. I was feeling okay. Next stop New Hampshire.

El Capitan' picked me up at the airport in Concord, and we repaired directly to his home in the woods. An exquisite place built out over a rushing trout stream. We hadn't seen each other in a few months and there was a lot of catching up to be done. He was curious about my scheme. He asked about Finn and Dove. He even thought he'd met Yousef at one point along the way. We talked and enjoyed a perfect martini as I sat at the kitchen bar and watched him prepare a pork roast with rosemary, cloves of garlic, and a variety of mysterious seasonings as the sun slowly set. The aroma was incredible.

After we'd polished off two martinis, we left the roast slowly cooking and walked out into the cool night, along a stone pathway that led to his wine cellar a short stroll through dark woods. He opened the heavy cellar door, found a candle just inside and touched a match to the wick. Warm light reached out and bathed an extraordinary collection.

We decided to sit for a minute by a small round table in the center of the cellar, surrounded by mysterious bottles. El Capitan reached for a bottle he knew well and prepared to open it right there, without further ado. We savored every sip. Conversation was cornered by talk about my adventure.

He was surprised by the depth of my financial plight. I told him how Diana and I had concluded that the best idea was to bring *Whitetail* home with a load of hashish.

"Of course, a grand idea. Exactly what you should do. I only wish I could go along. Time's getting away from me and everyone has heard all my old stories too many times. I need to log in a few more miles and cook up some new ones…I should go with you Pierce." He looked down at the bottle he held in his hand and shook his head, "I swear I should."

He poured the last bit of this nectar, and I told him of my adventure meeting Phillipe', and Yousef and Ahmed, and about the trip to the Rif. We laughed so hard that my vision was blurred by tears. I carried on with the story of how I didn't know what to do to roll a joint using a cigarette, and Phillipe got right in my face, thinking I was an undercover agent. Then, the story of Ahmed's father with his old shotgun, firing at the wild dogs, and his barn full of crummy reefer, sent us rolling on the ground. Our bellies ached, and more tears flowed, at first from our contagious laughter, but then from sweet memories of so many adventures shared. Another quick pour, and a final toast, finished the bottle. *"To then, now, and tomorrow, salute!"*

We decided to finish the evening just as the sun began to brighten the sky. I fell sound asleep and woke up about 10 a.m. with a monstrous headache, properly earned from the extraordinary night before.

El Capitan' was at the table with a cup of black coffee steaming up from behind the morning paper in the early light. There were two shoeboxes sitting at the end of the table.

I knew I was underway.

"I owe you $450,000. Why don't you let me talk you into coming along?"

"Next time," he said, with a big hug. "Good luck old friend, what time is your flight?"

Never, never assume there will be a next time.
Get going now…follow your bliss.

* * *

I borrowed a small suitcase and packed it with El Capitan's investment and checked it on the plane with me, bound for Atlanta.

I landed in Atlanta, and as soon as the wheels had touched down, a feeling of anxiety came over me. My departure from my dear friend had left an unusual melancholy. I needed to start running right now. Time was closing in and there was so much to do. I couldn't see how I was going to get it all done.

Diana was waiting for me at the top of the escalator that brought me up to the terminal. Oh man, was I ever happy to see her. She was always so striking. She loved me, and I loved her. She ran to me and jumped into my arms wrapping her legs around me. We stayed here like this, spinning and hugging as an irritated crowd bustled by. For a quick moment, my anxiety disappeared, and all was right with the world.

"Did El Capitan' get on board with the project?"

"Yes, he sure did. We looked over the plans and the charts for a long time. He was supportive and felt I'd have no problem making it all happen. He even thought he remembered Yousef from years ago. The guy has a good reputation. He was also happy to hear it was Finn who'd be helping me.

I shared with Diana my feelings regarding my trip. El Capitan' seemed a bit melancholy. Not sure why. We never talked about what was bothering him if anything. Probably just me, worrying about nothing as usual.

We went to the carousel to pick up the suitcase…an anxious moment. We both stared at the opening as the luggage popped through, then slid down to the carousel, bringing bags, boxes, and suitcases around. My bag popped through. I reached over and grabbed the heavy leather bag.

I was so happy to be home again. I didn't want to leave. Both cats came running to greet me. Diana and I all rolled around on the floor, laughing, talking, and touching, all at the same time. We lost each other for hours, satiating uncontrollable desires. No small part went untouched, bringing out the animal within, teasing again and again until we attacked each other. Something in both of us that had been left untended for too long came alive and wrestled hard, to the point of passionate pain. Controlled and inflicted with care, we began to devolve into shuddering erotic explosions, evoking screams of pure pleasure.

I opened my eyes, afraid to move. I lay still until I remembered where I was. A midafternoon autumn day was alive and kicking. My inner clock was out of tune. I hurt all over as I tried to untangle myself from the sheets. Was that blood on the pillow? My left leg had gone to sleep and showed no signs of reawakening.

Slowly, holding the edge of the bed, I pulled myself up and tried again. It worked this time. I stumbled into the kitchen where I found Diana, naked, making a salad of fresh tomatoes, basil and mozzarella bathed in olive oil. I poured a touch of olive oil in my palm and began to rub her back. She looked at me and rolled her eyes.

"Whew, I really missed you."

"You tried to kill me!" I said.

"Me?!"

We laughed, our sweat covered bodies squeaked as we kissed and hugged hard. It was late enough in the day for us to enjoy a bottle of Rose' with our meal. We sat naked on the sunbathed porch, shielded from the world by bushy palms.

Every bite was woven with incessant discussion regarding our next moves. We had so much to go over we didn't know where to begin. Before the sun began to take its leave, we'd gone over hours of details and made more plans for the next step. The Rose' put the finishing touches on our day, and soon, we were climbing the steps back to the battlefield, but there was no more fight in us, and sleep was our only quest.

Morning found us putting together a long list. Things I'd need for the trip. I couldn't get the sadness off my mind. I was already missing Diana, but nothing could be changed. Our lives were cast in this crazy plan. The last two days were slammed with preparation.

We shrink wrapped money in $5k packages and hid four in my jacket. Six more were tucked away in my carryon luggage to be used as the first payment for the hashish. This was to take place in the airport in Madrid. I worried that I might run into that same Guardia Civil. That would just be plane bad luck. Surely, he won't be there. Surely.

We prepared a sturdy Samsonite suitcase and packed it with twenty $5k shrink wrapped packages. We reinforced the Samsonite with sheet metal screws installed in a way under the suitcases metal trim, so they were impossible to see. We planned to check that bag all the way to Palma de Mallorca. This money was to be used in increments to fund the process of preparing the boat for the long trip. Thirty thousand would be hidden in *Whitetail*. This money would be left untouched until the time came to pay the fishermen their balance due at the time of pick up.

Dangerous? You bet. But the world in 1991 was much more innocent than it is today…in every way.

Diana took me to the airport on Thursday evening, the 26th of September 1991, bound for Madrid. We gave no audience to negativity, we supported each other in our endeavor, and worked hard not to give any life to sadness, loneliness, fear, apprehension, worry, and a million "what ifs", to include…*what if I never see you again?*

I finally picked up Finn at the airport in Palma de Mallorca on September 30, 1991. Our work was cut out for us – no time to waste. We were underway!

CHAPTER SIXTEEN
The Adventure Begins / We're Sinking

FINN WAS IN THE GALLEY working on a sauerbraten. He had purchased a beef roast in Mallorca which was now marinating in the pressure cooker while we were underway to Ibiza. He started his complicated preparation yesterday when we left Puerto Pollensa, and now, he was planning a grand menu to share with his Dutch friends, Millie and Hans, who lived permanently on Ibiza. They had invited us to join them for a meal; but none of us knew tomorrow was Finn's birthday. They came down to the port in a funky, light blue Citroen sedan with a canvas sunroof.

We locked *Whitetail,* climbed in the back seat and shook our way up a rutted old road where their lovely stone home awaited, overlooking the Mediterranean Sea spread out far below. Night had begun to fall. Their fire burned warm which immediately replaced the chill.

These were pleasant people. They appeared to have an idea about our mission. I'd asked Finn that he not spread the word, but judging from Hans' questions, I was sure Finn had shared more than he should've. Hans knew. He also kept alluding to the idea of him coming along for the adventure. He had no concept.

I explained as diplomatically as I could that there was simply not enough room for three people on the trip, but maybe we could plan another trip soon. The explanation seemed to suffice. I knew from experience that on a trip like this, two is company, and three's a mutiny. I didn't need another person to reckon with in the difficult, precarious world we were about to enter.

What a grand meal. There were turnips, carrots, and onions along with Finn's extraordinary sauerbraten. Millie had pulled a coconut cake together which inspired several hearty rounds of the birthday song sung loud and slightly off key. Champaign corks popped, bouncing off the ceiling and walls, as we washed the sweet cake down with glass after glass of the soft fizzy nectar. Very late in the evening, or perhaps very early in the morning, we rode back down to *Whitetail,* pulling at her lines, patiently awaiting our return.

The next day I called Yousef per our plan, promptly at 11 a.m. Was he prepared for us to launch? "No, not yet." This was a blessing. We needed a day to double check the boat and all her systems. We were so pressed for time in Mallorca while we prepared for the long voyage. *Whitetail* needed to be ultimately ready for the nonstop sail from Ibiza to El Jebha, and onward through the Strait of Gibraltar, out into the North Atlantic Ocean, bound for the Canary Islands and Lanzarote.

I planned to fiberglass the hashish we'd pick up at El Jebha into *Whitetail's* inner hull during that long leg, then we'd pull in at Lanzarote to refuel, and stock up on enough water and food to sustain us on the long twenty- plus day leg until we pulled in at the Caribbean Island of Antigua. At this point, we would have sailed over 4,000 miles. We would be poised to take a break, maybe even a month or so. This was part of my plan, to dovetail our departure from the Caribbean with the hundreds of boats doing the same, all heading north for the summer. They were known as "Snow Birds". We would blend into the crowds and eventually launch for Thunderbolt, on the coast of Georgia, a tough 1,700-mile sail.

The next day, at 11 a.m., I placed my daily call. Fantastic news.

I returned the receiver to its cradle, then turned and stood in front of the phonebooth looking up into the bright white autumn sky, I arched my back and spread my arms wide, squinting into the wispy Mare's Tails blown thin by powerful high winds, in the upper strata. They were, most often, indicators of stormy weather. I gave quiet thanks to the CSO, (Chief Spiritual Officer), for the news. Yousef had given the word for us to begin our adventure. My head spun with excitement. We were to set sail on the 400-mile leg to El Jebha . It was October 15th, 1991. We gave ourselves 70 hours to reach our rendezvous. This was based on an average boat speed of 6 knots. In four days we should arrive and be waiting offshore by 12 a.m.

* * *

We struck out on a south/southwesterly course, that would slowly evolve into a more westerly heading along the way. El Jebha lay waiting on the northern Moroccan coast in the southern part of the Alboran Sea, a small distinct body of water just eastward from opening to the strait of Gibraltar.

Passing by the mystical Old Town of Ibiza as we set sail for El Jebha

A cold hard wind blew a constant 25 knots out of the south and was determined not to be our friend. Ornery, steep, five-foot seas with a short fetch wanted to settle into a habit of bashing us on the nose. If these conditions persisted for the next few days, we were in for a rough ride. We would have little relief until we gradually, changed our heading to a more westerly course. That would make the boat's heading work well with the wind's direction. I would try and bend her that way as soon as we could, but I was wary of Cartagena's naval base there. Big boat traffic, like freighters and military craft, were likely to be more intense in that area, and I wanted to allow a wide berth. Also, as we closed on the north Moroccan coast, we'd have a little shelter in the lee of the mainland. But now, the weather was cold, windy, and rough with everything right on our nose, sadly a sign of things to come.

Finn was putting the finishing touches on a beef stew he'd begun while we were dockside in Ibiza. He was a master at cooking underway. Others would deem the feat impossible, but he never once complained, and our cuisine for the whole trip was first class. Fueling the machine was of utmost importance. I'll never know how he was able to balance hot pans on that wildly swinging stove. At times, he'd be looking down on the pan, then in an instant the stove would swing the other direction and he'd be looking up at the bottom of the hot pan. At first, I was concerned that he might hurt himself, but after watching for a while, it was easy to see that he was fluid talent. He'd done this before.

Every wave we met seemed to have it in for us. We worked to get the dodger (a canvas tent, that when mounted on its frame would give shelter from salt spray and boarding waves) properly tuned in so that it would help in our effort to keep the main cabin entrance, the cockpit and the helmsman as dry as possible.

With every wave that buried her bow, *Whitetail* answered with an erratic lurch. Her progress would stall for a moment from the confrontation. We had to steer manually now, since the auto pilot couldn't maintain the boat's heading in this sea. We worked out a watch schedule that would allow for rest between stints at the helm. Our eyes ached from staring into the dark unknown.

"Captain," Finn asked, "how 'bout a cup of coffee with a splash of brandy?

"Capital idea man, that sounds perfect. Just what the doctor ordered."

"Or maybe we should have a cup of brandy with a splash of coffee." He laughed at himself as he disappeared down the companionway to the main cabin below, but instantly reappeared.

Something was wrong. *Really wrong*!

Wild eyed, Finn screamed over the storm… *"GOOD GOD captain, WE'RE SINKING!!!"*

"What… did you say sinking!?" All other issues evaporated. These were the very last words any sailor wanted to hear, and sadly for many, they were indeed the very last they ever heard. I'm sure the sea floor is strewn with remnants and relics, watched over by the ghosts of these unfortunate sailors.

"Finn, grab the helm and let me see if I can find the leak!"

I grabbed our flashlight from the cockpit locker, and passed Finn coming up the companionway, on his way to control the helm.

"We have plenty of sea room," I yelled over my shoulder. "Let's head to starboard and take up a broad port reach. On this heading "Whitetail's" speed would be slowed, and her course altered, but her movement would be much sedated while we worked to find and fix this problem.

I dropped down into the main cabin. Cold water ran over the top of my sea boots and filled both instantly. I turned on the flashlight and saw things floating around that were normally stowed on shelves and in cabinets. I took off my boots. They had become heavy weights on each foot. I reached down and tasted the water hoping it would be sweet not salty. It was salty. There was a hole somewhere in her deck or hull.

I flipped on all the bilge pump switches. I remembered thinking when I purchased those pumps that I should have gotten the larger size. Now I wished I had a dozen. I worked my way up to the bow and opened the forward cabin door. The water in that cabin was deeper, and when I opened the door it rushed past and around me, throwing me off balance. Next to explore was the anchor locker. It was further forward up in the bow of the boat.

As I reached to open the door, I could hear water splashing from inside the locker. When I cracked the door open and tried to peer in, I was instantly hammered with a fire hydrant spray of cold seawater that tore the door right out of my hand almost knocking me over. "Oww!!" That was cold…real cold.

The flood began to abate somewhat as Finn got her calmed down on her new heading. I shot a beam from the flashlight into the locker, just in time to see another blast of seawater come rushing in as one more wave pummeled her bow. I wasn't sure what was happening and worked my way back through the flooded cabin. My main concern now was to ensure the water level was not above the air intake for engine. So far, the water wasn't getting to her diesel's intake, and it was ready to fire up if needed. Just for safety's sake I didn't want to crank her until the water level in the cabin was substantially lower.

I climbed out of the main cabin into the cockpit and told Finn what I'd discovered. He didn't say a word, jumped up, grabbed the light from me, and crawled up the deck to the bow of the pitching boat. After a long minute, he crawled back and fell into the cockpit.

"I see the problem," he gasped, "A wave has torn her hawse pipe cover off leaving the pipe totally open."

The hawse pipe is a five-inch hole in the forward deck of most boats that allows the anchor chain to pass through the deck into its storage area, the anchor locker.

"I have an idea," Finn said.

Instantly, he dashed down into the galley and out again with something in his hand. He cut his eyes toward me with a mischievous smile and held up and orange between his two fingers. He turned and crawled back up the pitching deck to the bow. A second later he was back in the cockpit with an ear to ear grin.

"Fixed," he said.

"How?"

"I stuffed that orange into the hawse pipe hole. A perfect fit. I'll just have to keep an eye on it."

He disappeared into the boat again. This time he was gone a bit longer.

"Yep, she's fixed."

He came out to a hard hug and a relieved captain. We gave a whoop and danced around the cockpit. We laughed. Finn said he was going to go below and find a big pot, so he could begin helping the pumps by dipping water from inside the cabin and pouring it down the galley sink which drains straight out to the ocean.

He dipped and poured buckets of water into the sink like a mad man. I kept the boat on as smooth a course as possible. After half an hour I looked down into the cabin and the water was about half as deep as it had been. Finn, with his big pan and his three pumps were quickly making a huge difference. The water level was way below the intake for the engine now. Another hour or so and we would have gotten most of the water out of the boat.

Morning came and showed us another day with cold white cloud coverage, and a hard wind out of the south. Finn produced that cup of coffee and made good his promise from hours earlier; there was much more brandy in that cup than coffee.

The boat was an absolute wreck down below and we both needed sleep. I opted to leave her on a course that would allow each of us a few hours to sleep, even though the heading wasn't ideal for getting us closer to our rendezvous.

I told Finn to find a place to lay down. I'd stand watch for three hours and wake him to take my place, so I could get some sleep too. The aft cabin was less affected, so Finn laid down on the berth. He was snoring before I stepped back into the cockpit.

A bit later, I crawled up on the deck to check Finn's orange. There it was in the hawse pipe, plugging the hole up tight. I couldn't think of anything that would work better so I figured we'd just leave it in place.

By 1 p.m. that afternoon, we both had a bit of rest and were feeling better. Finn put on a pot of rice and beans with onion and garlic, and a can of chicken. We then began gathering all the sheets, pillows and clothes that had been soaked with saltwater, wrung them out as much as possible, and hung them on the lifelines on both the port and starboard sides. We stretched the blankets and sheets over the boom. The wind set about drying our world, and we slowly took up our correct heading once again.

We had to be at our rendezvous by midnight tomorrow.

CHAPTER SEVENTEEN
El Jebha / Not Sure What to Do

I CHECKED WITH THE GPS to get our coordinates. The broken hawse pipe cap, and the time we took to regroup after that nightmare, had roughly cost us about five hours. We were going to have to push hard to make our deadline. We'd need to have our engine running to maintain speed and hold our correct heading to make El Jebha by midnight.

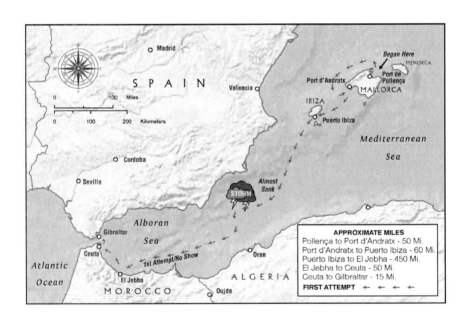

As we entered the Alboran Sea on our third day, we took up a heading that was almost due westerly. The sea state had become tolerable coming from our port side. The auto pilot happily steered the boat, and we were maintaining 7 knots with the help of the engine. We would reach our rendezvous, about 150 miles away, at two hours past midnight. Surely, the experienced crews on shore would understand the difficulties of a sailor's timetable and wait for us. I was pushing *Whitetail* harder than I liked.

The heat from the engine knocked off some of the chill and made it almost cozy down below. The winter sky from the past three days transposed into a brilliant blue, with a proper bright sun to boost our spirits. With a persistent 25 knot wind from the south and the sun's help, we were able to get most of our water-damaged interior dry again. We were excited and ready to take on our load.

Darkness fell. Our efforts paid off, and with help from the current running in our favor from Gibraltar, we weren't far away. The boat was prepped for the rendezvous and it looked as if we would be less than an hour late. Her sails were furled and secured.

All her sheets, which are ropes that control the sails like the main sheet, or jib sheet, they collectively fall under the heading of "running rigging" and are perpetually in danger of going over board and getting tangled in the prop, also known as fouling the prop, if the engine is running. In certain circumstances this can be critical to the point of losing control then losing your boat. Things were moved around down below to accommodate the bales of hashish. The plan was to get it out of the fishing boats and up onto our deck. We'd need to get the bales of hashish down below, safe, and out of sight before dawn when the spotter planes that had buzzed us several times during the past day, could fly by and easily see our load. Next, we'd pay General Lee, and head west for our passage through the Strait of Gibraltar in the early morning light.

The radar showed us to be about a quarter mile offshore. The GPS said we were right at the correct coordinates, and the clock showed us to be about half hour late. We vibrated with the tension. We stared in the dark towards the shore where we aimed our mighty flashlight and pulled the trigger three times.

We waited. No response.

The wind was blowing offshore and had pushed us leeward away from shore. I moved Whitetail back closer, checked our location, matched the shape of the shoreline indicated by the radar with the one indicated by the paper chart. They matched. Our coordinates showed us to be in the correct spot. Three more flashes at the shore yielded no response. Trees and houses lit up when our bright light passed by them. Our eyes ached. The sweet smell of land graced our senses. We spoke in whispers.

Another pass with Whitetail, another three flashes… nothing. No response.

Not sure what to do. Not even sure how I should be feeling. It was around 3 a.m. on October 20, 1991. I was wracking my brain trying to figure out what happened. A dozen scenarios crossed my mind, but none quelled the anger, disappointment, and frustration I was trying not to feel. Finn was quiet. There wasn't much to say. I decided to go to Ceuta, a Spanish enclave on the north Moroccan shore, to contact Yousef to see what happened and what we were to do.

"There must be a logical reason," I told Finn who was at the helm. He headed further offshore, then turned westward where Ceuta lay, just inside the mouth of the Strait of Gibraltar.

A few hours later, we entered the harbor at Ceuta. The sun had come up bright and clear, but as the next few hours came and went, a thick tumbling, ominous cloud cover built up and obscured the blue sky. We were the only boat in that nasty commercial harbor. The only place for us to tie up was against a wall of tall greasy bulwarks, made to accommodate large ocean-going freighters. Finn had been here before, so I asked him about the source of an extraordinary stench.

"Chickens."

"What do you mean…chickens?"

Finn explained that Ceuta is home to several large chicken processing plants, and when the wind is from the south, as it is now, the smell is absolutely intolerable.

"I agree," I said. "It's giving me a headache. Pull up beside the bulwarks. I'm going to climb up there," pointing to the top of the 25' steel wall, "and see if there's a phone."

He nodded, and we tied her to a low pad eye welded to the wall. Finn was adjusting the fenders to try to keep *Whitetail* away from the steel wall. I set about trying to climb the wall, covered with black grease. I found myself thinking of all the squirrels I'd laughed at while they tried to climb my copiously greased birdfeeder pole.

Somehow, I think running on pure anger, I climbed to the top, grabbing hold of the small greasy handles. The whole front of my yellow foul weather jacket was black with grease, as were my bibs. My hands had a permanent coating of creosote.

I looked way back down to *Whitetail* where she bobbed in the ink black oily water.

"Good luck captain," Finn yelled.

I turned and was off with a wave to explore a concrete block structure that looked like a restaurant. The place was closed. A scraggly old dog took up with me, following me everywhere but never coming close. Another half hour left me wondering why this place was so deserted. Nothing made sense. Then I noticed a phone on the side of a pole near the back of another concrete block structure. I picked up the receiver, and surprisingly there was a response. It was about nine in the morning. My hands trembled as I dialed Yousef's number.

"Yezzz?"

"Yousef, this is Pierce," working to stay calm, "What's happening? No one was waiting to meet us last night, so we're in Ceuta now."

"I have been awaiting your call. I am so very sorry. I've never seen a situation like this before. Something terrible has happened, but I can't talk on this phone right now. We will need to change your pickup point. Also, we may need some time before we can reschedule. I need to get more information for us to work with. Call me in two days at 5 p.m., I hope to have some answers by then. I am so very sorry these problems have happened." I wondered what had happened. I needed answers.

"I'll call you in two days Yousef. Come up with some explanation. I want some answers."

I slammed the receiver on its hook and turned to walk out of the phone booth only to discover the receiver was stuck tight to my black creosoted hand. In my anger, I had gripped the receiver unusually tight insuring a firm bond between the phone and my hand. I finally managed to get the receiver back on the hook and pried from my sticky hands. I felt sorry for the next guy to pick it up.

In confusion about this new yellow monster whose entered his world, my new dog friend cocked his head one way, then the other, "What is this, where did it come from, what did it want, and where was it going." He never took his eyes off me. He stood by the tall steel bulwarks and watched me as I slid down the greasy walls. A more precarious journey than the one climbing up. Decidedly more precarious. The detestable aroma of chicken parts clung indelibly to me.

"I don't think I can endure this place another minute."

Finn nodded and said, "I can see why, but most importantly, I can smell why."

"Let's get going right now so we can enter Gibraltar before it gets dark."

Trying not to show any of my simmering anger or anxiety, I told Finn what Yousef had said, and how we are to call him again in two days. He spoke not a word as we fired up our trusty diesel and untied from the wall. Finn silently began to pull the fenders up from the side of the boat. They were totally covered with chicken fat and they tainted everything they touched. The stuff was impossible to get off.

At that moment, the first sign of human life appeared. Three super skinny little kids started hopping around and dancing on a green lawn on the other side of the little turning basin. My old friend the dog even got into their excitement and hopped around, animated more than I'd seen before. The little boy's long boney arms flailed in the air. The dog spun around and around and barked, chasing his tail. The kids pointed wildly at us.

"They want the fenders," Finn said. "They've done this before. I don't think we'll ever be able to clean them up, you wanna let them have 'em?"

"I'll pull near to the shore over there where they're dancing, and you'll have a good chance of throwing those fenders to a better home."

Finn made a big show of the effort, driving the little kids and the dog crazy with excitement. He took each one and swung it round and round in the air, while singing some obscure Greek dancing tune, until he finally gave it a huge heave over the water and into excited waiting arms.

He did this four times.

We made these kid's day. It was nice …they made ours.

Then it started to rain.

Then the rain poured hard. Really hard.

CHAPTER EIGHTEEN
Gibraltar / Dynamite

___

WE ENTERED THE STRAIT OF GIBRALTAR AT CEUTA, heading north, about 4 p.m., bound for Gibraltar, only 15 miles to the north. The current was tearing along from east to west. Giant freighters were coming through. When they confronted one of the monstrous waves, white spray exploded into a mist that blew fifty feet into the air.

Finn and I were exhausted, suffering from lack of sleep and anxiety. The moment we stuck one toe out in the strait, things got crazy. We were asking *Whitetail* to do the impossible by having a heading which put us moving perpendicular to the waves. These waves were about ten feet tall and steep sided with a short fetch between. We would ride up on a wave all the way to the top, where we could see almost all the way across the strait. At that point, we could see huge freighters and tankers with white spray blowing high in the air. Then we'd slide down the other side into the hole at the bottom between the waves. The things would get quiet, and the wind would cease to blow. Finn and I were barely able to hold on, so we jammed ourselves tightly in the cockpit seats with cushions. Oddly, the auto pilot would hold our heading in this situation.

When we were at these low points dozens of small spinner dolphins put on a show for us. They would wait for *Whitetail* to hit the low spot between the waves, then they'd leap out of the side of the wave, sail through the air above our bow across the open space, and dive into the wall of water on the other side. They did this over and over again. We laughed at their antics, welcome moments of distraction.

* * *

October 21, 1991 was here, and the days were shorter. Darkness was coming as we approached the entrance to the harbor at Gibraltar.

Our crazy sail from Ceuta came to an abrupt end as we entered the calm waters of the harbor between Algeciras and Gibraltar. The harbor was mysteriously quiet without our dolphins and the radical movement of the boat that we'd experienced for the past three hours. We followed the navigation lights and worked our way starboard, the direction of the marina. I was up on the bow trying to read the lighted buoys that would guide us in.

Abruptly, a distant roar in the dark began to get louder. I could tell it was coming towards us, but there were no nav lights to be seen. The roar was even closer now, uncomfortably close. I strained my eyes in hopes of seeing lights that would identify what this was. In an instant, it was right in front of us about fifteen feet away running wide open with no lights. I don't think there was 12 feet between us. It was only a few feet away when it passed us, close enough for me to feel the spray from the wake that rolled *Whitetail* back and forth, making her main halyard clang against the aluminum mast. A halyard is a line made of rope, wire, or a combination of the two which raises and lowers the sails. Halyards are notorious in quiet anchorages for waking neighbors with their torturous clanging against the mast. Many a midnight brawl has begun because of these nuisances. A practiced sailor will tie the halyard away from the mast, so it can't' clang.

"What the hell was that?" I yelled back to Finn who was at the helm.

"Cigarette runners!"

"Cigarettes!?"

Finn explained that there is a booming cigarette smuggling business from Algeciras, a Spanish city, to the British city of Gibraltar which is conveniently just across the bay. The smuggler's small fast speedboats are painted flat black, not wanting to be seen. They run hard and fast in the night, with no nav lights. A lucrative business has been established. The promise of big money tempts kids to drop out of school and run cigarettes. It was a common concern in Gibraltar, and the authorities were working to stop the flow.

We moved slowly toward the marina in Gibraltar, then located the dock master's office, and pulled into a vacant slip. Nine p.m. came and we were worn out. When we cut the motor off, the quietness was tangible. We tied up, and without another word, waved to each other, climbed down the companionway ladders, and fell into our berths, wet, salty and asleep before we were under the covers.

* * *

The dawn came, grey and blustery, accompanied by a pounding rain that washed the salt off the decks. I was awakened by the roar of the rain on the cabin top. I stuck my head out of the aft companionway to be greeted by a tremendous explosion. What!! Then another. And another! Everything shook with these sudden detonations. I remembered Ahmed's dad with his shotgun. Out of the side of my foul weather hood I caught a glimpse of a fellow walking along the dock in the early morning rain. He noticed my perplexity.

"Dynamite," he yelled over at me. His accent was thick; I'm not sure from where.

"Why dynamite?" I asked.

Slightly put out, he carried on, "They detonate sticks of dynamite at the end of the runways at the airport." He pointed ambiguously over his shoulder, roughly where the explosions originated. He backed up under the overhang of a short roof at the end of the dock where he was able to partially hide from the downpour. "On takeoff the jet's engines have been getting clogged with seagulls that gather in huge flocks at the end of the runway. Over the years there have been numerous crashes from these seagulls clogging their engines"

"You'd think someone would come up with a better remedy," I offered.

"Like what?" he shrugged; arms out by his side, palms up, catching little pools of rain.

He looked as if he was patiently expecting my brilliant idea while he stood out in the deluge. I'm sure he was soaked, tired of this worn subject, and just wanted to say "goodbye" to this Yankee newcomer. He shook the pools from his hands then turned to go and disappeared into the deluge. "See you later!" was lost in the roar from the metal roof in the downpour.

In the distance, I could see the monstrous Rock of Gibraltar through the pouring rain. When the rain let up, I wanted to go see the Monos monkeys high up on the rock. The monkeys had been introduced by the Moors, who kept them as pets when they ruled the Iberian Peninsula, between 711 and 1492. Its estimated, because of British protection, there are more than 300 of the creatures living there.

* * *

At 9 the next morning, Finn was up and moving around in the galley. The first aroma of coffee drifted to my cabin at the stern of the boat.

"Halloooo Mr. Captain," he called, "are you up yet?"

"Where'd you hide all that hashish we took on board the other night?"

He laughed at his joke and handed me a cup. Sometimes it'd be impossible to improve on a cup of coffee. Our cabin was warm and dry as the rain continued its merciless onslaught on the deck above.

A knock on the cabin top called us to the companionway.

"Good morning gentlemen."

I invited the crisply uniformed British customs agent to join us inside, out of the pouring rain. I thought that he may have overheard our "not so funny" joke. I couldn't tell, certainly his countenance lent no clue. But, in any event, the sad truth was, we honestly had nothing to hide. An ironic twist.

"Welcome to Gibraltar," he said with a crisp Brit accent and a disarming smile. He wore a dark blue uniform with a white shirt and a black necktie.

His long yellow slicker, glistened in the rain, completing the package. He looked briefly around the boat. Water pooled where he stood on the wooden cabin sole(floor).

"Lovely interior joinery."

"Thanks, she's a pretty boat. How 'bout a cup of coffee?"

"I shouldn't, I've had my quota for the morning. When you can, please come visit me in my office, to fill out some paperwork. Bring your passports, and the boat's papers.

He turned to climb up the companionway ladder.

Pouring rain swirled around him, "It's hard to stay dry, isn't it?"

He disappeared into the deluge, then turned, "When you come, bring any firearms you're carrying. They'll be locked in our safe here in my office. We don't need any more guns floating around loose in Gibraltar. There are enough already. You'll retrieve them on your departure."

* * *

My first stop after coffee and discussion with Finn regarding our next move, was at the public bath on the end of the dock, where I took a long hot shower. I stood there with hot water running on my neck, vowing not to stop until the hot water ran out.

I needed to speak with Yousef as quickly as possible. We needed to know what had happened off El Jebha the other night, and what our next step was to be. It was still early and pouring rain, pouring endless buckets of rain.

I hustled out of the shower, got dressed and headed down the pier back to the boat.

Back on *Whitetail* Finn had dozed off in the forward cabin. He heard me climbing down the companionway and sat up rubbing his eyes.

"Sup cap?"

I now lived in my foul weather gear. Jacket and bibs. I wore them everywhere I went. A historic low-pressure front had stalled just off the

Portuguese coast, and it looked to be settled in for a while. Everything was wet and cold. Out in the Atlantic the storm was formidable. The same wind was still blowing 30+ knots out of the north. Choppy seas were building. Bottom line…we weren't going anywhere.

"I'm going to find a phone booth and try to call Yousef."

I hoped that he might be anticipating a call from me. The prescribed time for our calls in the past had been 11 a.m. There was a convenient phone booth out in the rain, where the dock met the road to town. There was a small roof over the phone that helped deflect part of the persistent deluge. It was 11 a.m. and I crunched into the phone booth as far as I could, to try and get out of the storm. I dialed Yousef's number and took a deep breath.

"Yezzz?"

"Yousef, this is Pierce."

"Oh my God I've been worried about you! Why haven't you called?"

Wait just a blasted minute here, man, I thought. I'm the one who should be upset.

But Yousef carried on without a pause. I had never heard him upset, certainly not this upset. He was talking a mile a minute.

"Insane things are happening here. Things that I've never seen before. The King has suddenly started to come down on the hash trade in the Rif. He's increased police presence on the routes to and from Ketama. He's incarcerating men who in the past had already earned immunity."

The Commander crossed my mind.

"El Jebha is being effected along with El Hoceima, and Asilah over on the west coast," Yousef went on. "I heard that there are Spanish planes buzzing the coast and following the routes of some of the boats. I thought that you might have been picked up in all the confusion. I have been very worried."

Thoughts of the plane that had buzzed us just south of Ibiza, and then followed us for a while, came to mind. He came back the next morning for another look. Had we taken the load off El Jebha that night, we'd be sitting low in the water and he may have been curious enough to be more aggressive. The next step could have been a Spanish boarding party. I laughed at myself… man, that was great, I'm so happy they didn't load us. What a turn in perspective. Who knows?

Meanwhile, Yousef carried on explaining what he thought had happened and why.

"We think that European pressure on Morocco to cut our hash production and distribution has increased substantially. I hear it has something to do with pressure from this new European Union that is forming. The situation began back in the mid 50's." He continued in an animated state, "The people of the Rif were responsible for substantial assistance to the King of Morocco in our successful battle for independence from the French. In gratitude, the King allowed the people of the Rif to grow marijuana which would be pressed into hashish and sold as a money crop since their terrain was ultimately unkind for cultivating conventional crops. This arrangement worked well for decades, but now, the Italian mafia and the Columbian cartels have found value in these old safe hash routes into Europe. They've begun using them for moving hard, deadly drugs like cocaine through Morocco into Europe. These new drugs are now falling into the hands of the kids of the Casablanca and Rabat elite."

As I listened, I thought this is beginning to sound like a perfect storm. Not good.

"Rumor has it that one of the King's daughters had a close friend who almost overdosed on cocaine at a party. She barely made it to a hospital in time to save her life. King Hassan II was infuriated that the old system was accelerating out of control, and his trust being misused. This, coupled with pressure from the new European Union, provoked the King to retaliate by beginning his personal War on Drugs."

Yousef was obviously deeply concerned.

"Yousef, what is the likelihood of getting the hash I selected up in the Rif a month ago moved to the coast for pickup?"

"Pierce, I would like to say otherwise, but you must know, in truth this will not happen."

"Are you able to get 600 kilos of hashish to the coast at all, and if so, what quality could I expect?"

"There may be a chance that we can get part of a larger load that's been waiting for pickup but hasn't been collected yet. I'll look into that this afternoon. The only possible place for the pickup now is Asilah on the west coast."

"I will call you tomorrow at eleven to see what progress you've made."

"Okay, and Pierce, listen to me, don't talk to anyone about this at all, and be extremely careful. There are people in Gibraltar and Algeciras that are dangerous, and work for the government. Don't make friends with anyone at all and don't talk about hashish with anyone. We need to get you out of there as quickly as possible. I've heard Phillipe has been caught and is in jail in Marbella. I'm worried about Peli and Julietta. It's a dangerous time, like never before. All the roads from the Rif to both coasts are now being patrolled by unusually aggressive motorcycle police on their Moto Guzzies, and they're playing now by a different set of rules. Payoffs are no longer get-out-of-jail cards...call me tomorrow."

✳ ✳ ✳

Uncanny timing. I was trying to get my little load on board and get the Hell out of there. All my efforts to get a superior product on board had been wasted, and I would certainly never see my selection again. Our first effort at el Jebha had failed.

I shuddered to think of being caught by the Moroccan or Spanish police. I dreaded the thought of the inside of a Ceutan Jail! Yousef seemed duly concerned and was trying to get more information and a feel for what was happening. I'm certain he wanted to get me loaded and out of there.

Was the possibility still attainable? I was going to find out. I had to.

CHAPTER NINETEEN
Asilah / The Good News

Ohhh, my head began to hurt.

As the conversation with Yousef intensified, I'd found myself pushing my body tightly into the phone booth and holding the receiver too tightly against my ear.

I hated to give Finn the news. I stepped out into the incessant downpour and realized that I was hungry, real hungry. It was about noon. I couldn't remember the last meal I'd had. No doubt freeze dried or canned.

I stepped from the dock over to *Whitetail*. She gently rocked with my weight. I slid the hatch open. Finn appeared from nowhere into the galley, rag in hand, broad smile on his face. He backed away, arms spread wide, as he proudly looked around the beautifully cleaned and dried cabin. She looked like a new boat. I was properly surprised, pleased, and amazed.

"Incredible. I can't believe my eyes. Thanks. Get your gear on hombre. Let's go substantially diminish that restaurant's food supply while we watch the rain trying to sink us."

He popped out of the companionway pulling on his jacket, lighting the way with that broad smile.

"We've got to touch base with the customs officer," I said, "or he'll begin to wonder."

We hurried down to the end of the dock again, and I knocked, then opened the heavy door to the customs office. The same officer who'd come by the boat this morning looked up from his desk.

"We're starving. Would you mind if we stop back by with papers and passports in about an hour?"

"No problem," he assured us. "Enjoy your meal. The pork tenderloin is particularly good."

"Thanks, we'll be back after we get refueled."

I backed out gently pulling the door closed.

"What'd Yousef say?" Finn whispered as soon as we were alone. "I'll bet I can tell **you** what he said."

"I doubt it Finn. Believe me, you've never heard anything like this before. Let's get stabilized with a meal. The situation is really complicated, and I need your opinion regarding our next step."

We left our soaked gear at the doorway, and found a table there with the lunch crowd, in the busy café, overlooking the marina. The very attractive waitress brought two small warm dry towels when she came to the table. I noticed we were the only two customers in there with warm towels.

"What'll ya have, sailors?" she asked, with an accent from somewhere north of here, maybe Irish.

"A fella on the dock recommended that we try your pork tenderloin,"

"I know who that was. Comes in 'ere most every day. A good fella."

"And for you sir, what'll it be?"

"I'll have the same, sweetheart," delivered with Finn's most meaningful smile.

The pork roast was the best. We put away two orders each. When the chef heard how long we'd been without a proper meal, he came out of the kitchen to have a look at us. He embellished our plates with a little of everything in his kitchen. As my hunger abated, I began to gain control of my runaway mind.

We ordered another beer to wash down a piece of the best bread pudding I have ever had. Must've been about two in the afternoon.

Then, over a double espresso, in the now nearly empty restaurant, I quietly recalled Yousef's story to Finn. He shook his head and succinctly summarized the situation.

"You just can't trust these people,"

But trust wasn't our issue now. It was too late for that. The question now was what were we to do? The only acceptable option from my point of view was to make another pass at the pickup by sailing south along the west coast to the village of Asilah. There we'd pick up whatever Yousef could get for us. Quality of the product was going to be a crap shoot. But something is better than nothing…isn't it?

We donned our foul weather gear. It was about two in the afternoon when we headed back out to the customs office, which was located at the end of the pier. I now dealt with a constant tremble of paranoia, and every person I met was surely out to get me. The customs officer was very pleasant. I thanked him for the tip on our meal, and for being patient with us about checking in.

He looked out his window. "Well gents, with this wetha I'm not exactly overwhelmed with long lines of boats to deal with. You can't see anything through all this rain."

I wondered how I could broach the King of Morocco's "War on Drugs." I was looking for confirmation on Yousef's story. I used the cigarette smugglers for my entre.

"So, these cigarette smugglers almost ran us down in the early evening last night. I understand they make rather good money for their efforts?"

"Oh yeah, they make enough to drop out of school. Illegal tobacco and cigarettes are much more expensive in Spain than they are in Gibraltar. Almost twice the price per carton. It's a real problem with Algeciras being just across the bay."

"I hear there's always been a historic flow of drugs from Morocco across the strait into Spain, France and Italy."

"Yep, it's become a way of life. Most of the smaller operations involving the fishermen are just overlooked. It's the big boats and payoffs that the authorities are gunning for now. This new European Union is beginning to crack down in all areas. There's a new sheriff in town. I heard the police have detected over 500 offenders carrying illegal tobacco from Gibraltar to Algeciras. There's fear of a growing involvement with organized crime. There's also been a noticeable increase in smuggling cocaine and other dangerous drugs. The authorities are expressly serious about stopping this."

"I hear the King of Morocco has always been supportive of Moroccans producing hashish."

"Yes, I've heard that too. It's just a way of "being", that is for the most part harmless. It keeps a big portion of the country's younger population off the streets."

"How long do you expect this might carry on? Do you think these changes being made right now will last, or do you think they will lighten up?"

"I've been with British customs for 12 years now. All this hoopla is a function of pressure from that new European Union. As it stands, small time smugglers are caught, and tried. Most spend a little time in jail. But as the loads grow larger and harder drugs begin coming across the strait, combined with our most serious problems, smuggled guns and stowaway refugees, the pressure is on and surveillance is increasing. Arrests and punishment will undoubtedly be on the rise. More work for me. Our offices here are usually the first to know of any big changes. We've always looked for smugglers. And there's plenty sitting around in jail cells to prove it. They say this cocaine is very bad. I had an old friend who seems to have done a bang-up job of ruining his life. He's gotten all caught up on cocaine. That stuff scares me."

Suddenly he leaned forward and glared at me, "You're not a smuggler, are you?!"

He leaned back in his chair, pointing at me, laughing at his joke.

I nervously joined in. I laughed with him.

Finn broke the thin air and appeared, dripping, with a black plastic bag carrying our 12-gauge Mossberg shotgun, our stainless 38 Smith and Wesson, and a file with all our information and the boat's papers. I began filling out paperwork. The agent took the two firearms and locked them in the office safe. "Nice shotgun." He presented us with a receipt, so we could collect our guns on departure. He kicked back in his desk chair, and with his feet comfortably on his desk, he casually looked over our passports.

"German and American, where are you two going?"

"I've kept my boat here in Mallorca for years, and just recently decided to sell her. Finn, my friend here, has offered to help me take her home."

"Where's home?"

"Atlanta, Georgia."

"Never been there."

"Don't know why you'd ever go there unless it was home. If you go to the US, go to the coasts of Florida."

"That's what I hear. See you gentlemen in the morning. The wife will come looking for me soon if I don't get home for that cup of tea. Enjoy your evening. Maybe it won't be raining in the morning."

* * *

The next morning, I was waiting at the phone booth when my watch touched 11 a.m.

I played with the sound of the of the torrents hammering the back of my jacket. If I stretched my back tight in my jacket, the rain made a higher note. If I relaxed, it sounded a lower refrain. I was working on an oblique version of "Jingle Bells" when Yousef picked up.

"Alooo", he said.

"Good morning Yousef, please tell me some good news."

"I do have some news for you. There is a large load already in Asilah, on the west coast of Morocco, about 30 miles south of the strait. It is waiting there for a freighter to come pick it up. However, because of the circumstances, everything is stalled now, and it would be suicidal to try and transfer this large load. The men there, tell me that you can have 600 kilos of that load if you'd like, and it will be ready for you to pick it up tomorrow at midnight. It will be safe working with small boats and a smaller load. Your coordinates for the rendezvous are Latitude: 35° 27' 54.79" N / Longitude: -6° 02' 2.94" W.

"Fantastic!"

My whole outlook on life shifted gears. I felt lightheaded when I turned around, taking a blast of rain in my face. I was thankful to the COG, (Chairman of the Gods). I did my best moon walk back to the boat in the pouring rain. I'm sure anyone who saw me figured I'd finally been driven mad by the incessant storm.

I stood by *Whitetail* and noticed a new wind direction was now pressing her against the dock. The wind had veered around to the northwest; the first change in over a week. The change would help to make the cranky seas in the Portuguese Current lay down a bit, making our heading to the south-southwest easier to maintain.

I hopped aboard and shared this great news with Finn. I was surprised when he didn't reflect my enthusiasm.

During these days, while we waited for the weather to lift, he'd been working on plans for his house addition in Greece, and missing Monique badly. Understanding that, he still didn't have enough money to complete his house project unless we could keep our plan alive through all phases to completion. The proverbial, "rock and a hard place."

"I can't do this without you, Finn," I pleaded, "and we won't make one thin nickel unless we ratchet up, and you give me everything you've got with your usual enthusiasm."

A quiet hour later, true to form, Finn slowly pulled himself together, and we set about getting *Whitetail* ready to go to sea again. I heard him whistle the theme from "The Good the Bad and the Ugly", and after a short break, the "Bridge Over the River Kwai" complete with a rhythm accompaniment performed with what sounded like a spoon and a stainless mixing bowl. He choreographed his moves while he prepared stews and soups. He disappeared without a word to return shortly with whiskey, wine, beer, canned and dried goods. Coca Cola was in the mix. There's no substitute for that fizzy black liquid sugar when you're feeling a little tainted by the motion of the ocean.

There was also fresh fruit, VHT milk, bottled water, one lonely chicken, and a variety of ingredients to keep us alive while we headed for Asilah to make our pickup. From there we'd head to Lanzarote, another island in the Canary chain, lying about a seven-day sail westward with luck.

There, we'd prepare for the long Atlantic crossing to Antigua.

We spent the rest of the day, preparing the boat. Even though it was still raining, the storm had diminished, and excitement began to take hold as we topped off the diesel tanks and secured the eight jerry cans to the lifeline stanchions. Five were for water, and three were for fuel. I was planning to set sail from Gibraltar for Asilah at 4 p.m. I wanted to strike out early enough to clear the strait into the Atlantic while it was still daylight, so we could see what we were up against. I needed to get a feel for the seas and wind and get past some of the freighter traffic before night fell and our world turned black.

It was 3 p.m., Thursday, the 24th of October 1991. We sat down below at the main cabin table and

savored an early dinner. No one could cook like Finn on a sailboat. We complimented every bite of a roasted chicken with carrots, onions, and potatoes. Our attitudes were up and ready.

I wondered about the quality of the hashish I was about to load on board. I desperately needed a superior product to make this all work. But now, I found myself in a position where I had no idea what quality hashish I was about to load.

"Are you ready?"

I checked in with the friendly port captain regarding our departure.

He seemed sad as he slowly looked up from the top of his desk where his arms lay on a stack of random white papers. The faint wisp of a smile caressed his face, "Yep, just as soon as that wind veered, I knew you guys would be the first to leave. I don't blame ya. Rainy days here in Gibraltar can get to the bottom of the best of us."

I signed the paperwork and retrieved our guns. With an "adios y bon vida," I backed out of that heavy door leaving a small piece of me behind and went to the boat to stash our firearms and have another look around *Whitetail*. Next, we threw off the dock lines, pushed away from the dock, and slowly motored out into the turmoil that persisted in the Strait of Gibraltar. I patted her binnacle and told her I loved her.

"Hang in there dear friend, I'm going to fix you up like a new boat when this is all over."

She kicked her stern up and over an errant wave, as if to say, "I'm all yours Cap let's do this!"

* * *

The tide was in our favor, running westerly with our course, and the freighter and tanker traffic wasn't too bad. We picked up on four off our starboard bow, entering the strait from the west. Their bows collided with the seas and shot huge spumes of white spray high into the air. Off our port bow there was a fishing boat moving westward, out into the Atlantic with us. Freighters were our concern now, but as we moved further south, big fishing boats could become an issue.

The problem was that these huge boats often couldn't pick us up on their radars. A small sailboat is easily overlooked by these scanners mounted high up on the bridge. We set the perimeter alarm on our radar to four miles to cover us in these tight quarters, until we cleared the strait and entered the Portuguese Current. At that point, we'd change to a slightly more southerly course, where we'd pick up speed and have a bigger body of water to monitor. We'd move our perimeter out to twelve miles once we determined it was safe.

This was wonderful sailing. The wind was blowing at about 25 knots out of the west and pushing us on a fast-broad reach. We were flying with help from a hefty current pushing from our stern.

A light misty rain continued as the first sun we'd seen in days, began to drop lower in the sky. Bright red colors without names painted the seas around us. The sun peeped out from under the lowest clouds for a brief cameo appearance. These clouds drifted along leaving colored trails low along the western horizon. The sky was red tonight, a delight. The thinning clouds promised clear weather was on its way. George Winston contributed the perfect musical score.

As it got darker, it got cooler, and we bundled up in blankets to stay warm.

"Mr. Finn let's have a cup of coffee and a proper celebratory shot of cognac."

"Whaddaya say?"Ahhh, sailing"...if you know what I mean.

We were right with the world. Conversation ran high and laughing was easy. We wondered what all those people were doing in their little houses along the coast. As we sailed by, their flickering lights reached out to stir our imaginations. They left the two of us with a lonely feeling as we passed by in the darkness of the open sea.

We were early for a change, so I steered slightly to starboard off our course to slow our pace. A big fishing boat that had been following along beside us, began to come closer and closer.

"Finn, what's he up to?"

I thought for a minute that they may have our load on board, but we were nowhere near our rendezvous coordinates. I worried that he may be the police but canned that anxiety since we were regretfully still without any hashish on board. The trawler steered closer and closer to the point that he was only about thirty feet off our port side. He slowed to keep time with our speed. I stayed our course. He gradually came so close we could see four men, silhouetted by the fleeting sunset. They all waved their arms, frantically pointing at their bow.

What in the world could they want?

They shined a bright light on a guy high up above us on their bow, with something in his hand. He swung the gift around and around over his head with one hand while the other pointed comically at the object, then back at us.

"They're going to throw something," Finn said. "I'm going to motion for them to let it go."

Finn went up to our bow and braced himself against the bow pulpit to get a better look at our new friend, now only twenty feet from our side. I could smell his diesel and feel his impact on the water between us. Suddenly, the fellow on their bow let go of the long thin object he had been swinging over his head. It sailed through the air, spinning, end over end. Finn stepped back and balanced on our forward deck, just in time for the gift to come out of the dark and hit him in the chest. He fell to the deck, square on top of the dark green moray eel who must have been forty inches long, heavy, and thank goodness dead.

A resounding cheer came from the fishing boat, followed with a hearty round of applause.

Finn managed to hold the Morey Eel up high for them to see. Another round of applause and cheers erupted. I grabbed our horn, always at ready under the dodger, and sent them a couple of long blasts in thanks. The smell of their powerful diesels wafted back over us as they pushed their throttle, and pulled away, in the darkness.

Not knowing exactly what to do with our new companion, Finn dropped below, wrapped the eel in a rag, and put it in the bottom of our icebox. We figured we'd try to cook up an eel dinner one night. There was actually a recipe in our "Fishes of the Atlantic" book.

* * *

A few hours later we were converging on a handful of lights that glowed on the horizon. The halo surrounding Asilah, came into view off our port bow, about half an hour away. Our friends on the fishing boat had inadvertently taken us further offshore than I had wanted. I turned her slightly to port and fit in smoothly where I'd been before their visit. I wanted to take on the load with our heading facing northward, nose into the wind and current to give us more control, so I sailed past Asilah on our port side, then after about half an hour, I spun her bow heading into the waves and wind.

Our ride instantly became tumultuous. As we approached the coordinates for our rendezvous, *Whitetail* starting bucking like a bronco dodging a rattlesnake. We prepped to drop our sails and start the diesel. Finn hopped up on deck to start bringing in the sails. The diesel rumbled to life. We furled our foresail and reefed the main on the boom. *Whitetail* liked that. She was less affected, and more manageable with this arrangement.

Motoring gave us more control. When I turned to go downwind everything became comparatively calm, but when I turned her northward to regain our coordinates for the rendezvous, her movement changed dramatically again.

It was ten 'til midnight. Time to try and connect with our load. We fired up our spotlight and fired off three healthy blasts into the night.

I called on the VHF, "Yankee to Rebel, Yankee to Rebel, come in Rebel."

I felt we might be getting too near the shoreline again. Finn held her best he could while I hopped down to the navigation table to compare our location on the radar, with our GPS coordinates and the chart. We were in the area, but we'd moved slightly away from the shore. We steered her back toward the shoreline.

The time now was 10 after midnight. We hadn't seen a response to our flashes, so we fired three more.

"Can you see anything at all?" I yelled at Finn.

"Nothing."

We were so close to the shoreline I could smell the little fishing town. Oil heaters and firewood. As quickly as we tacked, we fired three more bright flashes toward the coast.

"Yankee to Rebel, Yankee to Rebel, come back Rebel."

Still nothing.

The elation that had built since our departure from Gibraltar began to plummet. We continued motoring up and down the coast in front of Asilah for the next two hours. Repeatedly, we'd pound into the wind and waves motoring northward, and then we'd quietly drift southward past Asilah with our light flashing and radio trying to make contact. I began to get paranoid that we'd be noticed by the wrong people if we kept this up.

The unavoidable hard truth was, we weren't going to be loaded this night. Finn did his very best to feel better than me. "I'm just going to say this one time," he began. I knew what he was going to say. "You just can't trust these people."

He was right. Why couldn't they just respond on the radio? Something like, "come back tomorrow night," or "wait 'til dawn," or "we can't come out with the seas running so high," or, or…dammit, anything!

Going back to Gibraltar, headed north, would be a tough sail against wind and seas, and I felt we'd garner unwanted attention if we returned there so shortly after our departure.

Discouraged, I felt a need to be alone, to regroup, to make a new plan. I sounded like a fool to myself. Hah…make a new plan, that's funny. I needed to meet with Yousef personally as soon as possible. I needed to know what the situation was. Was it even possible at all? I was totally distressed.

I decided we would go to Puerto de Mogan on the south coast of Gran Canaria, and give the confusion in Tangier, and in my mind, some time to reset. So, we unfurled our sails and in 25 knots of wind from the north, we headed *Whitetail*, southwestward on a comfortable sea. Asilah, and some small part of me was left behind.

The autopilot held our course perfectly. Finn and I didn't speak at all. I knew his feelings although I didn't know my own. I found three extra strength Excedrin then sat out on the bow, while a family of dolphins kept me company rolling over on their sides looking up at me see if I was okay. Tears blended with the soft salt spray. The dawn came, slowly, gray. The rain had finally let up sometime in the night. Thick morning clouds scudded overhead and reflected dark green in this big Ocean.

I needed *all* the King's horses and *all* the King's men, before it was too late.

Diana, where are you this miserable morning?

Finn fell sound asleep on the cabin settee. He didn't move.

CHAPTER TWENTY
The Canaries / Puerto de Mogan

FINN BEGAN TO BANG PANS around in the galley. I hoped he was thinking beef stew. I was ravenous. I'd fallen asleep, or rather, passed out on the bow while *Whitetail* made her way towards the Canary Islands. I lay there a minute more, watching the wind in the foresail over my head, as it pulled us along. I checked my mind, my body, and my spirit, for signs of permanent damage.

The time was 1:00 in the afternoon on November 1st, 1991. A cold autumn afternoon. The cloud cover was changing. It looked as if we may see the sun soon. We hadn't seen a bright sunny day since we left Mallorca over 12 days ago. In a few words, things were bad. I guess they could get worse. Oh yeah, wait a minute, that's right, I remember now, they did get worse, a whole lot worse.

I held onto the lifelines and walked carefully aft across the undulating cabin top then dropped into the cockpit and looked down into the galley below.

"Good day captain," Finn said, turning towards me. "From the looks of you, a bowl of stew is in order."

I nodded, swallowed for the first time in hours, and shrugged my shoulders

"I'm honestly not sure what we should do now."

"Well let me tell you Cap, right now, you and I are going to have a wonderful sail to the Canary Islands. A sail most people just dream about. And dammit, we're going to enjoy this sail, we've earned it. We will answer all these questions in your mind and in mine. I don't think the answers are going to be all that difficult to find. And what have we learned here? You just can't..." he stopped, grinned, and dramatically pointed at me, I took it, "Trust these people!"

We laughed, and I began to feel better. Finn pushed a bottle of Rioja Cab at me with the opener. In the next 15 minutes, I had a bowl of the very best beef stew on the earth, a bottle of earthy wine, and a ray of sunlight lit up our cockpit and our attitudes. In a matter of minutes my whole world changed again. Finn put on a Grateful Dead cassette, and we sang along with all the tunes we knew so well. We opened another bottle and we began to sound pretty good. *Whitetail* was wondering what had come over her crew, but I know she was happy too. Things really can always be worse.

Recharged after our wonderful meal we rushed around getting all the wet things hung out to dry. The sun had a great effect on our outlook. At this rate, we would pull in at Puerto Mogan in about 6 days. I figured we'd come in from the north, between Gran Canaria and Tenerife, another island in the Canaries, and head slightly back eastward to tuck into this new port on the south-western side of Gran Canaria. We should arrive there on Friday the 8th of November 1991.

For the next several days, the weather was our friend. A steady blow of about 25 knots kept up its force and direction from the north. We flew along and recuperated from our disappointments to the point that we could calculate our next steps.

On the morning of our sixth day we could see the tall mountains of the Canary Islands. We were booking it. There's nothing like a landfall. We were about four hours from our destination. *Whitetail* was beautiful and sparkled in the sunlight, reflecting hours of elbow grease, scrubbing and polishing her every part. We were quite attached to her.

Mid-day the wind gods threw us a curve and began to blow like a banshee. Thank goodness the wind maintained the same direction. I imagine 40 mph was a conservative estimate before we entered the channel between the two islands. Hurriedly, we shortened sail. The two foresails were partially furled, and we doused the mainsail completely, and tied it securely to the boom where it wouldn't unravel as the wind continued to pick up steam.

The mountains on each of the two islands made a huge wind funnel between them that increased the wind's speed to gusts as much as sixty mph. A constant forty-five knots from our stern sent *Whitetail* faster than she'd ever gone before. The winds were so strong they blew the waves flat, so the sea state was not too rough. The log (boat speedometer) hit ten knots and stayed there. We felt like we were going a hundred miles an hour.

Suddenly, an explosion erupted at the bow of the boat, followed by repeated pops like rifle fire. One of the whisker poles that held the starboard foresail out to catch the wind, had rebelled at this new, never before tested, pressure from the wind, and broke loose from its fitting on the mast. Like one of Robin Hood's arrows, it launched, up and up, out of sight, and finally plummeted into the sea 300 feet off our stern.

I instinctively started to turn us around to retrieve the expensive pole.

Finn screamed at the top of his lungs. "No, no, no, forget that pole!!" I couldn't hear him very well, but I knew what he was saying, and I knew he was right. I waved a forefinger touched to my thumb, so he could see I understood. Had I been able to turn her around, our lives would have been in jeopardy, as would the life of our boat. The pressures and dangers of a wild wind are unbelievable and unforgiving.

Finn set about trying to corral the loose starboard sheet, which was cracking like Lash Larue's bullwhip, only a million times deadlier. He jumped into action and moved carefully to the bow as soon as he assessed the problem. If he'd been tapped by the powerful snapping line, it could easily have been the end of Finn. He managed to slip past the angry sheet which was still attached to the clew of the wildly flailing sail. It was recoiling and popping like a mad Cobra. He carefully moved out onto the bow pulpit where he was able to wedge himself in between the stainless tubing. He then began turning the sail's furling drum by hand, inch by inch, reeling in the loose line and the errant sail. I tried to help him tame the monster by putting light pressure on the sheet wrapped around the winch to take up any slack in the line, at the same time being careful not to counter Finn's efforts. The furling line was so taught, like a steel rod, and difficult to budge. Finn would manage with both hands to turn the drum as little as half an inch. While I pulled in the line at the same time using the handle at the winch to take in any incremental progress we were able to gather as a team.

We still had use of the port sail, a small, heavy working jib, held out by its own whisker pole. This sail was pulling hard and helped to give us steerage. With this crazy wind, the mast itself acted like a sail and added to the confusion of steering. I hung on tight, steering *Whitetail* best I could, going way faster than I felt we should, staring at that high-field lever on the fore deck, praying that she'd hold tight under this extraordinary pressure. After several anxious minutes Finn began to make headway, turning the furling drum by hand, an inch at a time. As the line got shorter, the violent flailing of the starboard jib began to subside as Finn and I made headway, and slowly furled the sail home around the forestay.

We were now approaching the bottom of the funnel, and it was time to head eastward off to port and hopefully hide from the capricious wind in the lee of Grand Canaria. This was going to require dismounting the sail from its whisker pole, then moving the sail to starboard and taking up a port tack. The "lee" is to wind, what shadows are to light. Peace from a storm can be found hiding in the lee of an island. A race can be won or lost if your competitor is able to put your sails in the lee of his boat and sails. This racing tactic is called "stealing your wind". Often your whole sail plan is based around staying and working in the lee of an island. Alternately, a race can be won by staying out of your competitor's lee. Don't let them steal your wind!

I remember times in the Bahamas when I'd pull into the lee of an island to escape the ravages of a nor'easter; a "rage" they called 'em. Sometimes a week or more would pass before the "rage" would blow out allowing me to carry on.

I headed *Whitetail* eastward as much as I dared to avoid an accidental jibe. The incessant howl of the wind for the past four hours abated instantly as we began to enter the lee of the mountains of Gran Canaria. The time had come for our dreaded jibe. When you jibe, you are changing the boat's heading by moving her stern through the wind's direction. In heavy winds this can be disastrous when the sails fill making a "goose wing" shape with the rear edge of the sail, the leech. You must control it as best you can with tension on the boom. The mainsail will explode with a loud pop when the wind fills in the sail on the new tack. The boat hates this and will let you know with a loud explosion and will heel way over, often with the mast almost parallel to the sea. Sails and masts have literally been lost when this maneuver is used, either on purpose or accidentally when the sea may move you where you do not want to go. We wisely decided not to take the chance with a wild jibe, but employed another tactic called "cranking your motor". This is when you turn the key until the motor cranks, then go about trying to save your ass.

Our trusty diesel rose to the occasion. Finn grabbed the end of the whisker pole, and at the right lull, disconnected it quickly from the clew on the small foresail. I steered her hard to port, trying to make the maneuver as smooth as possible. Here smooth is a relative term. Smooth?! It was all pure hell. The sail blew through the opening behind the forestay, almost wrapped around the jack stay, then flattened out with a loud "pop". *Whitetail* dove hard to starboard and buried her bow picking up a truck load of "green water" that rushed down her starboard deck partially filling the cockpit with cold water.

Whitetail shook hard in complaint, but all her fittings held. We were now blasting along headed off eastward on a port tack toward Puerto de Mogan, only a few miles away. As we moved further into the lee of the island and things calmed down, we easily furled the staysail and tied it firmly to its home on the port lifeline. Our stalwart diesel was the hero.

Finn came back from the foredeck and fell into the cockpit totally exhausted. His hands were raw, and every muscle in his body ached. A hard hug, and we both fell into nervous laughter, then we both screamed to high heaven, a howl I'm sure the god's heard loud and clear. Thanks! The loose starboard sail remained safely furled on its roller thanks to Finn's valiant efforts. We motored into the harbor at Puerto de Mogan, then tied up at the first empty space, happy to be there…alive and safe!

People from around the marina came by to visit.

"Where'd you come from? Did you get hit with any of those winds prowling around out there?"

Whitetail at the quay in Puerto Mogan and we still hadn't taken on any hashish

"Not too bad." I said, "The wind was blowing hard the whole time, about 35 mph until we entered that blasted funnel between Tenerife and Gran Canaria. Things changed quickly there; I'd guess it blew at least 60 plus miles per hour. "We were running in front of the wind, and the seas were blown down flat, so it was a lot like a ride in a 427 AC Cobra…totally outta control."

They all laughed at the analogy and considered us lucky. Early that morning a monstrous wind gusting over 75 mph, had blown two cars off the docks into the basin. Everything was affected but no major damage was found yet, except for the two cars. The first of November 1991 the last month of hurricane season, was upon us.

* * *

Puerto de Mogan in the Canary Islands. The day after the windstorm

Puerto de Mogan reminded me of a Disney movie set. Giant yellow, purple, white, and pink hibiscus bloomed everywhere in profusion, hung by vines with great green leaves. They reached up the tall stucco walls and wrapped themselves around iron balconies that hovered high above the cobblestone streets. The weather was almost warm, and the clean Atlantic air was alive with the excitement of sailors coming and going on their way to the Caribbean for the winter.

I stumbled along the pier toward shore, catching myself before falling, missing the rolling deck under my feet. I called Diana as soon as I could find a phone.

"I'm so relieved to hear your voice," I said the moment she picked up the line. "I miss you more than you know."

I had no good news for her, except the basics. "We're alive, still kicking, and *Whitetail* is still afloat."

Diana's temper always simmered not far under the surface. A fuse blew when I told her about the night off Asilah.

"Good God…what in the world are they thinking? You say there was no response at all?"

"No sweetheart, nothing. I still haven't spoken with Yousef yet." I laughed when I heard myself say, "You just can't trust these people."

There was so much to tell, so much to discuss. I had an idea that required that Diana be involved in the scheme, hands on. I wanted her to come out to the Canary's but couldn't ask her until I'd worked it out with Finn and Yousef.

"I have an idea that may save our project. How's your money holding out? I have a plan that may work for everyone involved."

I needed to speak with Finn regarding his next move. I knew he was wanting to go back to Greece. His departure would change all our plans completely. I didn't know another person who could replace him. I needed to be able to depend on him for this next phase.

The next morning, Finn and I settled into one of many enchanting restaurants in town. Fork in one hand, knife in the other, elbows on the table, Finn talked and ate at the same time. The tomato, spinach, parmesan tortilla disappeared in an instant.

It was time to talk…head cocked, he looked at me intensely.

"Cap, I hate to tell you, but I need to get back to Greece quickly." He waited for a reaction. "I've promised Martina that I'd be done with our room addition a month ago. I'm planning to get a flight out as quickly as possible. If you can rekindle this project, come up with money, and find a source for better information regarding the pickup, call me, I'll come back. I still need the money."

The stark reality that I kept both to myself and from myself, was… money was disappearing like water on a hot griddle. The $150k investment capital from El Capitan was diminishing quickly. Sixty thousand had been set aside to purchase the hashish. Thirty thousand being the initial deposit in Madrid, and $30k being kept in the main cabin's head liner only to be touched when the day came, and we took aboard our hashish. At that time, General Sherman will give General Lee his $30k balance due. All the new equipment, sails, instruments, radar, GPS, auto pilot, along with general prep work had added up to $30k which was more than expected.

As I think back, *Whitetail* had been asleep at her dock in Puerto Pollensa for over two years. A tough pill to swallow for any boat. The unexpected extra time in Gibraltar, and now the time here in Puerto de Mogan, was quickly polishing off roughly another $10k at light speed. My new plan, which included yet a third run at a pickup on the Moroccan coast, was going to cost at least an additional $30k, what with all the plane tickets, motels, meals, and transportation, and boat expenses. *Whitetail* desperately needed sail repairs and rigging repairs from damage incurred during the rough sailing we'd experienced, most likely another $20k. El Capitan's repayment as well as Finn's payment would be taken from the proceeds of the sale of the hashish, as would anything left for me, should such fortune befall. My life now was spent preoccupied with the flow of cash, woven in with the maintenance of a dozen credit cards, with balances high enough to make your nose-bleed.

Looming ahead would be the long and costly sail to Antigua and funding the time we'd need to stay there waiting to move north to Thunderbolt with the rest of the "snowbird" fleet. At least another $30k. I knew I was going to have to approach El Capitan for another installment. I hated that, but I would never have believed that things could have gone so awry. But I couldn't give up. Maybe I should have. But for me, giving up was just not an option, not by a long shot.

"Also, Cap," Finn continued, bringing me back from my worrisome daydream, "we're pretty sure the hashish you selected up in the Rif is no longer there waiting for us. In- fact we know that. What if they loaded us with something worthless? Under the circumstances, I'm not sure they can even get any hashish worth a damn down to the coast, north or west. It's all very risky, more so than I've ever seen it." I knew he was right. But, at this point, right vs. wrong had no say in the matter. It was pure desperation that held the key.

Still my compromised mind could only think *I've got to unravel and restart someway.* Would that be giving up? I just couldn't do that. Any sketchy thought that lent validity to the decision to keep on trying, was moved to the front in the line. There still seemed to be so much to lose if I abandoned the project. Money was pouring out like an open faucet, and at this moment I didn't even know how we were going to pay, when it came time to leave Puerto de Mogan.

One thing I did know, I needed to put Finn's plane ticket on my last credit card with any money left on it. I rented a car and took him to the airport, where he held me at arm's length, looked hard at me, and gave me an enduring hug. Then, true to form, he backed down the loading ramp with that smile that diffuses all negativity.

"Adios Cap, hasta la vista," he employed his best Schwarzenegger.

I watched until he disappeared; I was alone on the earth. I could not call Diana until I had time to think through my situation and figure out a new scheme that would keep me and the plan alive. The long ride from the airport back to the boat gave me time to feel my loss of one great partner. My heart was heavy. November 22nd, 1991 was here, and I felt like I'd jumped from the frying pan into the fire. Things were changing quickly, all in the wrong direction.

* * *

First on the list was to talk with Yousef Abboud.

I waited a few more days before I made the call. I really needed to keep myself together for this conversation. I couldn't lose my temper.

The phone rang.

"Alew."

"Yousef..."

"Please let me explain," he interjected before I could say another word. "I'm afraid it was my fault this time. The fishermen were there on the shore but couldn't connect with you via radio. They said their radio wouldn't connect with yours, and they didn't want to answer your light signals if they weren't planning to go out to load your boat. They saw you turn away from shore at 3 a.m., so they went to their homes. They were calling me at 4 a.m. to tell me what had happened. The pressure everyone is feeling from the government's crackdown is taking its toll."

I tried to stay calm.

"Yousef, look here, while I appreciate everyone's concern, things would have been a great deal easier if in your planning you might have insured that the fishermen on shore had a VHF radio, and knew how to work it. Just a wild and crazy idea I came up with.

Also, I assumed that someone on shore would understand English or Spanish, or fuckin' pig-latin. I guess the language that night was Arabic. How presumptuous of me. Everyone has a grip on Arabic don't they Yousef? I just needed a little warning, so I could brush up on my Arabic, to be able to tell you to go fuck yourself Yousef."

I was getting angrier.

"Okay, Yousef. That's done. Over. Kaput. But I'm not giving up now. I am coordinating another plan, and I'm coming back to Tangier to visit you sometime in the next few weeks. I have no choice but to keep on trying, and for that reason Yousef, short of just killing me, you don't have any choice either… you are going to keep on trying. Hang on just a second, let me check on a few things here on my list… Did this phone work? Could you hear me? I could hear you? You're understanding my English, aren't you? Last minute I thought about Swahili, but English seemed to work for everyone during the planning stages. Okay then, we've had a very progressive, solution focused discussion, and have checked a few things off my list so we can be sure you understand my intentions. Are we understanding each other Yousef?" I was yelling. I'd gotten louder and had begun acting like an idiot, throwing my arms around as if anyone cared.

"And Yousef," I shouted, "let me tell you, I am not going away!" And I meant it.

✳ ✳ ✳

The new idea that was brewing was straight forward. Likely the only thing to do. Simply go back, make another plan with Yousef, and pick up my fuckin' hashish.

I called, and Diana picked up the phone.

"Hey Baby, I'm sorry. I know you don't want to listen to me rant and rave, but this is just so infuriating. It should have been so simple." "No problem sweetheart. The solution really is simple. There is only one thing for us to do. Figure out how we can get that damn hashish aboard *Whitetail* and somehow stay the course. Also, the money problem is becoming more severe with every day that passes. The whole budget is blown with all the delays, false rendezvous, and boat repairs due to bad weather. The cost rises every day. I am concerned that when we reach Antigua, we'll be needing more just to fund the final leg to Thunderbolt."

I could hear her nodding.

"I do believe that I've got a plan that will work. I want to sit down with you here in Gran Canaria and go over it with you. Your input is invaluable. You're going to play an integral part in the scheme. You're the missing link."

"All right Pierce," she said. "I'll be there as soon as I can. Call me in a few days and I'll have flights and dates. Diana was great. She could dig in the trenches with the best of 'em.

I hung the receiver up and immediately began to relax and feel more confident as we began detailing a travel plan. A few days passed and I called Diana. She planned to strike out from Atlanta, around the 4th of December 1991. She planned to spend my birthday December 9th, Christmas, New Years, and her birthday January 9th with me on *Whitetail* in the Canaries. She would have time to finish up some modeling work in Atlanta that would bring some cash to our rescue. She also planned to get three months' rent in advance from our tenants, in return for a ten percent break in the rent. They thanked her profusely for the opportunity. Incredibly she managed to rent our little garage apartment to friends who wanted to be in Atlanta for the holiday months of December and January, while she'd be with me out in the Canaries. And with impeccable timing, some creative gunslinger of an investor, bent on taking advantage of the distraught via obnoxiously high interest, bumping the ceiling at 28%, sent us a brand-new unsolicited credit card with a surprisingly substantial limit of ten grand.

We tried it out immediately and put Diana on a flight to Gran Canaria on December 6th, 1991. I was as excited as a teen in heat. I couldn't wait to hold Diana close. We'd been apart for way too long.

I spent my time repairing and detailing *Whitetail*. She was spit shined. She looked like a new boat, inside and out. I'd settled into a nicely situated slip and spent a good bit of time with an interesting guy from Belgium and his wife, a nice-looking sports model from South Africa. They had met me and Finn while we were all weathered in together during the gales in Gibraltar. They were on their way to the Caribbean, where she, incessantly, taunted his nonchalant attitude, talking about her dream of "getting it on" with an islander.

"Specifically, a big black guy with a huge dick."

I thought the idea was kind of sexy, but talk is cheap, and fantasies are generally less disappointing if left just that…fantasies.

"The deal is, you must share it all with me," Michael, would tell her. Then he'd just laugh it all off until the next time.

I never did find out what happened, or who killed who. I often wondered.

On December 6th , Diana exploded from the arrival gate, the loveliest woman in the world. She saw me, yelled, dropped her bags, and ran to me, leaping into my arms. We supported each other, like we always had, holding each other close. Tight. Never to let go. Our eyes spoke, we said nothing, laughing through warm tears. The rest of the world evaporated.

People stared, then smiled.

The world was ours for the next three days. We experienced each other like never before. Our bubble went unbroken. We were in love, and we were ecstatic.

Extraordinary how life changes. Things you bet your life on…literally. Things you know to be never-ending. Intangible things that don't require collateral.

The sky forever remains bright blue. Right?

CHAPTER TWENTY-ONE
"Are You Crazy?" / The Sooner the Better

ONE MORNING, after an extra cup of coffee, I broached my thoughts with Diana regarding our dilemma; how we got here, and what can be done to fix it. I'd been mulling it over in my head for weeks, and I now felt confident with a revised plan.

We sat down at *"Whitetail's"* main salon table with pens, pads, maps and calendars.

I began.

"Okay sweetheart, the situation in Morocco is dire. The preposterous timing of this new War on Drugs in Morocco, and its effect on us, is absurd. Ironic. The complications generated include the indigestible idea that we may not get anything at all. I simply must do all I can to keep that from happening."

"Agreed," she said. "So...?"

"So... I'm going to write a note to El Capitan' explaining our predicament and ask that he invest another thirty thousand dollars. We'll need for you to meet me in Antigua with that money."

"But wait a minute," she interrupted. "How am I going to..."

"I don't feel comfortable asking him to invest more money before we have the hashish safe and on board. Then, I feel, we can be assured our success, and the successful return of his investment -- with profits."

"But...hold on…"

"Sweetheart, please bear with me, I need to blurt out the whole plan at one time. If I slow down to explain what will be answered by the next sentence you may lose me to confusion. Okay?"

"Okay..." she consented, "Sorry..."

"No apologies necessary," I said, understanding how crazy my new plan must sound to her."

"This is the way we'll set about putting the plan into motion. We'll buy tickets for you from Puerto de Mogan to Tangier. Then after I make the pickup and I'm on the way to Lanzarote, you'll leave Tangier and fly to Madrid, then New York, and onward to meet El Capitan' in New Hampshire. There you'll await my phone call.

"I need for you to consider all of this deeply in detail, and I don't want you to have any fear of saying no."

"Well…tell me. I'm braced."

By the time you arrive in New Hampshire, we'll have successfully taken on the load as you will have coordinating the pickup from the shore with Ahmed, Yousef and the fishermen. You are our shore side representation. Our contact. Then, Finn and I will fiber glass the hashish into the hull while we're underway from Asilah to Lanzarote. We'll pull into Puerto Calero on Lanzarote, in the Canaries, where, at that point, we'll have a boat load of hashish prepping for the sail across the Atlantic to Antigua. I'll call you at El Capitan's home from Puerto Calero in Lanzarote to confirm we have the load safely on board. You will give El Capitan' the note from me, explaining what has happened and what we need to do. Then, presuming El Capitan' is willing to increase his investment in the plan…you will take the thirty thousand to Atlanta. I feel certain he will make the investment, but I don't want to ask him until I've got the load on board in my hands."

Next, you're off to Atlanta from New Hampshire, with the additional funds. You'll spend about three weeks recuperating and insuring things there are in order. We'll be sailing across the Atlantic Ocean. Once we're in Antigua, about a 25- day sail, you'll fly down as quickly as possible with the $30k, and I'll pick you up at the airport."

"Whew! I'm glad to hear that part..."

"Finn and I should be heading back to the African coast from Puerto de Mogan, sometime around the middle of January. We will most likely run into famously disagreeable weather at that time of year. Everything will be coming from the wrong direction, including us. It'll surely be a sail to remember.

Diana listened intently, seriously, and without distraction.

"To get all this started, Sweetheart," I went on, "you and I will need to go to Tangier and meet with Yousef in person as soon as we can. I have ordered two ICOM VHF handheld radios from the chandlery. They should be here in about a week. I have yet to confirm Finn's help. He is, of course, an integral part of this plan. He's my next phone call. He simply must come; it can't be done without him."

Diana still hadn't said a word, unusual for her. Looking intently at the tabletop, slowly nodding her head, she looked up with a mischievous smile.

"Who else would agree to this lunacy?"

She was right. In fact, she was the only one on earth for the job.

Next, we walked together to the phone booth, talking a mile a minute. I called Finn and told him of the new plan, emphasizing that we'd have Diana on the coast when we came for the pickup. After a few questions regarding timing and funding, he, with some reluctance, agreed to come back. He was still in the midst of renovating his house and needed more money to finish. So, with a promise of the same original $40,000, Finn agreed to give it one more try. He'd be back in two weeks. "Give me a call and confirm when you have an arrival date. I'll pick you up at the airport at Puerto de Mogan. The earlier the better."

Excitement was beginning to boil, and we pressed ahead, once again considering ourselves invincible.

* * *

The next day Diana and I hopped a flight to Madrid from Gran Canaria, caught a train to Algeciras from Madrid, and took the ferry over to Tangier.

It was December 9, 1991, my 44th birthday. I was certainly old enough to have known better. I booked our room at the Hotel les Almohades, where we promised to have a proper birthday meal later. The Hotel restaurant was a very nice, white-tablecloth, kind of place, with uppity waiters, black hair slicked back flat on their heads, who knew what they were doing; in more ways than just one. We reveled in a rare moment of relaxation in the eye of a tornado.

I immediately called Yousef Abboud from our room. He was obviously surprised to hear from me, but pleasant. When I told him, Diana was with me and we were in Tangier, his pleasant tone stumbled; he was obviously taken aback.

"Do you really have a plan that will work?" he asked.

"Yes, but we must meet as quickly as possible, so I can tell you about it in person."

He stammered, "Well, I... can you... recuperating,

Come by before dark?"

"Yes, we'll be there in half an hour."

Diane and I had a cup of thick black mint tea with a wonderfully sweet bread, while we took a moment to relax on the ancient marble patio amidst tall palms. The hotel cat, "Marmot", kept a close eye for any crumb that might set itself free and make its way to the floor. We then hailed a taxi that took us up the hill to the narrow street that led to Yousef Abboud's ancient wooden door. After knocking with the heavy iron ring, the door creaked open, and a man I'd never seen before, motioned for us to follow. We climbed the now familiar stone stairway and entered Yousef Abboud's smoky little room.

Yousef stood graciously, calmly smiled, then took Diana's hand gently, while resting his other hand on his back, and bowed elegantly. He invited us to sit with him on the rug covered floor.

"I'm very curious about your new plan," he began, without further delay.

"First, Yousef, I want you to know, face-to-face, that moving a sailboat around rough water and bad weather is difficult, time- consuming, expensive, and dangerous. There's no room for mistakes or miscalculations, and the consequences for error are never negotiable. A mishap at any moment could mean loss of life and / or boat.

I felt better ranting in person and was prepared to continue.

But then, without a glance or a word, Yousef picked up his phone. I could hear the exasperation in the tones of both voices. Even though it was all Arabic I understood pretty well what was being said.

He hung up. I went on

"Diana is going to be my representative on shore until I get loaded and headed westward."

His brow raised while his dark eyes grew wide. He cocked his head, leaned forward, and looked incredulously at me…only me.

"*Are you crazy*!?"

Diana and I just stared -- unflinching, stunned, but determined.

"Yousef," I broke the thick silence, "We are going to do this. It is just that simple, so please help us and let's get on with what we need to do. We don't need your affronts; we need your help."

Yousef's countenance changed, he shook his head, leaned forward, forearms on each knee.

"You must understand the severity of your demands." Morocco is not like the US. Right and wrong are often determined the minute they are questioned."

"Now, please believe I will work with you to get your hashish loaded on your boat, but understand, the ancient system we plan to affront with this effort, may not take it so kindly. We will find out."

I wasn't sure how to take what I imagined to be a pseudo threat.

"I will put your wife in the care of Ahmed. He will keep her safe on the shore." He continued as if Diana wasn't in the room, "Should we be able to find this hashish, what would be your time frame for pick up."

"The sooner the better."

CHAPTER TWENTY-TWO
I Am Salma / The End of an Era

Diana's birthday was the 9th of January, so I made a quick decision to schedule the pickup on the 17th.

"The 17th of January, will give us about five weeks from today to get our end together, find Finn, and depart from Lanzarote for the rough seven-day sail heading back to the African coast."

I thought to myself that this would give Diana and me Christmas, New Years, and her birthday together. Too, it would also give Yousef sufficient time to find the hashish.

I dreaded asking the next question.

"Might the product that I selected so long ago up in the Rif, possibly be the product I'd be picking up?"

"No."

"Can I be assured the hashish that I was now getting, would be close to the same quality as that which I'd first selected months ago?"

"No, I cannot possibly know the quality of this new hashish," he continued in obvious frustration, wagging one long crooked finger back and forth, stirring the smoke in the air. "Under the circumstances, I would feel fortunate to find a small order like your 600 kilos, good or bad, anywhere in Morocco. There is a scarcity of ready product."

I knew that he just wanted to get rid of us and that the quality of the hashish probably made very little difference to him.

Then he brought up another very real problem.

"If we can find this hashish, it's going to be tough to find fishermen willing to move the load from the beach to *Whitetail.*

Now, it was time for my patience to be tested. I fought to control my anger.

"Yousef, this is your world! You know the ins and outs of this business. I'm totally reliant on you to pull together what's left of this miserable experience, and simply give me what I came to get."

Diana smothered a little laugh with a faux cough. I knew that laugh all too well. She always laughed when I got mad.

"Pierce," Yousef replied, "please believe me, I want to help you. You must realize that overnight our whole world has changed drastically. Our world been not been shaken this badly since the middle 1950's. It makes me so very sad. This would never have happened six months ago. We have here the end of an era."

I thought it might be time to bring up the $30,000 I'd given him months ago, peanuts in his world. But I decided to leave that discussion for later. To bring it up now could potentially push his frustration over the edge. Mine was already there. A tantrum never solved anything other than getting your ass kicked. I needed to keep my cool or I could stand to lose it all.

Yousef Abboud had changed. He was no longer the cavalier, smug businessman, spouting "this can all be done, no problem." Our surprise arrival with a new plan, fueled by determination and desperation, didn't fit his agenda. I honestly don't think there had been any attention given to our little pile of hashish, which I'm sure had been sold long ago, and was likely nonexistent at this point. I felt as if I'd been written off as collateral damage. To him the $30k due was nothing, a drop in the bucket, and hardly worth consideration in the scheme of things. I also didn't want to give life to these problems at this point. I ignorantly continued to assume that I was going to get some part of what I came for… 600 kilos of damn good hashish. Tenacious is the word.

He picked up the phone to make another call. Arabic began to flow quickly again in a low serious tone. I had no idea what was being said, but his vacant look gazing into nothingness as his nodded for no reason, left me little confidence. I wondered again should we run for it. This was perpetually an option, then perpetually not an option. The machine was beginning to turn again, and to quit now was not an option, only a tempting misleading way out, with multiple faceted monstrous losses being the return.

He quietly hung up the receiver, stared down at his rugs for a moment, then looked up with a deep sigh.

"We must all go now to meet with the person who is in charge of this business here in Tangier."

What? In charge? What was he talking about? Yousef Abboud continued, "when the King had gotten so angry, agreements changed." For some reason, the "Commander" came to mind. Perhaps his exile was generated by this "War on Drugs".

"I'll be as involved as before, and you'll still be doing business with me."

Diana, still quiet, was cool. Listening intently, she showed no signs of concern.

Yousef Abboud stood to leave motioning for us to follow. We walked down the steep steps and out and into the same cool evening we'd left earlier. It was almost dark. From nowhere, Ahmed pulled up at the helm of a rusty old Fiat. Yousef Abboud climbed into the front seat and Diana and I in the back.

Ahmed leaned around and said, "Hola, buenos tardes." I was glad to see him. Yousef was quiet, occupied with deep thoughts. Ahmed nodded at Diana when I introduced them, "Ahmed, this is my wife Diana." She is here to assist you with facilitating the loading of our hashish. She will insure we make contact with the fishermen on the coast when we come to collect our hashish.

Yousef Abboud and Ahmed conversed nonstop in the front seat of the car speaking only Arabic, punctuated by emphatic hand gestures, and shrugged shoulders. Diana and I didn't say much, but we held hands tightly as we bounced around, up and down, narrow, twisty, little streets. We came to a new, contemporary 30 floor apartment building. Everything in the foyer was white marble and glass.

The four of us stepped into the elevator. A button with a number high up in the building was pushed. We stepped off into a long, well-lit hallway lined with a variety of artwork, sculptures, plants, and doors, all lit creatively. We walked along, not speaking, until we came to a door left slightly open. Following Yousef, we all stepped in one at a time.

Inside, the room was dimly lit. Along the wall to our right stood three large serious men. Dark, pockmarked faces, with black hair combed straight back, sculpted to their heads. Their feet were slightly apart, hands folded in front, clothed as if they'd come straight from the golf course. I noticed one had a small handgun in a Bianchi, tucked into the middle of the back of his Sansabelts.

Yousef knew them all and nodded with no discussion. They acted as if they didn't notice us at all, but I knew they watched our every move. Pleasantries were nonexistent. The room was still and quiet. Someone in the background touched a wall switch, and the dim light brightened imperceptibly. I tried a little too hard not to appear surprised, when there, on a pile of rugs, spread on the floor, appeared a very languid, sultry, and somber woman.

Her skin was dark, her hair was black, and her eyes even darker. She wore Moroccan garb, a colorful wrap. She exuded a presence that blended power with intellect. She looked me up and down, unabashed, approaching disdain. Then she met Diana's questioning eyes; a long minute lingered while she assessed what she saw.

She addressed Yousef Abboud in Arabic with a surprisingly harsh tone. It sounded as if she may have said, "Abboud, you idiot, what the fuck did you think you were doing?" Yousef Abboud sensibly nodded in agreement, slightly shrugging his thin shoulders. There was no doubt this woman wielded power, and everyone in that room respected her. She then looked at Ahmed. A slight smile made an evasive appearance, and she slowly shook her head on a level plane with patient motherly understanding, never saying a word.

Somehow, Diana and I were here in a place where we might not belong. Undoubtedly, "Bull Shit" wasn't tolerated here, and humor rarely paid a visit, if ever. This all had a profound effect on me. I realized just how serious I needed to treat the circumstance. The smart ass in me went into hiding. This was no game…it was life moving along as usual in this corner of another world. We were all expendable. Every one of us.

Then she spoke to us in perfect English, and introduced herself, calmly, in the raspy voice of a smoker,

"I am Salma."

A pause.

"I understand you have had some mishaps in your efforts to do business with us here in Tangier. Is this correct?"

I looked at Yousef Abboud who stood to my right. He nodded with assurance for me to speak. Although, in my present circumstance, my mouth would open, nothing would come out. No one smiled.

"I beg your pardon, "I croaked," a glass of water, please."

"Would you prefer wine?" Salma asked.

"I'd better stick to water for the moment."

After a sip, things began to work again, and I told her very matter-of-factly, in great detail, with no emotion, the story of our involvement in Tangier to date. The "pissed off" part of me" had stayed behind in Yousef's little room and was not in attendance here, thank goodness. Suicide never struck me as a way to go. As I spoke, she looked unwaveringly, a-emotionally, at me, and when I had finished, she slowly shook her head, while she stared at her lap, hands folded. Without moving, she said something quickly, abruptly, unkindly, again in Arabic, directed toward Yousef Abboud.

Whatever she said had impact on him. I'd never seen him with such a retreating countenance. In an odd way, I felt sorry for him. I hoped that no negativity would befall him. I thought of the Commander.

Salma leaned back, looked over her shoulder and whispered to someone standing close in the shadows, just behind her. Things got slightly brighter. She looked directly at me for a long uncomfortable moment. Then in a slow and deliberate manner, she chose her words carefully.

"Alright sailor, now you listen to me carefully. You listen well. We will load you with 600 kilos of hashish in five weeks on the west coast just south of Asilah. You will make contact at midnight with your radios and lights at the same coordinates as the last time. While I don't approve of your wife being there without you present, I feel she will be safe on shore with Ahmed. She will certainly be a burden for Ahmed and Yousef Abboud. But they will be responsible for her safety.

"You and your wife will communicate with your radios at the time of your pickup. If for some unfortunate reason there is an insurmountable problem, and we cannot load your boat on your first evening's pass, you will simply repeat your approach until we are able to accommodate you. This process can sometimes require several days depending on the weather. Please employ your knowledge as a man of the sea to consider what may be happening on shore if the sea is very rough. These hard- working fishermen are simply human."

She paused again to sweep the room with her penetrating glance.

"After you have loaded your boat, you will pay the balance due of $30,000 US cash to the fisherman who asks for "General Sherman". There are many men who would slit your throat for $30,000. Always remember that, discuss nothing, and look at no one. You then will immediately set your course westward allowing for no further contact with these fishermen. Once all of this is done, your wife must, without hesitation, leave my country… immediately."

She looked directly at Diana.

"Ahmed will escort you to the ferry. Your unfortunate experience to date is not the fault of the fishermen, or the men of the Rif. These are hard workers. Your problems are the result of poor planning on your part, and ironic timing. You have not properly prepared for all the circumstances your smuggling business creates. Yousef should have worked with you more closely. Also, our people are used to handling much greater quantities, and while the workers want to respect you and your small load, their managers' treat your efforts with less care and respect. They have no reason to care. They don't understand. They will never have a boat like yours. To them you are a fortunate man. Yousef Abboud should never have entertained your interest."

"Now, times have changed, and our government is playing very serious games. First, they tell us they will allow us to grow Cannabis to make Hashish, which we have done for decades. Then they, with no warning, close all routes in the mountains and patrol the coast with military planes and boats. They have locked away many of our people, and the ones still working are justifiably fearful. Your initial contact to Yousef was with one of my favorite people, Phillipe. I am sorry to hear that he has been apprehended off the coast of Marbella, and currently resides in a jail there. His fate is uncertain. I am trying to put a solution together to help him if I can. Cash in the right hands still has tremendous power."

"I am very sorry to hear Phillipe is in trouble," I said. "It was an honor to meet him."

Again, I couldn't get the Commander off my mind.

She continued.

"Now you madam," addressing Diana singularly with a stern look, "You must remember that you are in a Muslim country and you must take extra precaution while you are visiting here, especially since you are, by the nature of your business, rubbing shoulders with a pack of ruffians. You do exactly as Ahmed instructs. You must act and look like a tourist. You must not confront anyone for any reason while you are here. Make no friends.

Times like these bring out the very worst in people, even friends and family."

"When you leave your hotel, make sure that you are in the care of Ahmed. You can trust him with your life." She moved as if she was about to stand up. The whole room seemed to rustle, and everyone stood a bit straighter. But then she settled back down to her comfortable nest there on the floor, and in Arabic said something low and almost musical directed towards Diana and me.

We followed Ahmed and Yousef Abboud's lead, and without a word turned and walked back into the hallway. I felt as if I wanted simply to thank her. I stopped at the doorway, turned halfway back around, and spoke before anyone could react to this affront.

"Thank you, Salma." A nod.

Not a word was spoken as we walked to the elevator and pushed the down button. The doors opened and we all stepped on. I couldn't shake the feeling I had. Diana didn't want to talk to me around Yousef Abboud, and my confidence and trust in him had sadly diminished. He sensed this and when he spoke it was lacking his cool demeanor.

"I too will work to insure you have no more problems."

I thanked him and felt again almost sorry for him. Evidently the burden of our ordeal fell on his shoulders. Of course, it would. Ahmed and Yousef drove back to our hotel and dropped us off. When we were getting out of the car Yousef spoke again.

"Pierce are you certain that you can be back in five weeks."

"Yes, of course, I will be here".

"Will you?"

CHAPTER TWENTY-THREE
Happy 44th Birthday / Christmas Came

DIANA AND I WAVED GOODBYE to Ahmed and Yousef as they pulled from the hotel. We turned and walked up the wide marble steps, hand in hand. I had so much on my mind, my head was spinning. Our meeting with Salma had been unexpected and uncommonly intense.

On departure I left Yousef with the plan that I'd get in touch with him in about four to five weeks and let him know we were leaving the Canaries heading back to Asilah for our third try at a pickup. "Third try Yousef!" The sail would take about six to seven days depending on the weather.

Finding the comfortably appointed hotel lounge we fell into a couple of blue leather chairs beside a little round table, lit by a flickering candle. I needed to slow it all down a notch, and a glass of Maccallan's took on the task. Diana followed suit and shortly we each ordered another round.

"Happy Birthday, sweetheart, I love you."

Wow! I'd forgotten it was my 44th birthday!

"You did so well in there." "Thanks Baby, what do you think about our situation?"

She looked thoughtfully out at the cars, the people, and one lonely camel parading by our window. Diana was beautiful when wrapt in thought.

"I'm not sure. We most definitely are on a better track with Salma on our side. Clearly, she's way up the ladder of this hashish hierarchy; and I imagine they want to satisfy her bidding."

"Yep, I agree. Our association with Salma is definitely to our benefit. She seems to wield a pretty big stick around here."

Our waiter stopped and suggested that we enjoy one of their wonderful meals. Diana told him it was my birthday. "Ohhh, well then, with a deep bow, please allow me," he pulled Diana's chair back for her and asked that we follow him to a quiet table in an exquisite dining room with a corner all its own. Our waiter, with exaggerated movements, motioned for his assistant to gather up our scotch glasses, get new napkins, and follow us. Nose in the air, he led the way to the special table he had in mind.

I had to laugh when Diana looked over her shoulder as we followed along and mimicked Finn's famous words, "You just can't trust these people."

I thought it might be nice to try and break that stigma ......being my birthday.

Sadly, I was to find out the very hard way, that not all birthday wishes would come true.

"Sir," Diana beckoned the waiter and looked at me with smiling eyes. She never turned back towards him, but continued to look deep into my eyes and said, "Sir, we would like to trust you implicitly to design a lovely meal for us this special evening,"

Another bow, "Yes, of course, shall we begin with a lovely bottle of cabernet."

"Okay Sweetheart," I continued after the waiter went about his business, "How do you feel about your involvement to help get our hashish?" Diana responded confidently, "I could easily feel, and often have felt, more paranoid on an evening's walk in south Atlanta. I can certainly represent us with Ahmed running interference. What do you think?"

"Yes," I said... " Everything seems perfect."

I raised my glass for a meaningful toast; a cling, a knowing smile, and the scotches disappeared, thus etching our future with the gesture…such a small part we presume to control.

Our enthusiastic server was again by our table. "Your wine," he boasted, white napkin folded over his forearm. The opener appeared with a click from midair, and the cork popped loudly. Expert hands poured a small pool in my glass. I spun the tester 'round then sniffed. The wine appeared to be all we'd expected, and with a confirmatory sip, and an affirmative nod, he filled Diana's crystal goblet, then mine, and proclaimed:

"This evening, especially for you, our chef will prepare our famous roasted golden beet salad served with dandelion greens, and dried local black figs, followed by your main course; chicken tagine with almonds, apricots, and olives, served over a bed of pearl couscous. Then, your postre; our chef's own date and apple cake with orange blossom glaze, finished with an espresso, to be selected from our collection from around the world."

"Oh my, yes, that sounds simply wonderful," Diane concurred as our waiter spun happily away.

I thought to myself, we should have birthdays more often, and strive to maintain faith in our fellow man.

* * *

The next day, after a delightful birthday evening celebration, we set about on our trip. After our meeting with Yousef and Salma in Tangier, Diana and I passed through the airport in Madrid on our journey from Tangier back to Gran Caneria. We had confirmed another commitment from the Moroccans, and a new plan had been born. I felt comfortable calling Finn from Madrid. I had been worried that he may have lost interest in the adventure with all the difficulties we'd endured to date.

He answered, "Bon jour Cap. Do you have another plan for us?" We talked about the plan and Diana's part. He seemed enthused, even excited about the possibilities.

"Yes, yes, well done, that all sounds like a perfect plan."

I breathed a monumental sigh of relief when he agreed to go for it again. Finn needed the money to finish his ever-expanding room addition. Several weeks would be needed for him to prepare to get back to Puerto Mogan from his home in Greece. He wanted to spend his Christmas in Greece. I suggested that he spend New Year's there too, and plan to be in the Canaries on the tenth of January 1992.

"I will be waiting for you. I'll have *Whitetail,* prepped and ready to sail from Puerto Mogan back to Asilah where we'll meet with Diana on shore and pick up our contraband. She will then travel to New Hampshire to visit El Capitan and await our arrival in Antigua. Finn and I will carry on with *Whitetail* to Lanzarote in the eastern Canary Islands. We'll rest there for a couple of days, take on fuel and finally head out across the Atlantic Ocean, hashish on board bound for Antigua. Then we'll meet Diana in Antigua to retrieve the badly needed $30k supplied by El Capitan as additional investment to enable us to carry on. Finally, our last stop will be at Thunderbolt, Georgia to unload our cargo.

"Fantastico!" His contagious enthusiasm seemed not to have waned.

But, I worried about Diana and the part she would play. I dreaded the weather that was sure to be against us. I wanted to trust the Moroccans but had no proof that they were trustworthy. At times, it all seemed so impossible, so ridiculous. I questioned my logic. Lack of money was the impetus for the whole affair. All I could do was put one foot in front of the other, one step at a time.

Options were nil.

On our flight from Tangier to Madrid and back to Gran Canaria, Diana and I, went over our plan again and again.

We would continue our stay in Gran Canaria through Christmas, New Years and Diana's birthday on January 9th. During that time, we would prepare Whitetail for her voyage and collect Finn on his arrival.

Our sail eastward was sure to be rough as it would be against the flow of the Portugal Current and the prevailing winds. The sail was likely to take as much as seven days each leg, bashing through wind and waves the entire way.

Christmas came. Before I knew it, I'd be setting sail again, headed eastward, back to Morocco for my third try. One more insane chapter to play out.

Whitetail was happily bobbing in the marina, tied in her slip waiting for her big day.

* * *

On January 8th, 1992, Diana and I picked Finn at the airport at Las Palmas on Gran Canaria. Finn was a welcome sight, as his broad smile came walking through the gate after his flight from Greece. I laughed to myself remembering the last time, seems like a lifetime ago, when I picked him up in Mallorca. He had showed up, with that banjo under his arm. He was determined to keep it aboard, but we had no room or time to deal with banjo lessons on the trip. Thank goodness the banjo was now back in Greece.

The voyage promised to be grueling at best…but I never could have dreamed what was about to happen.

Finn's ever capable, optimistic way was sure to be a welcome addition to this next leg back to Asilah. Finn remembered Diana's birthday and presented her with a delicate copper bracelet he'd gotten in Greece. She was thrilled.

The three of us spent most of that day on *Whitetail* going over our plan, trying to find safety nets that we could rely on if needed. We stocked up on groceries and fuel, with the intent of departing in a few days. I called Yousef and told him we were headed his way, and that Diana was to be there in five days to meet us at the pickup site. "We are ready." he promised.

Diana planned to take a taxi from Puerto Mogan and make her way to the airport bound for Madrid, where she'd wait three days before moving onward to Algeciras via train. She'd take the ferry across the strait to Tangier and meet with Ahmed and Yousef to prepare for our arrival. Diana and Ahmed planned to standby and listen for contact from me when we entered the VHF radio's range of reception, likely on the 16th, 17th, or 18th of January 1992. We would try to make contact on these nights at 10 p.m. and 11 p.m. But if for some reason we might be running a day or two late, we'd continue with the same program each evening, until we made radio contact.

After loading the 600 kilos of hashish, we would take up a south westward heading, bound for Lanzarote, the easternmost island in the Canary chain. Lanzarote, a peaceful, less populated island, would be some 600 miles back, roughly along a reciprocal course. It would take us about six days to get there.

On making landfall at Lanzarote, we would have sailed over 1400 miles nonstop in very rough weather. The total miles we'd accumulated under our keel since first leaving Mallorca three months ago, would be about 3,200. During the six-day sail from Asilah, to Lanzarote, we would fiberglass the contraband into the hull. This was planned while we were still in Mallorca, and I had purchased enough quantities of fiberglass mat, gallons of resin, hardener, white paint, brushes, putty knives, gloves, face masks, and a variety of solvents. Each one seemed more toxic than the next.

While at Lanzarote we would need to take on stores and fuel. *Whitetail* would most likely be stressed when we arrived, so we'd need to go over her in detail, prepping her for the long leg westward to Antigua in the Leeward islands of the Caribbean. With luck, we'd be sailing for 21-days, nonstop 24 hours per day.

CHAPTER TWENTY-FOUR
Second Wind / Small Pleasures Redefined

LATE IN THE DAY, almost dark on January 10th, 1992, Finn and I set sail for Asilah from Puerto Mogan. We'd had a pleasant, somewhat melancholy birthday celebration for Diana the night before. Another time span was about to begin when Diana and I would be apart with minimal communication. I was sad to be leaving her and the mystical Puerto de Mogan.

Diana stood, dimly lit by a streetlamp at the end of the jetty. As we passed the breakwater at the opening of the harbor to the sea, she danced, kicked her heels, waved and threw kisses. Finn and I waved back heartily, and I shouted, "I love you sweetheart, I miss you already!"

I promised myself, no more foolishness when this is finally over.

This was the last run. I meant it.

My words blew back to hit me hard in the face as the wind immediately gained substantial force out of the north once we cleared the breakwater.

Knowing how I was feeling, Finn came up from the dark cabin with a bottle of scotch. I took a welcome slug and felt the whiskey warm me from deep inside as it ran through my body. Some part of the cold sad night ran from the healing libation and we began to put our minds on our mission.

"Alright Cap, we're off to do this thing, and there's no turning back. We're just gonna go and get 'er done."

"Thanks Finn. Of course, you're right. I just get tired sometimes, and I know you do too. If things had gone as expected we'd have been home, two months ago, counting our cash, and figuring out the next sail."

Useless hindsight. What good is it?

We were poised to take a heading that would put us at odds with both wind and current for many days and nights. On clearing the breakwater, we left the lee of Gran Canaria on a northeast heading. A cold 30 knot wind out of the north-northwest hit us hard. After about four hours, we were able to tuck into the lee of Lanzarote for some small shelter. But once we cleared the northeast tip of Lanzarote, we were hit full brunt by an ornery sea and brutal winds. This unruly pattern continued for the next four days. Somewhat hardened by our recent experiences, we settled into our familiar watch routine and the intuitive ducking of waves and spray when the sounds and shudders of *Whitetail* gave us warning.

We carried on. Our recharge from the few weeks of peace at Puerto Mogan began to wear off. It wasn't long before the salt began to crust on our faces and beards. A lesser idiot might have turned back. But a real live, card carrying idiot, would just keep on banging his head against the wall, employing the logic, something's got to give.

* * *

Suddenly, on the fifth night, a most unusual event countered our plight. We were about sixty miles off the coast of Casablanca when the thick gray clouds that had laid heavily on us for the past four days abruptly pulled apart. An opening appeared, a huge hole in the sky, instantly filled with the light of a brilliant full moon. The moon light was so powerful that it cast shadows of ourselves around the deck and on the sails. We made duck shadows on the sails and quacked and laughed like little kids. For just a moment we forgot where we were; forgot what we were doing. The moonlight was so clear and bright that it even felt like it had gotten a bit warmer. Our whole attitude lightened.

Just as the moon tore a hole in the clouds, the wind veered from the northwest around to the east. The seas, with their momentum built up, were slow to change their direction from the north-northwest, and an unusual circumstance developed. These seas piled up on each other in front of the new wind which was now coming out of the southeast. They became much steeper with a much shorter fetch. I took up a close-hauled starboard tack pinching to the northeast when I had the chance. This tactic also put the waves more on the port quarter, which made the motion of the waves more tolerable.

We carried on for hours and became more familiar with the flow of the ocean from the northwest, coupled with the strong wind from the southeast. While these waves and winds required constant attention, they oddly didn't pummel us too badly on this heading. We were flying along in a most unusual configuration... essentially the wrong direction relative to the wind and waves.

We'd been at sea for six days. This heading change, due to the wind shift, could possibly cost us another day in passage time. We should now be about 2 days from Asilah. There was no time for any problems. We both were completely exhausted. Finn, who was nodding in and out of consciousness elected to get a moment of badly needed rest. I felt that while the present combination of wind and wave was radical, it was not particularly dangerous since the motion was somewhat repetitive. The time was right for one of us to take a break. Finn kept his foul weather gear on, and was to standby, ready to hop if I needed him. He disappeared below, and a minute later, a hand holding a large cup of hot chocolate emerged from the dark companionway.

"Try that on for size Amigo."

There was more whiskey in the cup than chocolate. Finn knew what we needed.

Thanks... small pleasures redefined.

* * *

The next morning, the sun shone bright. The seas and wind were a constant spectacle. We'd soon be closing on the west coast of Moroccan, just north of Rabat. I hoped the wind might abate a bit in the lee of the mainland and calm this cauldron. The auto pilot refused to steer so now it all had to be done by hand. We had to play our cards perfectly. I hoped the wind might even change direction again. Certainly, it would one day…why not now?

We were on our sixth day with another to go before we reached Asilah, about 100 miles to the northeast. While the wind was at a perfect angle to allow us to head off a bit on a broader reach, we couldn't take advantage of this because the waves, coming from such a precarious angle, kept a close guard on our every move. They played with *Whitetail* like a cat with a mouse.

The morning of our 7th day, as the moon began to allow the day's light to take over, we were gifted a brilliant dawn. I thought I felt a slight change in the wind. Finn had awakened from his rest about an hour earlier. We sat in the cockpit cradling cups of coffee.

Finn froze, his coffee cup midway to his mouth.

"Did you feel that?" he asked.

"Yes, I did. I think there's a change brewing."

A change would be exciting, and no matter what it was, a relief. In January, off the Moroccan coast, winter was firmly in place. We had been wet and cold for a week. These are things you never get used to, things you don't want to get used to. Our spirits lifted with this stranger, the sun, as it rose slowly and began to shine brighter and warmer. We had only experienced cold, cloudy, and rough. In this bright warmth, with a cup of hot coffee, and the sense of an imminent change, I caught myself smiling. Finn saw me and pointed. He climbed across our cluttered cockpit, grabbed my shoulders, one in each hand, and shook me hard until we both broke into laughter. We laughed nervously out loud; we laughed at ourselves. Happy to be the fools we were.

We were lucky. Before the seas could get more serious, they began to lay down a bit as the force of the wind abated slightly. This was most likely because we were finally closing in on the shelter offered by the African coast. We were now about 20 miles offshore. Over the next few hours, the wind began to back around and settled in at about 30 knots out of the northwest again.

The wind had finally begun a truce with the seas This yielded a calmer sea state as it now worked to blow the seas flat thus lengthening their fetch (the distance between the waves), Whew, at last. We welcomed these changes and settled into a powerful sail on a port tack. *Whitetail* sprang forward with glee, like an arrow unleashed from a crossbow. We let her rip as she cut loose dancing through the accommodating seas.

A spectacular sail. We had an extra cup of coffee mixed with cocoa and a shot of rum. Again, small things with monumental impact. Warming to about 45 degrees, the new sunlight bathed us with confidence that things would surely be alright.

I passed out on the cockpit seat without a word to Finn. I had had no idea how tired I was or when I'd last slept. Hours later I woke up, struggling to remember where I was. I quickly glancing left and right and looked for a sign. I sat up and forced my eyes to focus. Oh yeah, I remember.

Finn was on the other side of the cockpit sitting up keeping one eye on me and the other peeled for fishing boats and freighters bound to and from Rabat. The auto pilot whirred with every move the boat made.

"I was beginning to wonder if you were still alive." he speculated.

"Look hard… are you sure I am?"

I must have slept most of the day. The sun was falling towards the horizon, and the feel of late afternoon wrapped us. Finn hopped up and began pulling the last few dried things from the lifelines. He whistled and sang while he worked. The seas had abated slightly, and the wind was steady out of the northwest at about 30 MPH. It was still cold, and my joints had frozen in the same position they were in when I'd passed out. I was the "Tin Man" with no oil can.

Slowly, I unraveled my body to stand in the cockpit. Catlike, I stretched long and hard. My eyes fixed on a hefty set of waves coming at us. I habitually braced for impact, and my mind raced trying to figure out what to do as these dark monsters bore down on poor *Whitetail*. Although the seas were still substantial beings, Finn had enjoyed the transition hours earlier, while I slept, as they began to let us pass over and around them with the help of a strong wind pushing them from behind. This wind held them down and kept their tops from peaking and breaking.

I took it all in with an air of bewilderment. I was still half asleep. *Whitetail* was moving with confidence. Her bow would ride up the steep front side of these visitors then roll over the rounded crest with her nose up and her stern not far behind. The auto pilot whirred at every request, and Finn was dancing with a huge pot of something steaming on our gimballing stove.

The cool evening air was upon us, and the sun, low in the west, made every wave look dark and ominous in the shadows. Red skies and red clouds spread across a cobalt backdrop while the sun, now hidden halfway by the horizon, hastened its departure. I climbed below and turned on the chart light. I rubbed my face hard and roughed up my totally errant hair. I spread the chart out while the GPS communicated silently with the satellites to confirm our location.

Looking over the charts, I picked up our location with the help of the GPS. We were sixty miles south of Asilah and about 20 miles offshore. I stretched my frozen neck 'til it cracked, threw my head back and offered thanks to all the powers for our fortune and our safety. Whatever Finn had on the stove smelled extravagant. In the steaming pot on the swinging stove was Finn's famous beef stew concocted with components from the freeze-dried locker, beans from one of many cans, and a bag of dried fettuccini mixed in. Cuisine never tasted so good. Never felt so good. A celebratory bottle of wine was lodged behind a cushion. The wind began to behave, and as night came, both it and the sea settled into the first reasonable sail we'd experienced since our departure from Mallorca two months' ago.

We were thankful, very relieved, and excited about all that was to come. *Whitetail* was feeling her best. She clipped along, showing off. The seas, coming out of the north, were not aggressive, and a pleasant 20 knot breeze just off her port bow caressed us.

That evening, we reveled in the world as it was…Perfect.

CHAPTER TWENTY-FIVE
You Just Can't Trust These People / Can You Hear Me?

Our morning on day number seven was different. The sky was light grey yet very bright. The sun was a white and fuzzy, held at bay by the clouds. A cool 30 knot wind out of the northwest had picked up speed since dawn. The seas remained agreeable, coming from their favorite direction, out of the north. They were being flattened as they ran before a brisk wind.

This morning, I didn't trust them. The damage from the prior two efforts was far from healed, and now, everything combined reminded me of my feelings during those efforts, so hollow…so hopeless. We shared an eerie feeling as we set about putting gear in its place and straightening the boat readying ourselves for the unknown.

We'd been dry for about 24 hours, and rarely comfortable. I put on clean dry clothes and a warm heavy fleece sweater. I donned my old favorite, trustworthy red Patagonia good luck parka. El Capitan' and I had bought two of them one day on the ski slopes in New Hampshire while we warmed up in the Ski Shack. The dry clothes next to my skin felt luxurious. Dry socks in my sea boots were a forgotten thrill. My feet began to un-wrinkle. I poured a hot cup of coffee and bounced up into the cockpit to see if I could tell what the weather gods were going to dish out today. Never say you're ready for them. When you least expect it, they'll show you tricks like you've never seen before.

Through the night, we had closed in on the coast as we made headway to the north. We were now about 15 miles off the western coast of Morocco, intentionally out of sight of land, just a few hours south of Asilah. We needed to stay invisible until night began to fall. Thankfully, the seas remained somewhat flattened by the strong north wind. It was now blowing about 35 knots, and the day was still a hazy shade of winter. Occasionally, a fine mist would cover us. We tacked and flew back southward on a broad reach. We sailed along the coast for a few hours, keeping out of sight of land. We planned to tack back to the north when the night began to fall, coming ever closer to the Moroccan coast, and our rendezvous at Asilah.

As the pivotal moment of our journey rapidly approached, my anxiety and excitement grew proportionately. I worried about Diana, Yousef, Ahmed, Finn, the boat, the radios, me. I just worried.

Evening began to come as we finally tacked and settled into a close reach on our northeastward course with Asilah, a short 30 miles on the bow. We'd finished off the balance of the beef stew, and feeling the power of sustenance, I set my mind to the task at hand.

"Thanks Finn, you are a master chef. That pot of stew has set me straight."

"How do we look Cap? We must be getting close by now."

"We are. At our present speed and heading, we should be at our meeting spot in about four hours." It had been a long difficult time coming to this moment.

* * *

After another couple of hours, we were closing on Asilah. At 11 p.m., I turned on the freshly charged VHF and moved the knob to channel 44. We had decided to bypass the formality of initial contact via channel 16 as we didn't want to be noticed.

Diana and I had agreed that channel 44 was a good choice since it was easily remembered. I was nervous like a kid in a school play as I spoke into the radio.

"Hey sweetheart, can you hear me?"

Static.

I adjusted the squelch knob and repeated my effort.

Static.

I listened so hard I was hearing things in the static that weren't there. Maybe a small garbled voice? Finn, loomed over me, listening just as hard. We closed a bit closer on the shoreline. We were less than a quarter mile off. It should be easy for Diana to pick up my radio signal and easier to see our spotlight.

Then, suddenly, clearly, like a bell on Sunday morning. I heard Diana's voice.

"Baby, can you hear me? Can you hear me?"

I knocked the radio to the cockpit floor as I lunged for it in the dark. Fumbling,

"Yes, yes, I can hear you Baby."

"I love you," she said.

"I love you too." I shivered at the sound of her voice. "I'm here at the location where we'd planned to meet."

"Yes, I can see you."

"What is the status of our loading process?"

"Ahmed is right here beside me," she said.

Diana had a tone in her voice. A tone I knew so well. Something was wrong.

"They've been trying to contact the suppliers and the loading people for three days now with no luck."

Everything pent up inside my chest went out with my next breath. Calmly, controlled, I ventured another question.

"What does it look like at this moment?"

After a short conversation with Ahmed that I could overhear but not understand, she answered.

"Ahmed says he's been in contact with the necessary people, but they won't be able to load you tonight."

The old temper monster pushed his way past all logic and up to the front row.

"What the fuck is going on with these people!?"

Diana knew the direction I was headed. She implored me to calm down. "Please Pierce, you must not give in to your temper now. Please get control of yourself." The following long silence reminded me how futile and counterproductive my anger was, only working against our efforts and my health. My face and ears burned red, and my eyeballs itched in my fury. A heavy hand grabbed my shoulder. I'd forgotten Finn was even there. My world had become very small. This was not the time to lose control.

We steadied *Whitetail*. She was bucking like a nervous thoroughbred in the shifting gusts and shallow water near shore. Her sheets banged against the mast. We could hear the waves as they rolled into the shore. We were too close. Finn jumped below and confirmed we were in less than 10' of water. I decided to turn away from the shore into deeper water, while we sorted out this mess. The radio crackled.

"Baby, Ahmed says that he will have things worked out by the morning. He says the weather is going to be calm at the mouth of the strait, and for you to move the pickup to a place just under the light house called Cap Spartel on the southwest corner of the Strait of Gibraltar, at ten in the morning."

I felt this was just another ruse, another delay. I felt fucked with and my temper sored uncontrollably.

I growled into the radio though gritted teeth, "If they can't get their shit together in the morning, I'm done with these assholes. You tell them that I'm going to ram this boat into this shore, get off, and walk up this pile of rocks to come looking for those sons of bitches personally."

I'm sure they were laughing at the thought of *Whitetail* ramming the beach, followed by one worn-out sailor clamoring over the rocks, steam blowing out of his ears to pursue the likes of what he may find.

Nothing I could scream or yell…no words I could put together had any positive effect on me. I was one sad dude and it looked for all the world like I had just been royally fucked over, and now…I was tied to the post.

"Ahmed has heard you," Diana said, in an incredible display of understanding and diplomacy. "He promises personally that he will have the load to you in the morning."

I tried to calm down, and with this promise, I began to breath once again. What choice did I have? Cool it man, be as cool as you can.

My whole body, and what was left of my brain hurt.

"Okay sweetheart, we'll be there at ten in the morning."

I told Diana I loved her and asked that she assure me that she was OK.

"I'm fine," she told me. "I can see you heading out to sea. "Please be careful…Ahmed is a good man, and he's taking very good care of me and doing all he can. I plan to be back in Madrid tomorrow night. I love you with all my heart."

"I love you too Baby."

Click.

All was quiet. The sound of the ocean moving under *"Whitetail's"* hull was the only sound as she took up a starboard tack on a beam reach headed west. The aftermath of my explosion could be cut with a knife. Finn had dropped down below when I'd started my tirade. He knew I was hopeless, and we had no power nor control. He then heard a fool screaming into a radio and hopped back into the cockpit to try to calm me down. His silence spoke volumes, and we spoke not a word for hours until the dawn began to break in the east. Ohhh man, my head hurt…really hurt!

With Cap Spartel only three hours to the north, I set us off on a broad reach westward for the rest of the night with the idea of tacking back in at dawn to the new rendezvous at the mouth of the strait of Gibraltar.

I tried to lie down, but my chest just wouldn't stop pounding. I had no faith at all in these Moroccans. I'd begun to presume everything the Moroccans said was a lie. I refused to believe anything they said, and there was no enthusiasm for any part of what was now supposed to take place. I prepped for another lie. Another disappointment. I felt hopeless. A feeling I would not shake for a long time.

CHAPTER TWENTY-SIX

Success? /

The preposterous part of the exploit had just begun

Morning arrived like a perfect winter's day. A quiet Sunday. The bright sun quickly dispatched the darkness. There was hardly any wind. The strait of Gibraltar was a mirror. The benevolent weather brightened our spirits.

"Hey Cap, meet me in the cockpit for a minute."

I pulled myself away from the charts and the GPS and popped into the cockpit for a surprise that was much needed. Finn was waiting in the bright morning sun, with his broad white smile as *Whitetail* ghosted along on an easy broad reach with a light breeze on a calm ocean.

Proudly, he offered a large platter with a monstrous omelet accompanied by all the accoutrements: grits, coffee, toast and even a bottle of champagne. As we savored that meal, we shared our thoughts from the night before.

"Finn, please accept my apology. The idiot who came to visit last night was no help at all. That was not the time to come unglued. I couldn't control my temper. I am sorry."

"Cap, please, no problem." He patted me on the back, laughed and said, "If you hadn't blown up, I would have. You did all the hard work and you did a straight up damn good job of it too. No apologies."

We set about prepping for the next phase. We began to make up funny scenarios of what might happen here on the brink of our third attempt.

Soon, with the help of the Champaign, we were laughing at ourselves until we hurt.

Finn proved to be an invaluable friend and companion through this whole affair. His moxie, his skills and positive soul, made the whole impossible ill-fated quest move along from chapter to chapter at its hobbled best.

Finn, dear Finn, you have to love the guy.

* * *

We floated on the breathless sea for what seemed to be forever. The Strait of Gibraltar was as smooth as a duck pond. There were a few small fishing boats. *Whitetail* stood out like a sore thumb.

At precisely 10 a.m., we moved to our prescribed meeting place, under the shadow of the ancient lighthouse, Cap Spartel. For some reason, Finn and I spoke in whispers. We stared eastward hoping to see movement. Suddenly Finn crouched and squinted intently to the east. He thought he'd seen something move along the shore. "Look, there Cap, do you see that?" He grabbed the binoculars, stood up and rested them on the boom to help hold them stable while he searched for clear focus. Then, sure enough, out from the shadows of the craggy rocks and boulders that line the southern entrance to the strait of Gibraltar, came a trio of small black fishing boats. They seemed so small I assumed they couldn't be the ones we waited for. Finn continued focusing and refocusing the binoculars.

"Yes," he said, "Cap, they're coming toward us."

I jumped to my feet. Sure enough, here they came, slowly, ever closer. As they neared, we could see that each boat had two fishermen in it. They putted along quietly in a spaced single file line. As the lead boat approached one of the men tossed a coiled line to Finn who was now standing on our port toe- rail. Finn pulled the old wooden boat up to our port side and nodded to the Moroccan. His bow lightly bumped *Whitetail*, not a word was spoken.

He looked each of us up and down without expression. Then he addressed Finn, "General Sherman?" Finn pointed toward me. I thought I detected a slight smirk.

"Por favor ," he pointed to an open palm, and rubbed his thumb and finger together.

I'd totally forgotten the balance due, "un momento." I dove below to get the money from its hiding place. I counted it with trembling hands and put it in a couple of plastic baggies. Paranoia struck me and took over my exhausted body. I reached for the Smith. Why not? Plenty of greater men who've come down this path in the past have bumped off the ocean's bottom, barely remembered, for a whole lot less.

I checked to insure it was loaded and stuck the revolver inside the back waist of my pants, then hopped nonchalantly back up on deck.

The men said not a word to us or to each other. I leaned down and handed the fisherman $30,000 in US cash. He didn't smile. He didn't count the money. He took the baggy from my hand, crammed it inside his heavy worn canvas coat, and in gruff Arabic he turned and instructed the others to unload onto *Whitetail.*

There were 12 black plastic bundles each looked to weigh 50 kilos. There was no provision or time to weigh them or to see what the product looked like. Finn and I took them out of the fishermen's brown, hard calloused hands as they hoisted them up to deck level. Not a word was spoken. The only sound was the bumping of their wooden launches against *Whitetail's* hull. Lack of eye contact was intentional and well-practiced. In minutes, our cockpit and side decks were covered with the heavy rough looking bundles. The fishermen backed away from *Whitetail,* turned, and disappeared toward shore in three directions.

That was it. Uncomfortably quiet.

I wanted a fanfare, a parade, confetti, brass bands…something. But the grand finale was extraordinarily anticlimactic. I'm not sure what I would have preferred, but after five months of fighting through some of the roughest most unforgiving winds and seas that *I have* ever seen, then enduring unusually high anxiety, bent on fueling adrenaline roller coasters, all the while dealing with a perpetual array of dashed hopes, and general trepidation, I'd finally, unceremoniously, achieved the first and most important aspect of my goal. I felt now, with the hashish on board, the balance of our effort should fall easily fall in place.

I'll never know why I thought that.

Dreams are made to be handed back in a hand basket.

I called Diana on the radio.

No response. Of course.

I tried again.

No response…but then, on the radio's speaker, sounding a lot like frying bacon, a little voice barely audible came through,

"Baby… baby I love you…"

I knew then she was alright. I wanted to tell her, "we've got it sweetheart; we've finally done it, I love you too!" But I never knew for sure if she heard me or not. Ahmed would share the "good news". I knew, he too, must be relieved.

Sunday, January 19, 1992, *Whitetail* was loaded with hashish heading westward, so I thought.

* * *

The balance of this outrageous journey had just begun.

CHAPTER TWENTY-SEVEN

Is Something Really Better Than Nothing? / BAT

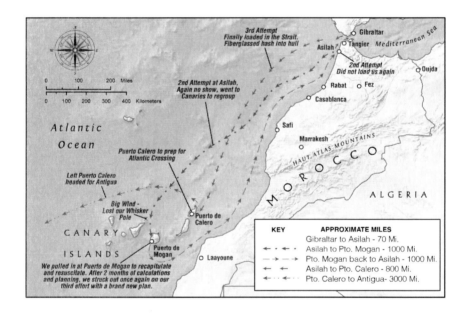

I PUT MR. SMITH BACK IN HIS HIDING PLACE and quietly gave thanks that I didn't have to make use of his talent. Then I set about employing a diversion I'd planned way back in Mallorca.

I'd purchased three large black letters at a hardware store. There was a "B", an "A", and a "T" in their limited inventory. I mounted them on a piece of plastic. I leaned over her stern rail and hung down over the transom. I covered her name, *Whitetail*, with her new name, "BAT".

BAT was of course a thin disguise, but you never know what just might save you, do you?

So, BAT, Finn, and Pierce struck out, across the vast Atlantic Ocean, headed southwestward, back to from where we'd just come, the Canary Islands.

Despite apprehensions, to say Finn and I were excited was an understatement. We would start laughing for no reason. You can't imagine how we felt. It was midmorning and I was physically and mentally spent. What with my severe anger, frustration, and lack of rest, there wasn't much left of me. I asked Finn to keep an eye on things while I dropped below for a few hours rest. "No problem," I don't remember climbing into my berth. Evening had arrived when I climbed out. *Whitetail* was headed the right direction for a change. The six-foot seas were coming as if choreographed from our starboard quarter, and the wind blew 25 knots from the same direction. The auto pilot whirred happily at every request. The sound of the ocean sliding under our keel added to the moment's perfection.

We planned to make landfall in Lanzarote in about six days. We needed to stock our food supply with fresh vegetables, dried and can goods, and a chicken or two in preparation for the long ocean voyage to Antigua.

Neither of us was ready to give up a watch for rest. We were charged up by all the possibilities that lay ahead. We made lavish plans for all the money we were surely about to make. I made list after list of all the people I would pay back with interest and bonuses.

"See, I told you," I would happily boast. It felt good. With every list, with every debt paid, with enough money left to begin a new business, the whole idea, the whole extravaganza, finally made sense.

The most common question, "What are we doing out here?" began to answer itself. The wind cooperated. The seas cooperated. We melted into goodness if only for a short while.

The next day, as quickly as the brilliant red ball crested the horizon and shed light on our scene, we set about prepping our contraband to be fiber-glassed into the hull. The sun moved higher, into the cobalt sky, and the wind began to pick up speed. All through the previous morning's rendezvous, the wind had ghosted along at about 10 knots. Then through the evening it had picked up to a solid twenty-five knots. The seas remained a tame four-foot swell, all from the north-northwest. It was cold, but we didn't care. *Whitetail (Bat)* rode the combination with ease and the auto pilot was on a favorite heading, a beam reach. I felt like we needed to get the hashish hidden away before the weather conjured up any new wild ideas. It was a job neither of us looked forward to. Also, I was never sure how far the Spanish and Moroccan jurisdiction could, or would, reach out to nab us if they were interested, or just bored. Again, we really were small potatoes, but I remembered the spotter plane that had followed us on and off for a couple of days.

* * *

"Well Cap, we better get down to real work. At this rate, we'll be on Lanzarote before we get the load glassed in."

We began by opening all the bales. They had been wrapped very well, and removing the black plastic and tape was just the beginning. Most of the morning and all afternoon were spent just to get through the first two layers and down to the hashish, which was pressed into 2,400, 250-gram pucks. Each puck was about four inches wide, six inches long and two inches thick. This would work out to our 600 kilos.

"Cap, unwrapping these packages will take more time than wrapping them. I wonder why they made this so damn complicated?" That question would not go unanswered as this catastrophe unfolded with us helplessly in tow.

Each individual "puck" was painstakingly wrapped with clear cellophane, clear plastic, tape, then more plastic wrapping, and finally tightly bound with shipping tape. We unwrapped for hours. We organized piles and piles of the pucks down below. We left the last two layers of wrapping on the pucks to help protect them from the ravages of the journey. I kept a few samples of different pucks to do a potency check when time allowed. I noticed there was no aroma coming from any of the opened bales. None. No spicy smell of quality hashish like I'd selected up in the mountains. I didn't bring this observation to Finn's attention yet. He was not a smoker and at this point he hadn't said a word about the obvious.

I put this painful truth out of my mind for now. There was work to be done.

We planned to line the interior of the hull with heavy black plastic, and then arrange all the individual pucks on top. We then covered them over with more heavy plastic, followed with a final layer of fiberglass mat soaked in resin. The last touch was coat of fresh white paint. I had no concept how difficult this was going to be. In fact, each aspect was almost an impossible task. But then, we had been hardened by impossible tasks, so with never a disparaging word we set about prepping for the next phase.

Customs officials would likely board and inspect us in Antigua and Thunderbolt, but not Lanzarote. Thorough inspections would be more likely to occur at Antigua, since we would have traveled from Spain to the Caribbean, a transition into a different country. It was a given that we'd be searched when we checked in at Thunderbolt, Georgia in the US, another country change, but right now, we had to prepare for our landfall in Lanzarote. We had five days to complete this project.

We pressed ahead, dauntless. We organized the pucks into neat piles in the forward and aft cabins leaving the main cabin open to access the hull under the teak flooring panels.

I was impatient to check the quality. I was hoping against all hope that this contraband was at least good enough to sell. I chose three pucks from three overtly different wrapping processes and opened each of them up. They were all the same, jet black and hard as a rock…maybe harder than a rock. In my experience, no component used in the legitimate hashish making process would yield a product like the one I held in my hand. A well-known ploy for the crooks in the business was to mix quality hashish with wax, henna, and occasionally camel dung. These and other fillers were used when a load requires bulking out for any number of reasons. The situation here certainly gave the Moroccans a reason to include any of these components. I only wished they'd included just a little bit of hashish in the mix…they didn't.

In my compromised mind, I blurred the obvious reality. Most of our load seemed to be the same hard-black configuration. I hesitated to begin the process of giving it a try, fearing the truth I was about to discover. I knew oh-too-well that what we had here seemed to be shit, and there was no way to change that. Shit is shit.

If, the hashish was even the least bit potent, the plan might still work, presuming Yousef Abboud's contacts in Canada would be able to market this hopeless product. It was not remotely related to the hashish I'd picked out up in the Rif. Not remotely.

Finn read my mind.

"Well, sitting around thinking about it isn't going to make water into wine, is it?"

I made a faux pipe out of tin foil and selected one of the pucks from the suspicious pile. I wrestled with the sticky packing that covered the puck. I take pride in a sharp pocketknife that I always keep ready in my left pocket. My old knife, although dangerously sharp, wouldn't dent this thing. I feared for the health of the blade. A jack hammer might have worked, or better yet, a stick of dynamite. Finally, with the claws of a hammer, I managed to break a small piece off the puck.

I was reminded of a rainy day a million years ago, on Sea Lion as I watched Phillipe, while he banged away with his hammer to pop a small piece off his cargo. What Phillipe had on board *Sea Lion* that rainy day, was not comparable to my trashy product. There was no spicy smell emanating from to this black mystery I held in my hand.

I put the little piece in the tinfoil pipe and fired up a lighter. The wind immediately blew the flame out, so I went below and tried again. This time it fired. I took a long pull on the pipe and held the tasteless smoke down deep inside. I didn't cough, there was no savory flavor. I waited…I felt nothing.

I turned the puck around and managed to hammer another sliver from the other side. I sat back and took another pull.

Finn sat in the companionway, closely watching my every move. This time I made sure to take real long toke. Smoke swirled around my head like the caterpillar in "Alice and Wonderland." Smoke filled the cabin. I held this one inside for as long as I possibly could. I watched as the smoke billowed from my lungs, followed by a couple of fancy smoke rings. I looked at Finn, who doesn't smoke, and slowly shook my head in the wrong direction. I looked down at the contraband continuing to shake my head. He had been absorbed and patient awaiting my assessment, watching my every move, my every facial change.

When the only verdict I could honestly convey became clear, Finn slapped both of his knees with his hands at the same time, stood up and rubbed his head hard. He looked up to the sky and spread his arms far apart as if he could conjure up changes that weren't available from the Gods that watch over fools like us.

Then quietly, without a word, Finn disappeared into the aft cabin where he looked like an old dog tried to find a place to lie down amongst the thousands of pucks of useless contraband. Lacking room, he went up into the cockpit and lay down, an arm folded across his eyes. He said not a word, there was no need. He didn't move for hours. I felt alone. I was alone.

The worst had come to pass. I fought to keep my thoughts from dwelling on the miserable future that now lay in wait for me. The only good news was it couldn't get much worse.

Oh no, did I just say that…please tell me I didn't just say that!

I selected more of the pucks and tested each one in hopes that this reality could possibly be written off as a bad dream. A terrible dream.

I paced around the boat. I so wanted to feel that old familiar altered state, characteristic of good THC. I felt nothing but a terrible headache. I lay down on the forward deck and wished that I could wish it all away. Unless some surprise miracle was about to save me from this reality; I had travelled into the Rif Mountains, selected 600 kilos of exceptional hash, borrowed tons of money from dear friends, sailed around winter oceans in wrong directions, risked my life, and tampered with my soul, all for a boat load of pure worthless shit.

What I had on board was useless, totally useless.

You heard right...***our load was not hashish.***

I was so disheartened; I hadn't even considered the possible value of the other two types with different wrapping. I thought maybe I should give them a try, but I hesitated. I'd seen them, and I knew what I had. The very best I could expect would be to try and get El Capitan's investment back and pay Finn. I would have to work the details out with Yousef Abboud. I would have to have his help dumping it. Every step promised to be an extremely difficult, dangerous, time consuming, complicated, unsavory task, which, with luck, would culminate with me losing my ass and everything else. Whitetail would have to find a new home, and I'd likely need to sell our house in Atlanta. There was no shimmering spec hidden anywhere in this muck. Howdy depression, Pierce is the name, come on in.

At this moment, I had little hope that the Moroccans would, for any reason, have loaded us with a viable product. Why would they? It was likely that they didn't even have any quality product left. I preferred to think that I'd been *inadvertently* scammed, rather than set up like a bowling pin and then knocked down. Somehow that idea hurt a little less. Talk about grasping for straws.

The wind continued to pipe up to its normal 30 knots, and the sea followed suit. We had to get this crap glassed over in the hull as quickly as possible. Any inspiration had hauled ass with the camels that left my load of hashish in the streets of Tangier. The thought of just throwing it all overboard crossed my mind. Why not?

Why didn't I?

I settled on the logic that "surely something is better than nothing."

Once Finn had come back to life from his nap, we began halfheartedly pulling up the galley sole (the floor of a boat's cabin). I stopped, and in exasperation fell back on a pile of pucks.

"Finn, what do you think has happened here? What do you think our next steps might be? I'm having trouble with the idea of pushing onward. Should we throw it all overboard?"

He laid back against the pile of pucks behind him. We could feel the ocean flowing by under "*Whitetail's*" keel as she slid off the waves that chased us onward into oblivion.

"We can end it all right this very minute, Cap" he said. "I can see the logic with that. But what I do know, is we've got ole *Whitetail* ripping along, and we are going to have to hit land at some point so we can get off. When we do, I think I'd rather have what we've got, no matter how awful it is, as compared to nothing. We'd hoped for a better product…but it's all we've got. I'm totally on board with your decision Cap. But, remember, if we don't try, you know what we get, don't you?"

Without another word, we began preparing sheets of plastic in the open floor to lay our camel dung out before covering it with more plastic, and finally sheets of fiberglass mat, which we soaked with gallons of two-part fiberglass resin. We endured our efforts with thoughts like, maybe some of the 2400 pucks were better than others, and maybe the untested pucks would be drop dead potent and create mythological fables to the effect that purveyors would give it a famous name and remember it for lifetimes. Or maybe this was the normal expectation for the Canadians. Maybe they'd be happy with what we have.

I pulled out several pucks and put them aside to test on another day. There would be plenty of time for that later. We had at least 20 days and nights at sea when a proper test could be done, and the result pondered and calculated. Right now, the evening coolness was setting in. Wednesday, January 22, 1991 came, and the seas began to mount.

CHAPTER TWENTY-EIGHT
Lanzarote / Two Ways Wilson... You Pick It

T HE *IDEA* OF GLASSING IN THE PRODUCT and *actually glassing* in the product were a million miles apart. It took us four horribly grueling days, working around the clock to get the project done. The space that 2,400 pucks of hashish demanded, required more care in the placement process than I'd anticipated. We not only had to remove the main cabin sole, but also the forward berth sole, the galley sole, the aft cabin sole, under the aft cabin berth, and even under the refrigerator, which had to be removed.

We began by putting down the first layer of heavy plastic to line the inside of the hull. Then carefully arranged two layers of the pucks along the interior of the hull and every available nook and cranny. Some areas held as many as three layers.

We then pressed ahead and carefully put a layer of plastic over the top of the pucks. We did our best to make the hiding places waterproof in case we began to sink again. As we continued, our shared belief in blind enthusiasm came for a visit. We began to feel immeasurably more hopeful regarding our plight. There was no reason for this...just perspective.

I took a moment to inspect and smoke a sample from another of the pucks I'd set aside. I thought I may have copped a buzz, but in reality, it was more easily described as a terrible headache. Basically, our hash was of no consequence.

It may have been kief at one time. Kief is the bottom of the barrel, so to speak. The least potent residue from the last sifted plants. At its best, Keif starts out as a virtually worthless bright green powder. But, my keif was also old, dried out and ruined. THC had taken a vacation when they pressed this powder into a puck. Whatever the maker of our hash had used to bulk out the load; likely dung or henna, or wax had turned it black and made it hard as a rock.

It seemed our entire load was worthless.

Finn parlayed, "Sir, how would you like to buy some really awful hashish?" I jumped in, "There's a special sale on camel dung today, and today only." The whole affair had gotten ridiculous.

Laying the fiberglass mat down over the top layer of plastic that covered the pucks, was tedious. We worked on this a section at a time until we were able to get the appearance we wanted. As hard as we tried, the boat simply didn't have enough room to hide the entire six hundred kilos safely, so we decided if we jettisoned one hundred kilos of these black pucks it would certainly be zero loss. This would reduce our weight to a total of 500 kilos hidden under the first layer of plastic. The decision would help *Whitetail* maneuver the seas with more agility as well as ensuring a better job of hiding our contraband in the hull with essentially no measurable loss. An interesting twist.

We celebrated as we tossed each of the four hundred black pucks into the Atlantic and watched them sink, spiraling out of sight into the deep blue water. Neither laughing nor crying seemed appropriate, but we felt this was the first decision we'd made where we actually had any control. When the last of the four hundred black pucks plunked in, we applauded each other with our decision, and laughed at how brilliant we were. Genius.

But now, we just weren't ready for this. We had no idea of what we were getting into when we began to mix the catalytic hardener with the resin, things instantly turned serious and extremely dangerous. When we added the precise amount of the catalyst to the exact amount of resin, we had ten minutes to lay the resin-soaked mat in place covering the plastic sheeting that lay on top of the hashish. When the resin "went off" and turned hard as a rock, it would get hot and produce visible smoke-like fumes.

These fumes from the catalytic process were unbearable. Our eyes began to sting, and tears poured. Our throats burned. Our nose hairs disappeared, and we got a buzz that was more of a kicker than a double shot of moonshine but no fun. In this climate, the typical stay below lasted around twenty minutes, when we could no longer endure the fumes and leapt out into the cockpit gasping for clean, cool, air.

To further complicate an already impossible situation, the seas had continued to swell. They were up to about six feet now, and the wind was blowing its happy thirty knots again. Our only blessing was the fact that our destination required a broad reach, and the autopilot liked this heading, so we could work in the hell down below while the boat handled herself.

The five hundred kilos left were just enough to make *Whitetail* bury her bow in some of the steeper waves. This would send copious amounts of green water along the decks, then into the cockpit to douse the poor soul there trying to recoup from a stint down below. Aware of the explosive nature of the fumes, we dared not create any flame or spark. We were intoxicated, cold and hungry, not to mention tired, mad, and ripped off. We both sported headaches of epic proportions. The economy size Paracetamol (Aspirin) bottle was close to empty. Our bodies itched, burned and hurt all at the same time.

Finally, one gray morning after two days and two nights of this hell Finn appeared in the companionway. He had one of our makeshift face masks pulled up on top of his head.

"We're finished," he said with a smile.

I fell back against the cockpit coaming and threw my blue plastic glove covered hands, over my head and screamed out loud with sheer joy.

We let everything settle for a day. We allowed ourselves to relax and begin the healing process. We had a meal of our usual fare, cold beans and pasta from cans washed down with cold hot chocolate. We always kept a bottle of wine open.

The fiberglass installation had taken the better part of three days. Now *Whitetail* hurtled along doing a wild dance with each wave that passed. Running one small headsail held out leeward by the remaining whisker pole on a starboard tack, she acted as if she was doing her part to make up any lost time. The auto pilot thankfully had held a course all this time, but due to our myopically compromised states of mind, we had failed to keep an eye on our location. The general idea had been to keep her headed on a southwesterly course. The radar's perimeter alarm continued to scan in search of anything that entered a 5-mile radius.

We scheduled applying a thick finish coat of white paint for the next day. The cabin air was still thick with fiberglass fumes. Painting didn't take long. The paint rollers with their thick nap, covered our work perfectly. Truthfully, I could say, it looked pretty darn good. We took the next day to recoup and let the paint dry, a process that took longer than expected with the humidity and the cold temp. We opened all the hatches and vents we could to lend as much air flow to the cabin as possible. The paint dried to a sticky finish. We were able to cover the sticky areas when we reassembled the interior just as the mountainous island of Lanzarote came into view. We had about another twenty-five miles to go. While Finn held my legs, I leaned far out over *Whitetail's* transom, and with a can of acetone and a scraper, I carefully removed three hard- stuck letters, thus removing her alias, *BAT.* Did the diversion work? I'll never know. It must've.

A happier *Whitetail* glided into the calm of the winter-empty marina at Puerto Calero on Lanzarote, the eastern most island in the Canary archipelago. On Tuesday, January 28th, 1992 about eleven in the morning, we tied up at the customs dock, the only boat there.

We tied her up and found a place in the cockpit to lay down, then passed out from sheer exhaustion, coupled with a serious dose of asphyxiation. Hours must have passed when, with a knock on the hull, a pleasant Spanish gentleman, in an unusually crisp uniform, spoke to me.

"Captain pardon me. When you've rested, please come up the hill to my office to fill out your paperwork." He pointed up to the top of a long steep hill.

"Yes, yes, of course." I immediately I fell back to sleep. I don't think Finn woke at all.

* * *

"Cap, Cap," Finn shook my arm.

I worked to re-enter the world. Hours had passed and I wasn't sure if the Spanish customs officer had been a dream or not.

"We've got to climb that mountain," Finn laughed, "no matter how steep."

Then he pointed upward at an uncomfortable angle. "I asked a gentleman walking along the dock a couple of hours ago, if there is a restaurant nearby, and he pointed up this hill, and said it's a grand place for a celebratory dinner."

"Remember our customs officer from this morning?" I said. "We've got to pay him a visit soon, or he may get suspicious." Finn quipped, "You know mate, we're in the fertilizer business now."

"C'mon Cap, I'll be dead before we get to this restaurant if we don't get moving soon."

He danced along backwards, winding up the hill, all the while teasing me to follow. He pressed me over and over to wake up and get going. "C'mon, c'mon, let's go."

I was unsure about my general state. My fatigue was amplified by my hunger and the anxiety of our first "check in" with a customs officer while our contraband rested quietly, now glassed into *Whitetail's* hull. It must have been a little after four in the afternoon when, in the brilliant winter sun, we climbed the stone path, up the steep hill to a small office. We knocked and were greeted by the same pleasant gentleman from my dream, who, with a sweep of his hand, bade us enter.

"Please do come in. I could tell you were exhausted, and thought I'd let you sleep on."

"Thanks, my friend," I said. "We are worn out. The weather has been giving us a hard time."

His office was stifling hot. It was difficult to breathe. I guess I'd been so cold for so long that I'd become accustomed to it. Of course, it could also have been the effect from spending three days inhaling fiberglass resin fumes. We all sat down.

The office had an extraordinary view out across the Atlantic Ocean to the northeast. He said that he'd seen us coming when we cleared the horizon and had watched as we made our way toward his port. Small boats like *Whitetail* were all but nonexistent in this part of the world this time of year. He was very curious; more from boredom than from professional interest. I felt no discomfort from him or his questions. I was never sure if he was the port official or a customs officer, or both. Lanzarote didn't have any restrictions on noncommercial boats coming and going. A casual inspection of *Whitetail* from the dock as we slept through the afternoon seemed to suffice.

Still, he was keenly interested in drug smuggling and was especially attuned to any movement westward from the African coast. With a raised brow, in an "Inspector Clouseau" way, he showed interest in Finn being German, me being American, together on a boat with British registry from the Channel Island of Jersey, flying a Spanish courtesy flag, in route from Mallorca to the Caribbean. It took a while to explain it all. Finn chimed in, and between the two of us, we did a fantastic job.

It went like this: We were old friends bringing my boat back to the US. We had engine trouble in Ibiza, and it took weeks of waiting on parts for us to make the necessary mechanical repairs. Even though this problem had thrown us late in the season to continue the trip comfortably, we decided to carry on to the Caribbean despite the promise of terrible weather. We were looking forward to a vacation in Antigua before we took her home to the US, when Finn would return home to Germany and me back to real life in the construction business.

We talked at length about the US, about Germany, about the boat, and the weather we'd endured. We, in turn, asked him questions about Lanzarote. He lit up, animated with his audience. His name was Leopoldo and he'd grown up in Lanzarote. He shared photos of his wife and kids. We were curious about his island, and he was proud to share his world with anyone who would listen.

Finally, a break in the conversation left room for me to ask where we might find a good meal. We were so hungry… we worked to ignore the thought of sustenance. A hand full of freeze-dried peanuts had held us for the past few hours. Leopoldo stood and apologized knowing we must be tired and hungry. Since we'd come from Mallorca and were now in Lanzarote, both Spanish islands, we had very little paperwork to fill out. We didn't mention our stop in Gibraltar. Most of the paperwork was relative to our entering and staying at his new marina here in Puerto Calero. We were one of three boats in the marina on this winter's day.

We needed to fill our tanks with diesel fuel, so he told us to stay tied up where we were for as long as we'd like, and he'd help us take on fuel whenever we were ready. Hands firmly shook all around and we went from the stifling little office back into the fresh, clean mid ocean air.

We stood there breathing in so deeply and exhaling so hard, that Leopoldo came out to make sure we were alright. "Oh, Captain, I forgot to ask. While you were sleeping this afternoon, I walked down to check your boat into the Marina. I noticed a very odd smell, something like paint that seemed to be coming from her." He painted the air with an invisible brush to make sure we understood. My mind vaulted from relaxed and anticipating our meal, to ultra-anxiety. A transition that takes a toll on me. I forced myself to be cool and wipe that "deer in the head lights" look off my face. I furrowed my brow and shook my head as if trying to figure out what the smell might be. "Oh… I know. We had a couple of days when we could work on her varnish, so we decided to put a coat on her toe rail and cabin trim." We kept Whitetail's varnish up to par during the trip and had taken a couple of days while in Puerto Mogan to add another coat. Your boat shows that you take good care of her. I get so many junkers in here in the summertime. It's amazing what people will take to sea. He turned and locked his office door and bade us to follow him back down the hill to Guiermo's Café. When we entered the Café a most gregarious brother gave Leopoldo a hard hug and turned to take us to a table by the windows. I excused myself to use the telephone I'd seen on the wall in the foyer. I needed to call Diana. As I passed by Finn, he opened his eyes wide, in question, and gave me a "Do we need to worry" look. I returned his question with a look and shook my head to say to indicate, "I don't think so." I felt we'd passed our clearance into Puerto Calero in good shape. I still was a bit shaken and wary.

Leopoldo came from back in the kitchen area, a small brown bag in hand. He slapped me on the back as he passed by while I was on the phone with Diana. "Buen provecho amigo," he whispered and waved. He was off, whistling on his way down the hill toward home. A phenomenal sunset surrounded him with colors rarely found on an artist's pallet. These colors sparkled and made music across the vast Atlantic spread out far below.

* * *

An anxious Diana grabbed the receiver before the phone rang twice.

"Sweetheart, are you all right?"

I told her about our ordeal. I described parts of the sail, the fumes, the arrival at Lanzarote, the pleasant customs agent, and the restaurant awaiting, where I stood staring in the doorway, mouth-watering, watching as Finn savored a glass of wine and a plate of sardines. Diana was so relieved she began to cry. I consoled her as best I could. I opted not to share the fact that we weren't certain yet about the quality of our contraband. I wouldn't do that until I was completely certain what we had on board.

I explained to her that we'd be recuperating here on Lanzarote another three days before heading to Antigua, and our anticipated landfall. This next part of the sail would take another 21+ days at sea. We decided that in 30 days she'd fly from New Hampshire to Antigua, bringing the much-needed additional funding. I must admit, although I truly loved Diana, and I wanted to keep talking; the platter of sardines and gnarly bread that Finn was devouring reaped havoc with my normally gentlemanly ethics. I told her I just had to go for now, and all was fine. I couldn't wait to see her in Antigua in 30 days.

"I love you baby!" I said and hung up.

Finn had not wasted one moment in his quest for sustenance, and while I was in the foyer on the phone with Diana, he began his repairs with a glass of wine and a baguette, then a plate of sardines for starters.

He raised his glass when I came in. He was feeling so good that he stood up and gave me a big hug, spilling most of his glass of wine down my back. No time for a menu.

"Senor, por favor...estafado de pollo, mas pan, y un otra botello de vino."

My trembling hand already had a piece of Finn's bread which was in my mouth before the waiter turned to head back to the kitchen. Ahhhh... unreal. Sustenance immediately began to run through my body with the first bite of this crusty baguette. Finn was all but laughing at me. I looked at him and shook my head, eyes wide with a mouth full of bread.

"Do you believe how good this is?" Our strength began to return right there at the table. Finn and I laughed and talked incessantly about our adventures. Neither of us allowed the stark reality of what was happening with the plan, to interrupt this once in a lifetime meal. Denial...it works.

* * *

I slept like a dead man. *Whitetail* bumped hard against the dock to wake me. I lay there staring at the wooden ceiling over my berth and pulled up my blanket. The reality of where I was, and where I was going, haunted my every thought.

I have a terrible habit of wanting to move to the places I love when I encounter them. It helps salve the sadness of leaving with the thought that I'll be back. It was a short stay, but the ways of Lanzarote that winter will always be a part of me. I've never been back…yet.

After another two days of taking on fuel and stores, and bolstering our energy, Finn and I were quiet as we slipped through the cold dark morning just ahead of the dawn. We took up a southerly heading, resisting the urge to head west. Old sailors who made their way along this path for hundreds of years said, "Head south until your butter melts, then turn westward."

After several days on our southerly heading, we got closer to the Cape Verde Islands. It began to get a bit warmer, then noticeably warmer. We doffed layers of winter clothing to greet the warmth, and finally spun *Whitetail* westward. It seemed that I had also managed to doff some part of my tenacious anxiety. I had arrived at the crossroads where you realize that you can go through trials and tribulations in "two ways". This is always your choice. You pick it Wilson.

CHAPTER TWENTY-NINE
Sailing Across the Atlantic Ocean

T HE WEATHER CONTINUED TO WARM DAY AFTER DAY. The wind blew constantly at 35 knots, from our starboard quarter accompanied by fast moving six to eight-foot seas. The weather was balmy. *Whitetail* kicked up her heels as she reveled in this perfect combination. We dropped the mainsail and rigged up a canopy over the dodger that would shield the cockpit from the sun. The two foresails were held out wing and wing, one with the remaining whisker pole, and the other tethered to the tip of the main boom, held forward with a preventer. We barreled along in this configuration for days while her stern rode up and down and the following seas passed us by.

We towed a large spoon fishing lure, nicknamed the "MG Bumper."

I'd mounted a stout bait casting reel securely to the leeward lifeline stanchion. We caught mahi-mahi daily and concocted one fabulous meal after another. Sadly, we often pulled trash from the lure in the middle of the Atlantic Ocean. There were a variety of plastics mixed with logs, old furniture, and huge floating containers. During the night, we feared these containers, some as big as *Whitetail*. Should they wander into our heading where we could ram them, they could cause tremendous damage to our hull sufficient to possibly sink us.

A freighter occasionally made a cameo appearance passing close by heading north, most likely directly to a U.S. port. Freighters in shipping lanes can be a very serious hazard to small boats. We kept our perimeter alarm set to a 10-mile radius. If the radar picked up anything within that radius, a loud alarm would sound giving us time to find the intruder and alter our course if necessary.

Finn and I were on top of the world. After about a week, we entered the fair winds out of the east. Our speed never slowed, day and night we barreled along…flying. We cavorted with monster fish that found company in the shade of *Whitetail's* keel. Some must have been fifteen feet long. We thought they might be some type of Sturgeon. They swam right alongside for days at a time.

On another day, a medium sized whale passed close to our stern out of nowhere. I was fearful he could become entangled with the taft-rail generator. The humming sound it made could have attracted him.

Repeatedly he would come directly towards us, picking up speed and riding the surface of a wave rolling under our stern. When he got near, too near for my comfort, he'd dive under the boat, just under the keel and play along, zigzagging back and forth in the turbulence made by the keel as it cut through the water. As a precaution, we pulled the generator line and the fishing lure into the boat and tied a length of line around ourselves and the other end to the boat. If for some reason this whale miscalculated and hit the keel, he would really shake *Whitetail* hard. Hard enough to easily knock us overboard.

The whale entertained us for hours. He wouldn't go away. I figured he thought he'd found a long-lost friend. He would dive under the boat and repeat the same routine, over and over.

Then suddenly he disappeared, and never returned.

We were alone again, skimming along on our own personal sparkling blue ocean.

Days slid by and turned into weeks. We'd been gifted by the gods with three perfect weeks of sailing on an ideal course. I guess they thought we needed the break. I'd never say openly that we deserved it, but dammit, we did. I found myself almost disappointed as we began to move into a calculable distance from our landfall. It seemed every day, as we neared Antigua, my spirits suffered a downturn. The dream was surely coming to an end and monsters slowly returned.

We caught the first glimpse of the island on the afternoon of our 21st day after leaving Lanzarote. At first it was difficult to distinguish it from just another large wave. Finn and I shared binoculars and stared at the hump on the horizon until we were sure it wasn't moving. We had made phenomenal time for a boat our size carrying such a heavy load. As long as the afternoon sun shone bright, we watched Antigua draw closer. We spoke little. An odd melancholy set in.

Then the sun began to drop behind the mountains, and the sky turned a bright orange. Unbeknownst to me, Finn had stashed a bottle of Champagne. A particularly good bottle, known for its tiny bubbles.

"Cap!"

He appeared in the companionway wearing a t-shirt that had a tuxedo screen printed on it, and a floppy hat.

"To us."

He sent the cork flying and poured two large celebratory glasses. With carefully worded toasts, hugs, and slaps on the back, we pretended not to see each other's tears as darkness fell.

We drew closer to Antigua and soon we could make out little specks of light along the coast and up in the mountains. After a moment of working with the GPS and the charts, I knew we were seven miles from English Harbor where I'd chosen to make landfall, and subsequently our home for staging the next step of this errant adventure. It was time to drop our sails.

Three weeks of immobility had made us as stiff as our salt encrusted sails. With some effort, we tied each one to the lifelines of their respective sides. We fired up our trusty diesel and rounded the eastern tip of Antigua, passed Green Island, and were shortly off the entrance to English Harbor. After we had rounded the southern tip, the breeze picked up the smell of land and presented it to us like a gift. The scent was exotic. Herbal. My head spun from sensory overload.

We motored ever so slowly and carefully through the dark. We passed through the opening in the high rock cliffs that have protected English Harbor from the ravages of the sea forever. Finn stood on the bow, slightly illuminated by the dim light mounted high up, on the front of the mast, quietly directing me with hand signals as we carefully and slowly, wove our way around and between a myriad of boats anchored there in the crowded harbor. We followed the lights at the docks until we felt we were comfortably near. Then Finn picked up a mooring ball and tied *Whitetail* to it. He turned, smiled, and shrugged his shoulders. I stood at the helm; hands cramped in place on the wheel. English Harbor was quiet. It was the middle of the night. No one knew we'd arrived, no one cared. A few loose halyards tinked against their masts in welcome.

We spoke in whispers.

All was still and silent. Magical. Done.

CHAPTER THIRTY
Antigua / English Harbor

Wℋᴇɴ ᴛʜᴇ ɴᴇxᴛ ᴍᴏʀɴɪɴɢ's first beam of sunlight found me, I was in total confusion wondering where on earth I was.

Oh yeah, I know. On *Whitetail.* But why weren't we moving, where was the sound of the waves caressing our hull. Why is the boat so still? Pulling myself up on my elbows, I shook my head until reality began to fill the voids.

I sat up a minute, confirmed where I was and stepped up into the rear companionway. I looked out onto a most exquisitely beautiful harbor, dotted with a hundred peaceful boats from all around the world. It was completely still, and the morning sun reflected so brightly from each hull that I had to squint to see. The water under our keel was as clear as a glass of drinking water.

Finn's head popped up in the forward companionway.

"Are we really here, Cap?" We looked at each other across the cockpit and laughed.

"Are you in the mood for a bit of breakfast?"

He responded with a look that said it all. In minutes, we untied our inflatable dinghy which had been strapped on the aft deck since we left Mallorca. Finn pumped away at the salt encrusted pile of folded grey rubber as it began to resemble a little boat. I released the outboard from its home on the stern pulpit and reunited it with our Avon dinghy. We washed up as best we could in our hurry and dropped down into the dinghy, now floating on water as clear as air.

We pulled the Avon up on the beach and turned to stand on solid ground, almost falling over at the sudden change from *Whitetail's rolling* deck. We had become so accustomed to anticipating her every move as she danced beneath our feet for the past several months, we didn't know how to recalculate our body's gyro. Laughing like fools, we swaggered along the beach looking like drunks while we looked for the first restaurant that could fry an egg.

Somewhere between that first smell of bacon in the skillet, and the last bite of homemade toast with fig preserves, I managed to banish the thought of 600 kilos of hashish lining our hull. Little yellow birds stopped by to visit on top of our table, rummaging for whatever they found edible.

Other patrons, mostly proper British couples, caught themselves staring at us with a look of disdain, and then quickly averting their eyes when we nodded. I'm sure we presented the despicable appearance of a pretty sketchy pair. Blackened by the sun, gaunt, dirty, with long hair and scraggly beards. Neither of us had looked in a mirror for weeks. We were the ones they hoped their daughters would never bring home.

After we'd eaten all the little restaurant had to offer, we went back to *Whitetail* to assess her general condition in the bright morning sun and identify any damages. I stopped by the marina office in the back of the cove to check on customs and the entry process.

It was late February of 1992, and the island was buzzing in preparation for a huge annual celebration, "Antigua Sailing Week." Boat slips at the docks were at a premium in English Harbor, the hub for all festivities. It hit me suddenly that we had no anchor or chain. Yesterday evening we were able to negotiate tying to one of the mooring balls, but I expected to be asked to anchor in Falmouth Harbor, the adjacent protected anchorage to the west.

As I walked into the office, one of the managers, behind a desk stood up, waved frantically at me, and motioned out the window to the docks below.

"Would you like to have one of the slips?" She whispered in a very British accent. "One of the larger cruisers has just called to cancel their reservation, and I need to get it leased instantly, right now, like yesterday!"

Thrilled at our fortune, I quickly accepted her offer. We moved *Whitetail* into her new home, stern to, right in front of the marina office. It was a wonderful way to polish off a successful Atlantic crossing.

* * *

Customs consisted of a visit to the office, a bit of paperwork and nothing more. Essentially our experience to date had been that we could have left the load resting in plain sight on the cabin floor. But we still had the fearsome US customs and the DEA to deal with. I was sure they would care a whole lot more than these peaceful easy-going islanders.

I called Diana, and all seemed well. She had met with El Capitan' in New Hampshire and was holding onto the additional investment funds he'd given her, till we could meet in Antigua. She planned to come south in about a week. I was to pick her up at the airport.

I was so excited to see her. During the whole trip across the Atlantic, I'd wished to have her there to share the experience with me. I'd even begun to plan the next crossing to include her. If only I could have had her there… well, things might have gone differently. But despite our efforts to control what time we're given here on earth, our lives, tend to go along as if fueled by a whim, certainly not the way we lay them out.

Finn and I settled into the festivities of preparation for Race Week. Every night there was a jump up on the high cliff called Shirley Heights that looked over the entrance to English Harbor. A Jump Up is the islander's equivalent to a Ho Down only fueled by rum, reggae, and reefer, as compared to moon shine, whiskey, and a square dance. We ate, drank and partied into the wee hours surrounded by famous people with huge yachts.

One-night Finn even ended up in an all-night billiards game with Keith Richards and some friends. Eric Clapton had a lovely sixty-foot sailing yacht a few boats down from *Whitetail*. He had celebrated his birthday that week. Rick Wright, from Pink Floyd was over in Falmouth Harbor on his lovely Swan 65' ketch, "Evrika".

I later had the pleasure of calling Richard a friend. He and a dear old friend of mine fell in love and married. For me, meeting him was the chance to spend time with a rare and talented artist and gentleman. He was plucked from this world way too soon. The world is sadly out one great man.

When we weren't partying the days and nights away, Finn and I filled those warm early spring days working on *Whitetail's* varnish and making mechanical repairs. We needed to get the masthead fitting for her inner forestay rebuilt at the sail loft. It had finally pulled away from the top of the mast after enduring constant stress from the beginning of the voyage and was hanging on by a sliver of stainless steel just waiting to let go at any minute. Her sails had also been compromised and needed about half dozen patches sewn in to reinforce the hard-worn places. I planned to have *Whitetail*, totally rebuilt when we finally got her to Thunderbolt, Georgia and offloaded.

The week went by in a flash as Finn cornered the girls, and I impatiently awaited Diana's arrival. She and I were going to take a couple of weeks off to spend time together onboard *Whitetail*.

* * *

Finally, she was there, running up the ramp from her flight at the airport, her brilliant smile lighting her way. She dropped her bags and jumped into my arms. Laughing, we spun around and around, out of control until we were dizzy.

When we got to *Whitetail*, we quickly dropped her lines on the pier and set sail to Green Island, a small private sanctuary off the southeastern coast of Antigua We hid out, swinging to *Whitetail's* new anchor and chain, sharing every imaginable indulgence. Finn stayed behind with his newfound friends.

I laughed at the memory of the orange's removal. It was there to stay and had no intention of sharing some dumb anchor's hawse pipe. For just a brief moment, my mind drifted back to the stormy night of our sinking. "Baby, where are you? You're some place far away." I popped back to the moment, and the orange finally yielded to my trusty knife and popped out on the deck, hard and dry in the sun. With utmost respect, I paid homage with a proper memorial service to this life saving citrus. I mounted the new chain and anchor in its place.

Diana and I carried on northward from Green Island to Barbuda, a flat, beachy, and almost deserted island. After a couple of weeks, we completed our circumnavigation of Antigua and re-entered English Harbor. It didn't take long to find Finn in the shade of a favorite bar, with two lovely women laughing, and hanging onto each arm.

Diana stayed with me another week, then left to go back to Atlanta and prepare for my arrival at Thunderbolt, Georgia. As we bade farewell at the airport once more, she turned to me and spoke very quietly.

"Baby… I'm pregnant".

"What?"

Surely, I must've misunderstood.

"Did you did say you're pregnant?"

Oh, my god…a child. Was this a good thing? Was this a bad thing? Certainly, an unexpected thing.

"I debated whether to wait and tell you when you got to Thunderbolt," she explained, "but I just couldn't keep the secret from you for another day."

Evidently, our tryst in the Canaries two months ago had yielded a sprout. A kid…I'd have to change a few things. Diana would be a great mom. It would be a new level of responsibility for me.

My head hurt as I rode back to English Harbor.

The bar was my first stop.

CHAPTER THIRTY-ONE
Thunderbolt / No one Blinked

"THINK YOU COULD PULL THIS LAST LEG OFF SOLO, CAP?" Finn said, grinning. "I could just hang in here a few more months with all the ladies, then catch a flight home."

Daily, we'd put off our inevitable departure for Thunderbolt, promising ourselves just one more day, then we'll go, just one more day. We'd found the time in Antigua to be captivating. I consoled myself, with the assurance that I'd be back before long to stay.

We finally broke away with the consolation that we'd stop in on Dove along the way. He had opened his new restaurant on the island of Anguilla. Yep, the same Dove who'd connected me with Phillippe a million years ago. Dove knew everyone along the Atlantic crossing paths, the western Med, and the Caribbean. And we all knew him. In fact, it was Dove who'd reminded me of Finn's potential availability to crew on my exploit.

I told Finn, "It will be a proper way to begin the end. We'll drop by to see ole Dove. I've not seen him in years, and I hear he's doing quite well."

So off we went, under the guise that we'd stop by for a free meal with Dove. We motored *Whitetail* out of English Harbor, leaving behind a small piece of our hearts. As soon as we were clear of the rocky cliffs, we hoisted sails and she picked up her skirts and began to dance to her own private reel, while the wind played the tune.

We were bound for Anguilla, 100 miles of perfect sailing to the northwest.

"Finn, isn't this incredible how easily we fell back into this routine?"

"Those girls have probably already forgotten me," he lamented. "I was so in love." Finn grinned; eyes glazed as he gazed far up into the endless deep blue morning sky.

"I'm sure they're in love with you too man." He winked at me.

Whitetail was flying along on a fast reach taking us ever further away from a beautiful dream.

"They'll be there, waiting for you when you come back."

* * *

At 2 a.m., May 3rd, 1992 we ghosted into Crocus Bay on Anguilla and dropped our new anchor in about fifteen feet of clear water.

A long night of quiet, uninterrupted sleep recharged our batteries, and we awoke to an exquisite scene. *Whitetail* was suspended on "air clear" water, as were about a dozen other sailboats, presumably all heading north after the festivities in Antigua. The early morning sun made everything sparkle. The bay was surrounded by tall cliffs, lined with shacks and open-air restaurants. It was early, and no one was moving.

After a pot of coffee and a morning swim, we went in search of Dove and his new restaurant. The first person we met on the beach pointed the way to "Basil's." Dove almost ran into a prominent palm when he saw us.

"Oh, my God! What is this? Kate, hurry, come look what the seagulls drug in. What did I do to deserve this?"

Kate, Dove's better half, and both of their kids came running to see what caused all the early morning ruckus.

"Pierce, Finn, c'mon in, sit down over there. Now, tell me what you're up to. I need a good story this morning. Where've you been. Good God, c'mon in."

We all sat at a large table in the empty early morning restaurant, and tall tales began to flow around on the gentle early morning breeze. I smelled bacon frying, and soon, plates of fresh eggs, toast from homemade bread with fresh butter and garden tomatoes were passed around the table.

Dove was shaking his head in disbelief as we shared some of the highlights of our misadventure.

"Only you guys. What an incredible tale. Well, if you lose it all, the one thing that no one can take from you are your memories. You should write a book."

"I'm very surprised at Yousef Abboud. To my knowledge, this is something that has never happened. I hope you have a dose of good luck when it comes to taking it up to Canada. Those folks up there will probably go for it."

We spent the day in their care. In the late afternoon, Dove began to prepare for dinner guests. Finn and I joined them at the restaurant for dinner. When the last guest was gone, we carried on with Dove and Kate for "after dinner" drinks. It was extremely late that night, when we sadly bid adieu and walked in the dark down the steep hill to the dinghy awaiting our return on the beach. We rowed out to *Whitetail* floating in the bay, bathed in the dim light provided by a billion stars. Our visit had been invigorating, but we needed to press ahead with an early departure on our last leg… home, to Thunderbolt, Georgia.

* * *

We sailed for 10 days with incredible exhilarating broad reaches that were then followed by hours of dead calm.

I became increasingly worried as we closed in on our destination. The futility of our exercise haunted my every waking hour. I lay awake worried and spent, tired of it all. I had been able to temporarily overlook my real dilemma, absorbed with the daily process of sailing a small boat across a big ocean. Now, the undeniable reality lurked. I could do nothing about these ghosts. The whole tribe came back to haunt me with a vengeance. It was time to figure out what really could be done with a load of highly compressed dung. Fertilizer remained at the top of the list.

The day was hot and still as I waited for a nonexistent wind to come and take us the last 500 miles. We motored for about two days pushing ever closer to our "finale". And as the final miles passed under our keel, I developed a hollow hopeless feeling that just would not go away.

Finally, we found ourselves at the entrance to the Wilmington River. In just a few miles, we ran aground on a low water mud bank. Then, while we waited for the tide to come in and set us free, we were digested alive by a welcoming party of four billion relentless No-See-Ums. When we began to float with the incoming tide, we fired up our faithful diesel and pulled off the mud bank back into the channel.

After 8 long months, and more than 9,000 miles, we tied up in Thunderbolt to await our final customs and immigration inspections, for entry into the US. I felt hollow.

* * *

It was May 20, 1992. I called on the VHF radio and requested entry. I was so tired and beaten by my own devices, that when the two customs agents arrived on the dock, I was at the point of simply not caring what happened.

The agents, a man and a woman, were a pleasant couple. They sat in our cockpit with stacks of papers for us to fill out. They asked where we came from, where we'd been, what we'd been doing, and where were we going. They were duly impressed with our abridged stories of coming from Mallorca to Thunderbolt. Our story was entertaining. They said most of the folks they saw came from Maine or New England, on their way down to, or on their way back from Florida, or they were jumping off to the Caribbean, or on their way home.

They marveled at the smallness of *Whitetail*. They couldn't comprehend two people sailing across an ocean in a boat this size. They sat in our cockpit for several hours talking, laughing, and filling out papers. They never even looked below. Evidently, the boat and our countenances conveyed no element of suspicion that would concern them enough to look more closely at us or the boat. They could never have imagined what lay just beneath their feet. The obnoxious smell had withered to a faint hint and was no cause for worry.

Once we'd cleared customs, I immediately called Diana. I could hear her on the other end of the phone, whirling around, dancing and whooping, overwhelmed with relief.

We were in port, through customs and finally safe and sound. She would drive down tomorrow. Finn was ready to get back to Greece as quickly as he could.

Diana arrived at about 8 a.m. after driving five hours from Atlanta. When the car door flew open, she popped out and ran straight and fast into my arms sending me staggering backward, almost falling. She grabbed me fiercely and burst into hysterical sobbing. She couldn't speak.

Something was wrong, really wrong. I looked over her shoulder to see if there was something chasing her. All this emotion was definitely not a reaction to our safe arrival. She said something through muffled sobs.

"I lost it..."

"What... lost what sweetheart?"

It took a few minutes of waiting and listening, for the news to sink in.

"Our baby is gone." unable to speak, she sobbed.

She'd miscarried. Our baby was gone.

We hugged a long quiet tight hug. I didn't let her go.

Finn quietly went below to pack for his flight to Madrid, then onward to Athens.

* * *

Diana was physically fine, but the loss left an irreparable sadness for what might have been and now will never be. The loss of our child was a terrible burden for her to bear. We did not expect, nor plan to include a child in our life at this point, and when Diana had gotten pregnant, she was excited and said she was ready to nurture this gift. Me, I had not been so sure, and even though I felt overcome and deeply saddened by our loss, our feelings were telltales regarding our choices on parenting. Maybe we'd try again, yes let's try again later. I knew, for sure, now wasn't the right time.

We went for a long walk along the Wilmington River and came to grips with this new reality. We spent the rest of the day together watching the red sun dip into the grass of the marsh. We found Finn and shared a good bottle of wine to accompany an unusually great seafood dinner, like you find at one of those funky little crab shacks along southern coastal rivers.

The next morning, Diana and I took Finn to the airport. He and I discussed money along the way. I promised to send his part of the money just as soon as the rewards for our efforts began to come home. As I spoke to him, I felt guilty, as if I was lying to him. I couldn't see that what we had in the boat would have much value at all. I only hoped I was wrong. If I wasn't wrong, then *Whitetail* would certainly be collateral damage as would everything else I had left, and then some. I hesitated to share the severity of this with Diana, particularly now with this new development.

Finn understood what I was up against. He knew I had been duped, and the value of the contraband, we'd fought so hard to get, was just about nil. At the airport, Finn and I shared a long hard bear hug, then stood apart, holding each other's arms hard, with a good long look. No one blinked.

Finn turned abruptly, and without a word, walked down the runway to board his flight. He skipped, spun around, and walked backwards with that million-dollar smile, both hands waving. I smiled back, I battled tears and pulled my sunglasses down to cover my sadness. I remembered when I first picked him up at the airport in Palma de Mallorca, banjo in hand. I never thought that I would not see him again.

* * *

Finn was gone. I immediately missed his energy. My world echoed in his absence. Our bond had been galvanized by impossible circumstances, and now I was on my own. I decided my best move would be to wait a few days for the Memorial Day weekend. Then the shelter of the Thunderbolt holiday crowd would help provide cover for the discreet removal of the contraband from *Whitetail's* hull.

Diana stayed a few days, but it seemed best for her to be gone when the time came to cut the load out of the hull.

"Sweetheart," she said to me, "don't you think it would better for me to stay and help run errands, and give you a hand with getting that stuff out of the boat?"

"Thanks, beautiful, but if something should go wrong, I would really need for you to be able to help and not get caught up in whatever goes wrong."

She reluctantly agreed, with the understanding that she would leave the following day. We were still in shock over her miscarriage, and found relief spending this last day together. We needed to be together. We worked better together. The sooner we could get this stuff to Atlanta and sent off to a new home, the sooner we'd be able to start putting our lives in concert once again. The thought was motivating.

The next day, as soon as we could rent a car, we put Diana on the road. I rented a storage shed at the marina and began the impossible task of unloading *Whitetail*.

First, I needed to remove salty sails, salty lines, worn out sailing gear, and rusty cans of unopened stores. Every one of them reminded me of Finn. There were cans of dolmades, mung beans, red rice, black rice, alphabet noodles, black and green olives, tomatoes in various configurations, white asparagus, white sausages, and dozens of other stores I'd never heard of. All the while I was arranging the boat's interior to allow for removing the contraband. I had a difficult time referring to it as hashish.

Memorial Day weekend, 1992 came on quickly with all the people, revelry, and noise I had hoped for. I began my project early Friday morning before it was light. My goal was to free the hashish from its hiding place. I used a sharp aggressive toothed hand saw with a stiff blade. I had employed a local machine shop back in Mallorca to cut the saw into a custom shape. It was fourteen inches long with the forward end of the blade tapering down to 3" with the corners rounded. This would allow quick cutting in hard to reach spaces. It performed perfectly.

The whole day Friday was spent carefully sawing the surface of the glass matting into small random shapes that would allow me to tear the pieces out in manageable sizes. Even though I had on a long sleeve shirt, a hat and a bandana tied over my mouth it was all no match for the fiberglass dust. I was covered with grit that seemed intent on getting under my skin.

On Saturday morning, while wearing thick leather gloves, I began to pull the sharp glass mat away from the hull to reveal the contraband. I pulled the brittle, prickly sheets of fiberglass mat away from the hull, and began opening the hiding places. When I finally peeled a piece out exposing the load, a rank sickening ammonia fetor crept up from the bilge. It filled the boat and choked me to the point that I was unable to breath. I hopped up into the open companionway gulping for air and began an incessant barrage of chain sneezing with a compliment of a few dry hurls.

When the first attack had somewhat subsided, I mustered enough courage to delve deeper and decipher the source. I held my breath, covered my nose and mouth with a dishtowel, and eased back down below. Further inspection revealed that the problem stemmed from the intake of copious amounts of seawater during the voyage. The imperfect fiberglass bond to the hull had formed small spaces where the fiberglass blend hadn't completely bonded to the hull. These gaps allowed the pucks that we'd laid in the lower area of the hull to soak up sea water for weeks. They'd turned from hard black camel dung into soft black camel dung. The dung had morphed into a mush with a foul ammonia smell bordering on intolerable. The layers of pucks on the lower level were totally ruined, but those stacked in the upper tiers weren't so wet and in pretty good condition.

I feared I'd lost roughly another 150 kilos to water damage. I consoled myself with the poor logic that it really wasn't much of a loss, since, had it been in perfect condition, it still represented the same useless commodity. One hundred kilos of which I'd opted to throw overboard in the Atlantic Ocean so the boat wouldn't be overloaded. I now planned to shovel another 150 kilos of stinking mush into the river at nightfall. So, it seemed, at this moment, I had a total of 350 kilos of seemingly worthless stuff that didn't resemble the superb hashish I'd selected in Ketama.

Good God, I thought. *What's next?*

If only I'd known. Again, it's better that I didn't.

I pulled the jagged fiberglass pieces from the hull and loaded them into old sail bags. An electric fan, a filter mask, and a bit of time for breaks to get out and breathe, rendered the smell slightly less caustic, then again, maybe I was just getting used to it.

Diana had driven my pickup truck from Atlanta to Thunderbolt. Its low camper cover was perfect for making the load discreet. I'd taken Diana to the airport for her flight home to Atlanta and kept the truck for my drive there once the contraband was loaded. With the help of the marina's hand truck, I lugged the sail bags, bursting from the weight of the fiberglass chards, one at a time, from the boat to the truck and slid them out of sight under the bed cover.

Exhausted, I slept in the aft cabin for a few restless hours and headed to Tybee Island, about fifteen miles away. There, I emptied the contents of the sail bags into a conveniently anonymous dumpster and stopped by Home Depot to pick up twenty-two large plastic storage boxes with lids and continued back to the Marina.

It was early Saturday morning. I was recharged. I went back to *Whitetail* and set about loading the same, now empty, well-worn sail bags, with contraband. At this point it was difficult to pretend the bags contained sails as they were extraordinarily heavy. But the folks milling about the marina this early morn seemed to pay no attention to me, absorbed as they were with preparation for their own celebration.

It had been five days now since Finn and I had arrived. I'd been so prevalent in the Marina I'd become a fixture, just another sailor working on his boat. As the day began to come into focus, groups of people, families, and kids, all began to nod and wave and wish me a happy holiday. I reciprocated in kind and went about my work as if it was just one more day in the life.

I worked like a Trojan all Saturday and far into the night. By the end of Saturday night, I'd managed to dispose the balance of the fiberglass pieces I'd cut from the hull. I'd thrown the useless rancid mush overboard in the dark of night, and moved the contraband, a little at a time, from the boat to my storage shed. I organized the 350 kilos or 1,400 pucks in the twenty plastic bins. Each bin weighed just under 38 pounds on my new bathroom scale freshly purchased from the Home Depot.

This undertaking was no easy feat. Using the marina's hand trucks, the process took ten trips from the boat to the shed, each trip with two storage bins, bout 76 pounds per trip. I used the marina's hand trucks. I had intended to make this move during the daylight, but I'd fallen behind, and it was about ten in the evening before I was finally done. I looked like I had been run over by fast freight.

"Howdy mister."

Adrenaline made a loop. Trying to pull my eyes back in their sockets, I turned and nodded at the security officer standing there. He'd materialized from nowhere. My mind went blank while I tried to quell my totally freaked out reaction.

"Good evening sir," I sputtered. "What great weather we're having for the holiday weekend."

I stared up into the darkness as if admiring the "weather." A few big moths fluttered around the parking lot lights. I needed to find "cool." I felt as if the guard knew exactly what I was doing.

"I noticed you been working like a dawg all day long. Down to your boat and back up here, down to your boat and back here. What in the world are you doin'? It's a holiday, shouldn't you be drinking a few beers and eatin' hot dogs and hamburgers?"

"Yes sir, you're exactly right. I told my wife when she left me here yesterday, that I'd probably work the whole weekend if she left me alone."

"My name's Tony," he stuck out his hand. "What all do you have going on here?"

"Mine's Pierce," I said, smiling as I shook it. "I'm sorting out a lot of stuff on board. After that bad weather I had, there is a good bit of damaged equipment," I explained, trying to stay cool. "At one point, I think everything on that boat was soaking wet with saltwater. Blankets, sheets, sails, tools, cans, everything."

"Looks to me like you could use a little help. I've got a couple of kids that'd help you out if you want."

"Thanks, I would have taken you up on that yesterday, but I think I've got it by the horns now. I didn't realize how much work it'd be."

I searched for a safer line of conversation.

"I've just sailed from the Canary Islands in this boat. I've got to pull just about everything out and see what I can save, and what I'll have to throw away. That sail over there for example," I motioned toward the open door of the storage shed, which revealed only the darkness inside the shed. "It was brand new when I struck out, and now, it's probably no good at all. The stitches around the clew have pulled out, and the dacron material is so ruined that most of the other stitching has failed."

"Well, if you ask me, you look like you could use a break." I'll bet I did appear to need a break. I'm sure I made a pretty rough appearance. Hot, tired, dirty, smelly, unshaven.

"Why don't you join me over at the club house for a dawg and a beer?"

He turned and headed resolutely to the busy club house, talking to me over his shoulder.

"Did you say the "what" islands…the Contrary Islands? Where the hell is that?"

I reconsidered, "You know, I'd better go lock up the storage shed and call it a night. Let's have that dawg for lunch tomorrow. I'm buying. If I'm not careful, somebody may take a shine to that stinking bunch of garbage I'm paying to store here."

We laughed and waved.

"I'll see you tomorrow."

I couldn't quit worrying about the guard. He honestly didn't seem to be that curious, but I knew I'd stick out in the crowd, and that wasn't good. I felt it prudent to join him for lunch the next day. You know the adage, hold your enemies closer. Mainly, I needed to get on the road to Atlanta as quickly as I could.

Dividing and labeling the contraband was confusing and I noted a rough count based on what it looked like. It was what it was…no good at all.

I locked the storage shed, threw my hands in the air, bent backwards, then forward to touch my palms to the ground. The sand stuck to my dirty hands. I was dazed. Time had no meaning. I peered into the darkness over-looking the river. I had no energy left. I was spent. Exhausted, I laid down on *Whitetail's* cockpit seats and fell into the world of dead men.

* * *

I awoke to morning fog, soaking wet, covered with a heavy layer of fallen dew. I was a dirty mess. I smelled bad. I stepped down below into a terrible mess. *Whitetail* only remotely resembled the beautiful boat she had been. It looked as if a bomb had been set off inside her cabin. Consoled by a cup of coffee, I wiped a clean spot on the main cabin table where my elbows could rest, and I began to look over my notes.

I couldn't think clearly about these things right now. Speculation was a waste of energy, and there just wasn't enough to waste. It looked like I'd lost everything and still owed about another $155k.

I spent Monday morning, Memorial Day of 1992, cleaning *Whitetail* and putting her back together again. I hoped that Mustafa, Yousef Abboud's son in Montreal, could sell this trash. He would have to be a miracle worker to move this stuff, but who knows? I chose to look at it as positively as possible. I worked on my perspective, and prepared to depart Wednesday morning, after leaving *Whitetail* situated at the Palmer and Johnson boat yard. The hash would live in a temperature-controlled storage facility near our home in Buckhead. I planned to show it to Mustafa in hopes he could sell it in what Yousef Abboud had assured me was a needy Canadian market.

"Mornin' Captain, I'm here to collect that hot dog we talked about last night."

I'd forgotten.

"Perfect timing Tony, I'm ready."

He had his cargo shorts, flip flops, and a Jimmy Buffet t-shirt on. He looked different today. I looked different too. Early in the morning I'd stood in the marina shower for half an hour. It was extraordinary, watching what had gone down that drain. I felt less threatened by this young man than I had the night before. I joined him for lunch at the clubhouse. Everyone knew him, and soon I was surrounded with a dozen people asking questions about everything.

Oddly, it was easy to embellish answers to their questions, spawned by curiosity without intent. Crossing the Atlantic is a ready topic, and the fact I'd done it in a relatively small boat seemed to make real, the dreams of many. I ended up staying the afternoon, drinking a few beers, and talking with a wonderful group of folks. I couldn't remember the last time I'd spent a whole afternoon not working.

It felt great. Regenerative. I reveled in my cleanliness. It was also the first hot dog I'd had eaten in a long time. Food of the gods. I made a note that I must have more hot dogs, more often. Everyone wanted to help in any way they could. Good people.

Whitetail had performed her role in our adventure flawlessly, and I'd promised myself that I'd leave her at the newly opened Palmer and Johnson boatyard in Thunderbolt to have her rebuilt from stem to stern when I left for Atlanta. She had taken the voyage on the chin, and every part of her needed attention.

It was truly a memorable Memorial Day weekend. Early Wednesday morning, I motored Whitetail under the tall Thunderbolt bridge and tied her up to the docks at the Marina. I went over a long list of things I knew needed repair and told the yard manager if they found other issues to please fix them too.

I walked back across the bridge and backed my truck up to the storage shed and loaded the 22 bins of mostly poop into the rear of my pickup and headed toward Atlanta.

Diana was waiting. She had found an air-conditioned storage facility near our house in Buckhead, and that evening when I arrived, we took the hash over and unloaded the bins there in the storage room. I sat on one of them as my head began to spin with thoughts of the last eight months, thoughts of money, and thoughts of the lack of money. Exactly the way this whole disaster had started.

We drove home and shared several days isolated from the rest of the world. We wondered which one of us our baby might have resembled.

It was an odd feeling to return to a place that remained virtually unchanged after I'd been on such a wild ride for the past eight months. I'd struck out in October of 1991, and it was now June of 1992. The smells of turpentine and oil paints from my studio, a few unfinished canvases, the cats, Fischer and Max, and the warmth of our place welcomed me home with open arms.

I settled in for a few days and settled down.

CHAPTER THIRTY-TWO
Ghost Economics Blinded by Reality / Nothing to Lose

Dᴵᴬɴᴬ ᴀɴᴅ ɪ were basking in the comfort of being safely home and together. The past months could have easily yielded any number of distasteful contrary outcomes. But after all that effort and risk, the end result was that finances still remained our paramount concern. Lack of money had been the reason for the whole project; love of adventure had been the catalyst. Nothing about the initial dilemma had changed. So, against my better judgment, I quickly, and with much apprehension, set about making the first few phone calls to begin the last step; liquidation.

My agreement with Yousef Abboud was to buy the product from him and bring it into the US. I planned to disperse the load incrementally to a wholesaler, presumably Yousef's son Mustafa in Montreal. Each portion of the load would be C.O.D.- paid for at the time of pickup. By selling wholesale, to Mustafa, Yousef would be able to compound their profits, and hopefully be more inclined to help prevent rip-offs and maintain enthusiasm getting rid of the hopeless shit.

I'm pretty sure the people Yousef was dealing with in Morocco on our third try were a last-ditch choice, and gave me whatever they could find, just to get me to go away. I believe Ahmed and his family and cousins really wanted me to take their hash that fit my needs perfectly. Certainly, that crop had been sold long ago. Recalling my conversation with Salma, I felt my losses were minuscule by comparison to the confusion that had followed the drying up of the flow of hashish to the bigger smugglers still waiting along the

Moroccan coast. The King's war on drugs had just begun, but even in its early stage, it proved effective.

Over the first several months at home, despite my concerns, I was feeling enthusiastic. When I'd contacted Yousef and told him of the circumstances, regarding how worthless the hashish really was, he simply responded by saying, "My son, Mustafa, can definitely sell it in NYC and Montreal with no trouble. Just let him get started with the process."

The relief from those confident words renewed my waning confidence. A plan was made and Mustafa with two of his friends were scheduled to arrive in Atlanta via Amtrak at the Brookwood Station from NYC. I prepared two suitcases, each carrying 25 kilos of carefully sealed and packed camel dung and met them at the station.

It was August of 1992, and we walked together out to the dark parking lot. Mustafa was a trim and pleasant young man in his mid-twenties. His two friends were from the same mold. They looked like three college students on spring break. Mustafa, like his dad, promised success and reassured me they'd be back in short order to collect more. They went off excited, back into the train station, and back to NYC, to ply their newly procured product.

I gave them the two suitcases feeling a twinge of guilt as I took the $40,000 (50 x $ 800) from him, knowing, that short of a miracle, they would never be able to sell that trash. But, what did I know? A kilo of hashish for $800 was certainly gift priced. It would set anyone in motion, scrambling to buy as much as possible. It was a price unheard of in Canada and the US. It was no mystery that if I could actually get $800 per kilo, and I had 450 to sell, then I could expect a return of $360,000. With that return I could cover my debts.

All my life, my brain unbridled, has always wandered off to the preferred side, no matter what reality dictated. I was slow to sharpen my pencil to corroborate these superficial calculations for fear that reality may get a foot in the door.

I called Yousef with the news of my successful rendezvous with Mustafa and asked if he knew of other possibilities for people who could sell this product. He connected me to an Australian fellow living in California, but that played out quickly. The guy never even displayed enough interest to buy a plane ticket to come see the product. Next, Yousef put me in touch with an old British friend who was coming to the States the next month. He said that once he was stateside, he would contact me by calling Yousef first. I never heard from him. To his credit, I felt Yousef Abboud was genuinely trying to help me with this mess. I sensed that he honestly didn't know how I'd ended up with such an inferior product, and he seemed sincerely apologetic about it. At this point there was no real gain for him in helping me. He could easily have cut me off and left me to my own devices.

But he never did.

Ten months passed while Yousef Abboud continued to dig deep for potential buyers, only to be thwarted again and again because of the despicable quality. As time passed, I regressed into an odd state. I became sure that the DEA was waiting for me every time I visited the storage building. Paranoia snowballed. Sleep became a premium. Hopeless solutions roared incessantly around and around in my head like motorcycles on the "Wall of Death" at the county fair. As my situation became dire, I pressed Yousef harder to dig deeper into his resources for a buyer. I'm sure he began to uncover dark places that even he rarely visited, and likely considered last resorts. I wanted him to dive into a pool commensurate with the product I had to sell.

Then, I'm sure as a last resort, Yousef set me up with Lupo Rocco in New York City, with the ominous caveat, ..."Pierce... be very careful."

Careful seemed a small price to pay to get this stuff out of my life. I definitely could be careful.

"Yousef told me you were going to call," Lupo said in a surprisingly pleasant voice.

We reminisced briefly about his dealings with Yousef over the years. He explained to me that he understood what I had, and he was certain there would be no problem moving it. He explained that his buyers in NYC were more interested in the uniqueness of hashish rather than the potency of the product, and they would buy it simply from interest in this difficult to acquire commodity.

I had to laugh. I am sure that "pressed camel dung" really is difficult to find, just about anywhere.

"Abboud tells me that you are wanting $800 per kilo. Is that right?"

"Yep, that's the price. I also want to be paid for it on delivery."

"You're going to have to wait about a day before I can get the money back to you. How much do you have?"

"Let's start with fifty and see how it goes."

"OK, so you're going to bring fifty kilos up here and I'll pay you $40,000 for it the next day. Abboud says you've got more."

"I do."

"How much?"

"Like I said, let's start with fifty."

"Okay man… whatever. Use this number to call me when you're coming."

"It'll be about five days"

"Just call me when you're coming."

Every little bit made a difference in our financial predicament. Diana was wonderful. She was tough, and she dug in with me through the whole ordeal, helping to navigate all the shoals and tempests that came our way.

* * *

It was November of 1992 when I loaded two suitcases, each with 25 kilos of the dung, and bought a plane ticket to NYC, using one of the last two working credit cards. My plan was to work in 50 kilo increments with this character. Ever the optimist, I felt sure that I'd have $40,000 tucked away on the trip home. I even began to feel the price was a gift and found myself wondering if I should have asked for more.

I landed at LaGuardia, nervous as a cat. I picked up the suitcases from the carousel, convinced all the other passengers collecting their luggage were working for the DEA. Every step left me on edge and paranoid.

I took a taxi to a quaint old hotel near Central Park. The hotel was steeped in character, and the ambiance trumped the incredibly small size of the rooms.

Whitetail had more space than this little cube.

CHAPTER THIRTY-THREE
Lupo / Be Cool Man

Lᴜᴘᴏ ᴀɴᴅ ɪ had set a time and place where he would send a taxi to pick me up. I didn't want him or any of his cadre to know where I was staying. I walked down the street a few blocks to his prescribed spot. A ubiquitous sinister black SUV pulled up to the curb, where the driver stopped, opened the black tinted passenger window, and motioned for me to sit in the back seat. I carried twenty-five kilos of hashish in a suitcase for Lupo and his buyer to inspect. I'd left the other suitcase, with the other 25 kilos, under the bed in my hotel room, with a "Do not Disturb" sign on the doorknob. Key in my pocket.

Apprehensive, I slid into the back seat, and told him where I was instructed to go. He nodded, said nothing, and never looked around. It wasn't long before I realized we weren't headed where I thought I was supposed to be going.

"Stop the car," I said.

The driver looked at me in the rear-view mirror, and smirked.

"Be cool man. I'm not stopping the car. Lupo told me to take you to a coffee shop he likes over on the Westside. I'm *NOT* pulling over, and that *IS* where we're going, *Okay!*"

I remained silent.

"Let me hear you say Okay... Okay!" he said.

"Okay."

I began to figure I'd be doing well to get out of this alive. Like the driver said…I MUST BE COOL. Wipe that stupid look off my face. Take a deep breath. What was going on? Where had all my judgment gone? I didn't even know what Lupo looked like!

The coffee shop was on a corner in a scruffy part of lower Manhattan. A part I'd never seen before.

When I reached for my wallet, the driver waved me away.

"Lupo's got you covered."

I still had my suitcase at my side. I stuck out like a sore thumb. I looked like a stranger, an immigrant from 80 years past, staring up at the tall buildings in amazement, shoulders drooped from the weight of my suitcase.

Inside the coffee shop there were a number of people, each more of a character than their neighbor. They all knew each other. The little square black and white tiles amplified every sound, and the resulting din made it difficult to hear, or be heard, especially since the language was from a different planet.

Steam from the dishwasher filled the room and there was a smell of old coffee and bacon. Regulars sat out of the way in the corners, wanting to be left alone, buried in their morning papers. Little spindles of cigarette smoke, animated by the morning sun, rose from behind several of the newspapers.

It looked like the Apaches were sending me a message… "Run white man, run!"

I sat down for a minute and thought better of ordering my habitual coffee. I didn't need to be any more tightly wired. I needed to debug my eyes, and act like someone I didn't know. A second later, the glass entrance door swung open and slammed hard and loud, cracking the glass window behind it. Everyone in the place jumped and looked. Some shook their heads and returned to their preoccupations, unaffected. The cook behind the counter threw both hands in the air and pointed with his chin.

"Lupo, c'mon ya' criminal, whaddaya tink ya doin.'"

Lupo raised his thick eyebrows comically and tilted his head from side to side while he shrugged and threw his hands into the air mimicking the cook. "Whaddaya tink ya doin', whaddaya tink ya doin, he says."

"Jinx, man, you shouldda fixed the damn thing by now…whaddaya want that I should do?"

He reached in his pocket and threw the cook what looked like a wadded up hundred-dollar bill. "Now, fix it dammit. I'm ain't gonna keep on throwing "C" notes at you every time someone opens that door. You got some kinda scam going on here wit dis door? You ain't cuttin' me outta any business I should know 'bout…are you Jinxy? I know that glass has been cracked for two months now."

"Common Loop, you know them C notes ain't to pay for dat door."

"Watch it you ole piece a greasy dried up bacon."

The café got noticeably cooler. Everyone in the place seemed to know what was going on.

I set about re-debugging my eyes. Be cool. I was surely a stranger in a strange land.

Everyone in the place was now staring at him. Even the most reclusive had peeked from behind their morning news to watch this borderline friendly banter.

Lupo clearly relished the attention. He was alone…I thought. Tall, fearless, heavy set with shining black hair slicked straight back, tight on his head. Maybe 45 years old with a dark complexion and dark eyes. A pale blue Cuban shirt with black slacks, and highly polished black Huaraches completed the image.

He moved quickly. His eyes assessed me, and in an instant, he was standing by my table, looking down at me; an artist of intimidation. Every person in the place followed his lead. Every head in the café turned to stare… they'd never seen the likes of me around there before. That's real cool Lupo,

I thought. I'm sitting here with 25 kilos of hashish in a funky old Samsonite, and now the whole place is staring at me.

He pulled back a chair without looking at me and sat down. With a loud snap of his fingers, he waved a waitress over. He showed her a familiarity as if they'd gone to high school together.

"Coffee," was his first word.

"Water," was mine.

We compared notes about our dealings with Yousef Abboud. It turned out that Lupo knew my friend, El Capitan', and another mutual friend, Ken. I felt some small relief at the discovery of any common ground. I evolved from totally freaked out, to just scared, working hard not to show it. After about half an hour, he finally got down to business.

"So, let's go look at what you've got there."

"That's what I'm here to do." We stood. He tossed a handful of bills on the table and we headed for the door.

I worked hard not to show the suitcase I was lugging, weighed over 50 pounds. The big, polished black SUV with gangster wheels, appeared magically in front of the coffee shop. As I climbed in the back seat, I nodded at the same driver I had earlier that morning. A surly goombah, also in the back seat, acknowledged my entrance with a slight nod.

I wasn't included in the ongoing conversation that was resurrected when Lupo slid back into the front seat. He and the driver kept nodded toward me in the back seat, motioning, but never looking. They spoke rapidly in an Italian/ English blend regarding affairs I felt it better for me not to know. I remained quiet, bolstering my waffling confidence.

I reminded myself that I could handle this. This is nothing compared to what I'd been through. I reminded myself that I was the one who'd gone into the Rif Mountains, procured the hash, then sailed across the Atlantic Ocean with it, smuggled it into the country, and brought it to Atlanta. Surely, if I could do that, I should be able to handle my situation with these ruffians.

Right now, I needed to begin a self-protection program. I needed to watch carefully where they were taking me and be prepared for anything.

My main line of defense was running. I told myself, if it became time to run, by-George, dawg, you haul ass. Don't hesitate. You pick 'em up and put 'em down. I knew I could outrun anyone in that car. Maybe even a "speeding bullet."

I watched closely as we headed south to SoHo where I assumed their buyer was to be waiting.

"Tone, pull this rig over right here."

Lupo never looked around, instead he watched intently out of the windshield. He held up a hand.

"Okay Pete," (Forgotten my name already. A good sign.) pointing to a rather pleasant looking restaurant. "You get out here. There are bars, restaurants and galleries around here to keep you busy." I thought I'd heard an insincere laugh. "I'll be back at this place here in two hours, to pick you up. I'll have your money when I return."

"Pete, I been watching you all morning, and I got the feeling that you ain't been toting around no hundred pounds in your little box," nodding at my Samsonite. "How much is really there? You told me you'd be bringin' 50 kilos, didn't you? I told my man here; I'd be showing up with fifty kilos. I don't like lookin' like no fuckin' liar to my peeps."

"There are 25 kilos in there now. If this goes well, I've got the other 25 in a safe place nearby."

"Aww, (condescendingly), he don't trust my skinny ass fellas."

No one spoke. He'd turned the rearview mirror to focus on me in the back seat.

"And now, I don't trust his ass."

"OK," I said, "let's be short with the theatrics. Do you want it or not? And yes, you're right, I don't trust you. Why would I?"

I couldn't believe it was my voice I heard doing the talking.

"I want the cash for this first half. After I get that, I want cash in advance for the second half."

"Get your ass out of my wheels. Now! Leave your little box. We'll be back."

I went into the restaurant, relieved to be free of Lupo Rocco and ordered a desperately needed vodka on the rocks. Then I had another. It began to rain.

I waited about an hour, then figured I may as well have a meal. By the time I had finished my meal and spent a bit more time over a couple of expressos, about three hours had passed. A rainy evening had begun, heralded by numerous streetlights coming on. The rain seemed to thicken as it poured down in front of the light from the streetlamps.

I began to feel increasingly like a bumpkin, hoodwinked and ripped off in the big city. It rained harder. I imagined myself as one of those inflatable clowns you knock over and they bounce back up…over and over again. I berated myself…but what could I have done differently? A fine blend of anger, coupled with my familiar old friend, "desperation", was brewing. I stamped myself as officially ripped off.

I called Yousef Abboud and told him where I was and what had happened. I needed Lupo Rocco's address, and a phone number. Yousef Abboud said to call him back in 30 minutes. I did, and he supplied me with the address of Lupo's ex-wife and kid. He was pretty sure that this was where Lupo stayed when he was in NYC. I hailed a taxi and asked the driver to take me to the south side of Central Park where the address led me to one of many exclusive high-rise apartment buildings. It was still raining, and darkness had fallen some while ago.

Somewhere between ultra-mad and ultra-scared, I walked up to the entrance of the palace where a uniformed doorman stood.

"Good evening," I said.

He politely looked at me.

"I'm an old friend of Lupo's in town for the evening and had hoped to catch him for a drink before I have to leave."

He told me that Lupo, Bruno, Laura, and Steph had stepped out for dinner about an hour ago. He was sure they'd be back before long. Would I like to have a seat in the lounge while I waited?

"That would be perfect."

I selected a chair facing the entrance and settled in for a short rest. I took deep breath after deep breath, I rehearsed what I was going to do and say.

The stupid look that I fought to erase, which was normally followed by gulping from a desert dry throat, was gone…really gone. The image of the fool, duped and ripped off, had evaporated. I was pissed! The kind of pissed that will get you killed. At this point, killed almost seemed preferable.

It must have been fifteen minutes later when I heard voices in the entrance laughing and talking. A woman came through the door pushing ahead of her a lovely little girl followed by Lupo and the guy from the back seat of the SUV this afternoon. I sat still, watching. When Lupo finally saw me, he looked away, then he did the classic double take, and bored through me with a look of disbelief, instantly eclipsed by anger.

"What the *fuck* are you doin' here!" he shouted.

Both he and his goombah were at a loss for the next move. He walked back to the door, then spun around and headed straight back toward me. His little girl had stopped in front of her mother when they heard Lupo's outburst. They now stood on the landing. The doorman came rushing in wild eyed, looking at everyone at once.

"You're way out of line," Lupo said. " You're really fuckin' things up for me."

"You're the one way out of line, Lupo," I snapped right back. "Didn't your Mama tell you how to act?"

"Stay with this fuckin' wart. I'll be back in a minute." The goombah nodded.

"Don't believe him," I addressed the goombah. "He told me the same thing this afternoon and never came back."

Lupo, shaking his head with a fixed jaw, took a hard, fast right swing at the air in front of him. Then, he kicked up his heel, spun around and walked up the spiral steps pushing the astonished girls, (his ex and their daughter), ahead of him.

The door man knew he had made a mistake.

"Should I call the Police"?

I shrugged.

"I wouldn't, if I were you."

I sat there with this gangster. We said not a word, while we sat waiting for the next 30 minutes.

Suddenly Lupo hit the top step running down towards us. I stood up, he was in my face, nose to nose, in seconds. The henchman stood and watched without emotion. He'd seen it all before. Lupo was so furious he was spitting on me as he screamed. What the fuck did this criminal think I was going to do? Obviously not what I did.

I spoke slowly through clinched teeth. Anger was my friend.

"Don't tell me your weak, fuck-ass mind has already forgotten what happened this afternoon? Have you no short-term memory left. I'm here because Yousef Abboud recommended you. You hauled me to the other side of the city like some third-rate dumbass, then took 25 kilos of my product and left me on the other side of the city, with a plan which you seem to have either forgotten or you're in the process of ripping me off. If I had to guess, I'd say you are in the process of trying to rip me off."

The volume had turned up a bit, and the doorman stepped inside, ever more watchful.

Lupo looked around.

"Step outside where we can talk."

We exited the lobby and walked down the steps to the wet street, the gangster on one side and Lupo on the other. We turned right at the first block and continued slowly down the side street. It seemed as if Lupo was considering his options. The light of the streetlamp faded as we walked further from it. Ultra-fear began to kick in. Lupo stopped, turned, and with arms flailing, began screaming again.

"You're an idiot! You have no idea what you have done. I am trying to get a visitation rights with my daughter. The biggest obstacle is that the court assumes that I dabble in various unacceptable business endeavors. You, showing up here now, has really fucked this up for me."

"You, Lupo," I shot back, "are the fucking idiot! Do you really think I give half a shit about all your crap? I honestly could not care less if you never see your daughter again! I don't even know you! You are absolutely nothing to me!"

He had begun walking slowly again. I followed. Suddenly he turned to face me. We stopped.

"How'd you find me anyway?"

"I called Yousef Abboud to check on your reputation, I called el Capitan' to check your reputation, I called Kenny to check your reputation, I called Dove, the contact that sent me to Phillipe, to check your reputation, and they all said the same thing; they all said you are a complete piece of shit and warned me to be careful. I understand why now. With a phone call, I got your ex-wife's address and gambled you'd be here!"

I began transitioning to just plain old wet and tired, and wanted this to be over. For me not an uncommon predicament.

"Lupo, tell me your plans. The way I see it, right now, at this point, you've ripped me off for $20,000 worth of hashish. I'm roaming around NYC at night, in the rain, trying to find you. Quite frankly, I'm sick and tired of this whole fucking deal. You're out here with me on a dark side street, trying to scare me I presume. I'm worn completely out, and I'm beginning not to care about anything. I don't even care if you shoot me right now."

I paused to take a deep breath.

"But Lupo," I went on, "you must know, that I am not the only person that has your ex-wife and daughter's address. There are two other people who are closer than brothers to me. You've never heard of these guys. Each of them now holds that information. They're only hours away, and I told them both to expect a phone call from me at 11 p.m. this evening. If they don't get that phone call, your little court drama will intensify dramatically. So, give my product back, or give me $20,000 right now.

Lupo pounded his trigger finger on my chest. His face was red…heart attack red. Blood vessels in his neck were overworking. It was his first physical affront. I braced for the transformation into a fist. The goombah was behind me.

"Look here, you complete piece of Italian horseshit," I growled now. "if you can't get a grip on yourself, I may just let 11 p.m. come just so I can sit back and watch the party. That little ole doorman will have his hands full. You know how it goes…the Police come, blue lights flashing, neighbors come out of the woodwork, everyone is wondering what's going on?"

The rain picked up. We were wet and getting wetter.

Lupo carried on. "If I wasn't mistaken, I'd think you may have just threatened me. I don't stand for that…ever, at all. I eliminate the threat first, then deal with the problem."

The way he spoke made me believe him.

"I personally cannot deal with you anymore. This here is Bruno," Lupo pointed with his elbow, hands in his jacket pockets. I was sure there was more than his hands in there. I wondered if it was a 38 or a 9. "He's gonna handle all this shit now."

Then he stepped around me to Bruno.

"Bruno, you listen, and listen good. This is your fuckin' problem. You made one hell of a mess here, and somehow, you've gotten me in it neck deep. This whole thing is a chicken shit situation that should not be happening. We're talking here about 40 grand for 50 kilos of camel crap. We don't need this now. You go tell those fellas down there, those guys you call friends, and you get this guy's 20 large tomorrow morning, early. I don't want no excuses. Any problems, and you tell that laughin' asshole that he'll be talking to me next. This guy here," pointing at me with his thumb over his shoulder, "has got 25 more kilos more of the same shit somewhere here with him. Pay him the 20 grand for the first bunch in the morning and pick up his other suitcase. See if you can do that without fucking it up. Get those assholes down there to sell it as quick as possible, for whatever they can get. It's totally worthless shit. I still don't know how I got hooked into all this. That damn slick talkin' Yousef Abboud. I'm gonna kick his ass too."

Lupo looked at me.

"It'll take a few days to dump that crap, and you know it's crap. So, this here is Bruno's number, you give him yours, and you guys work it out. Bruno, man, I'm not fuckin' around here. This is serious shit. Do not fuck around. Get it done quickly…like yesterday! Do you hear what I'm sayin'…do you hear me?! I'm outta here."

I turned, and for the first time, looked at Bruno as a person. His head was still nodding in affirmative response to Lupo's tirade. I would now be dealing with him. I heard Lupo's steps fade into the darkness. I was exhausted, and not completely sure whether or not I might be about to hear my last sound, that "Pop" of a spent round.

Bruno and I agreed to meet for coffee the following morning at 9 a.m. at the same coffee house where we'd met earlier this day. What a long day it had been. It seemed like years ago when I first met Lupo. Bruno was to have my money, and I'd bring the second suitcase full of hash. At that point, we'd figure out how and when I would be paid for the second 25 kilos.

I walked the seven blocks back to the hotel. I needed time alone, and a walk along Central Park in the rain seemed like just the remedy. I got back to my hotel, soaked and shivering. I stood in a hot shower while the water ran down my neck and conjured up recollections of the unbelievable evening. My God, what had just happened?

* * *

The next morning, at 9 a.m. I waited on Bruno at the little coffee shop. I noticed the glass behind the door had a long piece of packing tape zigzagging from left to right. I sat down at a table and put the suitcase with the hashish on a chair. The cook recognized me and yelled out.

"What'll ya have this mornin' my friend?"

"Coffee and one of those bagels sounds good to me right now."

"What's in them suitcases you been carryin' around witcha all da time? Knowin' Lupo, I'll betcha they're fulla hundurd dollah bills."

"Nope, just moving out of the hotel before noon and heading home. I wish it was full of hundred-dollar bills. Is that what Lupo normally carries around, cases of hundred-dollar bills? You better get that door repaired."

"Fuck Loop. If it wasn't for him the door wouldn't be broken in the first place. He's always leaving a trail of destruction wherever he goes." Jinx was gazing out the front window of his little diner, caught in a daydream, hypnotized by the bright morning sun. A smile contorted the wrinkles on his face with a memory. He shook his head came back to earth and looked at me. "Even when Loop was a little kid, I'd chase that idiot after he'd pinched a candy bar from the shop. He'd be laughing and calling me every name in the book, while he hauled ass down the alley. If I had the luck to catch him, I'd drag him by the collar over to his dad's warehouse down the street for a lesson. He'd be jerkin' and pullin' and sometimes he'd get away. If he got loose, the little bastard would turn around and threaten to kick my ass. If I could finally get him over to his dad's place, the ole man would thump Loop's ear, grab the candy bar and whack him hard on the back of his head with an open hand. Then he'd throw the wrapper at me while he ate the candy." "Now, get the fuck outta here ya bunch of delinquents." "Jinx, don't you forget our agreement. Anyhows, what da ya tink ya doin' running around the streets chasing kids for clipping a-piece-a candy. It don't look good Jinx, it just don't look good"

Jinx carried on, "I always hated it when Loop would circle back to my shop and get there before me. He'd have grabbed another bar before Jannette could throw a bagel at him. Man, she had a mean arm. Grew up with six bad brothers. Them stale bagels really packed a wallop. She should 'a been a pitcher for the Yankees. The 100-mph bagel. I still laugh at how red Loop's ear was. I know it hurt the little fucker."

A dose of reality brought me back from Jinx's story. Bruno had arrived 45 minutes late and sat down without a word. He then proceeded to tell me a long story about what had happened the day before. It seemed he'd rehearsed it well and wanted to spit it out before he forgot it. It went something like this. Their guy took the stuff and went to meet with another guy. While he was at the other guy's place, the car with my hashish in it had been towed for a parking violation. They had to talk to the police and finally got the car back complete with my hash. It was lucky that they had all gone to school with the police officer. It was too late when they went back to find me at the restaurant.

I didn't believe a word of the tale. To me, it meant only that Bruno feared Lupo enough to come up with a story to make it look as if they'd never intended to rip me off. Of course, they had intended to rip me off. Lupo had so adamantly berated their stupidity in the rain yesterday, and in no uncertain terms, outlined what Bruno and company were to do. Lupo was the undisputed boss. He'd left no choice but for Bruno to get his shit together, find 20 grand to pay me for the first suitcase, and work with me on selling the next 25 kilos.

I suspected that Yousef Abboud, knowing Lupo as he did, was keeping an eye on the situation. I'm certain he was the only person that Lupo would possibly have listened to.

"I've never seen ole Loop so surprised as when he saw you at his wife's place," Bruno said. "Whew, he was hot!"

These guys were all loose cannons. I wanted to get out of NYC as quickly as possible. Bruno had my money in a briefcase in the trunk of his car. He said he planned to give my second suitcase to a different group. While he thought it would eventually sell, everyone had complained about the quality. It was no good. With such a bad reputation it would take a bit longer this time. At the same time, he needed to move quickly before the new buyers got wind of the trash he was purveying. Then none of it would sell.

At this point I was so worn out, anything was fine with me. I desperately wanted to get home and regroup. I could leave NYC with $20,000 cash, and Bruno would owe me another $20,000 for the second suitcase, presumably within a week. When it was ready, I would fly back to NYC and retrieve the balance.

I had no other plans for that 25 kilos, so I figured why not leave it with him. I know, I know...there were plenty of "why nots," but my lack of success with this process led me to decide to leave it with Bruno, and take the chance of dealing with him, instead of the chance of flying back home with it.

I said okay, and Bruno gave me the 20K cash.

At last. Hallelujah.

* * *

On the plane going home, I perused my original plan and bolstered myself for a painful dose of reality I was about to lose my ass, and everything attached. The initial plan had been based on ending up in Thunderbolt, Georgia with 600 kilos of exceptional product, worth easily more than $1,500 per kilo for a quick sale. Had it gone this way, it would have yielded $900k gross return. After paying El Capitan' $ 510K and Finn $40k and covering endless expenses and repairs due *Whitetail*, which I figured would total at least $50k, I would be left with $300k to call my own.

Questionably worth all the danger, risk, effort, and pain.

But now, when I swap killer hashish for camel dung, and include the losses for water damage, these calculations take a sharp downward turn and the reality sucks. In the end, the hard facts were, I ended up with about 350 kilos in Thunderbolt after losing 100 to the Atlantic for weight and worthlessness, and another 150 kilos to water damage. This pseudo hashish, with a lotta luck, may be worth $500 per kilo, which is doubtful. I would consider myself fortunate to be able to give it away. But, for calculations sake we'll say $500 per kilo, I would gross $175k. I owed El Capitan' per our agreement, $540k ($180k x 3). I would have to ask him, if under the circumstances, he would be willing to let me repay him his initial investment of $180k. That would at least get El Capitan out without a loss in this failed fiasco. As I calculated the reality, the more it hurt. I insisted, no matter what, on giving Finn his total per our agreement of $40k. This would leave me negative $45k. I still had $35k due to friends, and at least $30k on credit cards. I was looking at a total loss of $110k and a boat in the boatyard that would cost at least another $50,000 to fix her up to sell. Where was I going to come up with another $160k? Now, sadly, *Whitetail* would have to be liquidated. I hoped we could hang on to the equity in our property on Peachtree Avenue. But most likely it would need to be sold too.

This fiasco was far from over, and it was highly unlikely that it would play out this way. The haunting truth that I had such a hard time accepting, was that the likelihood that this hashish might not sell at all.

Still, ever the optimist, I hoped for bad rather than terrible.

CHAPTER THIRTY-FOUR
A Roll of Quarters / He'll Forever be in my Memory

DIANA PICKED ME UP at Atlanta's Hartsfield International Airport. At first, she seemed unusually relieved. But, when we stood back from a long hard hug, a look of concern instantly clouded her face. It was so intense I began to worry about me. Despite my efforts, my eyes, deep in my head, surrounded by dark shadows, betrayed the desperation in my heart, and the exhaustion of the experience.

"Pierce, you're worrying me. Are you alright?"

"Sweetheart, I've got to get home. I am almost not alright."

She grabbed me and guided my way out to the car. She drove home. I longed for days alone. I needed to focus on saving what was left of me. Since I'd arrived at Thunderbolt, every little bit of money I could find quickly evaporated like water on a hot griddle. The $20 grand in the briefcase was destined to follow suit.

I dreaded getting in touch with El Capitan'. I called him and explained the circumstances. I told him the abridged version of all that had come to pass since our last meeting. It looked to me like the best I could hope for would be to work toward getting his original investment back. I did not want him to lose money on my ill-fated scheme.

El Capitan' was a true friend. It was this person that responded.

"I know you've done as well as possible under the circumstances could be done, and I would never think less of you for falling into such a trap. You know that we've always understood the nature of these investments. You can never tell what will happen. You either win a lot or you lose a lot. The best news is that you're okay…you are okay, aren't you?"

Silence.

He didn't push me to answer. I'm not sure I was capable.

"You and I need to get ready for a sailing trip soon, just for fun. Be thinking Camden. We need some waves and wind that we can call friends." We planned to get together as soon as the smoke cleared. He said, "At the least, I expect the long-detailed version of this adventure over a bottle of Cognac."

"Real soon I hope."

Friends in general are damn difficult to find, and harder to hang on to. It takes years of ups and downs and ins and outs, until finally you say, "Friend". Friends like El Capitan' are irreplaceable. Things happen as they do, and as much as we'd do anything to change them, it is impossible. We are powerless to change the past.

I miss him. He'll forever remain in my memory and in my life.

✳ ✳ ✳

Diana worked miracles to patch me up. She dug deep to find any infinitesimal speck of hope and then embellished it. She hung onto small facts like, we're still alive and kicking. We're together. She played down any negatives, such as the probability that Bruno, given the chance, would likely try to rip me off again.

I was fragile, breakable. A week passed. I finally called Yousef and told him what had happened. I could hear him shaking his head. Nevertheless, he assured me he had good news. In a few days, he was to meet with someone with connections in Miami. He felt certain that this fellow had enough business acquaintances that the sheer volume would bode well for him taking the entire balance of the load in one swoop. In this person's world, 400 kilos of hashish were a small drop in the bucket.

Yousef's news was all it took to get me moving again. The remote hope that someone might take the whole pile was impossible to comprehend. Diana seized this optimistic chance and held on tight.

Another week passed. My call to Bruno went unanswered. I called again and again and finally, apprehensively; I left a message. While it was cryptic, there was no doubt what I was talking about or the seriousness of what I was saying. We didn't use cell phones, pay phones were the tool.

Several more days passed. During this time, I was contacted by Yousef's new prospect from Miami. Romero Gonzalez was German. After our initial conversation I was left with a palpable sense of hope. He knew the right people and was certain that my proposal would be easily put together. I tried to sign up for Diana's cheerleading team. Romero would be in Miami in a couple of weeks and wanted to meet me in Fort Lauderdale.

The anticipation of this meeting with Romero lightened my negativity regarding the ordeal at hand…Bruno. He still hadn't called, despite my angry, borderline threatening phone calls. Another week of this, and I was ready to fly to NYC just to find him. I didn't know his last name or even where to start looking for him.

Then a light came on. If I could flush Lupo out of hiding, he would most certainly find Bruno for me. He had been so adamant about wanting nothing to do with our deal. I had an idea. I went to the library and found the Brooklyn White Pages. Lupo's last name was Rocco. Since I figured there wouldn't be too many Rocco's in the phone book, I planned to go down the list and call each number until I hit pay dirt and lured a call from Lupo. I settled into a phone booth in a quiet spot, list in hand.

My spiel went something like this, "Hello…I'm a business associate of Lupo Rocco's. Just recently Lupo took something from me that doesn't belong to me. It belongs to a group of businessmen in Miami, and it's worth a lot of money. I can't find Lupo, but it's extremely important that I do, because these businessmen want their investment back. Regretfully, at this point it is long overdue. I need for Lupo to call me ASAP to try and rectify this before it gets more serious. Please have him call me at this number."

I used the number for the pay phone, and figured he'd call while I was still going down the list. I ended my message with, "The group in Miami is getting restless."

I was into the list, about ten phone calls down, when I hit gold.

"Oh my", came the voice of a sweet older woman. "What has Loop done now? I am his aunt, his mom's sister. I think he's gone to Amsterdam, but I'm not sure. I'll get the message to his mother if I can..."

Oh, to what depths we plummet. I felt terrible worrying an old woman who I imagined already had more than her share of grief from her nephew, but it did the trick. Shortly, the pay phone began to ring. I gulped and picked up the receiver to hear an infuriated, irate, incensed, screaming Lupo on the other end.

"Didn't I leave all this mess with you and Bruno?" he screamed... I feared for his health. I didn't want to lose him to a stroke until I'd gotten what I needed. "If I ever see you again, I will kill you, do you hear me mother-fucker? I will kill you dead on the spot with my bare hands!"

I was sobered by his anger and his selection of words. I responded, calmly, mostly to quell the fear that welled up inside.

"Bare hands eh? If you get anywhere near me waving your bare hands around, I'll just blow your fuckin' head off and be done with you, you lop eared wop." Somehow, I was enjoying this. "You are every bit the rodent that people tell me you are. I'll look forward to confirming that in the future. Save yourself a heart attack and give me the measly pile of money you owe me. Save all this anger and crap and spend it on that halfwit partner of yours. He must be a relative, he shares your general shit for brains. For two weeks now, he has not returned any of my calls. I expected my money a month ago." I carried on, "You come up with the money you owe me... soon. I mean real soon, like yesterday. Then when I go back to NYC, get my money, and arrive safely back home, I'll leave you and your family alone, and with any luck, we'll never see or hear from each other ever again. If this doesn't happen quickly, harassment will escalate. It's that simple Lupo…it's that simple."

I had almost forgotten to employ my potential safety valve should something go awry. Silly thought…what could possibly go awry?

"Also, dickhead, don't forget I've taken the liberty to share all your contact info with some of my very best friends. They are a talented group of the world's greatest magicians. They are practiced in the art of making people disappear."

I hung up the receiver just before it fell out of my shaking hand. My knees didn't want to hold me up. I felt queasy. When will all of this be over? A job at The Home Depot began to sound pretty good.

I went to my favorite pay phone and called Bruno. I was sure Lupo would have called Bruno immediately. I'd hit a soft spot when I'd connected with his sweet aunt. Still no answer from Bruno, I left him a message to call me back in half an hour on this payphone. I went to fill the car with gas and came back to wait for Bruno's call. Most phone calls during this whole affair were made and received at random pay phones. Roll upon roll of quarters lived in my glove box to fund these communications. Even calls to Tangier were made with stacks of quarters. We thought we were tricky. Who'd ever figure that out?

With my windows open, I waited for over an hour. The phone finally rang.

Without a word of an apology, Bruno started by telling me in his smart-ass way that there would be no money coming this week. My fuse blew! Before I could collect myself, I unleashed a hard-right jab on the concrete wall where the phone was mounted. I'd forgotten the roll of quarters in that hand. Forty quarters flew everywhere and the pain from my screaming knuckles, impossible to describe, only hurt more as I shook my hand. I bent over double and jammed my poor bloody knuckles between my knees. Take it from me, never hit a concrete wall especially if you have a roll of quarters in your hand. That hand has never been the same. To this day, when I wiggle my fingers, I wish fire and brimstone on those fuckers.

I slowly stood up, the right leg of my blue jeans was soaked with blood, and when I finally picked up the receiver with my left hand …Bruno was gone.

Diana had so often absorbed the brunt of my latest catastrophe. She poured a bowl of warm water and added salt. Then she put a towel under my elbow to hold my injured hand comfortably to soak, while we talked about everything that had happened since I'd last seen her several hours ago.

"Real smart, why'd you do that? Those guys don't need to beat you up, you're doing it to yourself."

Why did conversations like this always make me mad? Probably because I didn't have any answers.

CHAPTER THIRTY-FIVE
Get Down! On the Ground! / Get Down Now!

Dɪᴀɴᴀ ᴡᴀs ᴀ ᴍᴏsᴛ ᴡᴏɴᴅᴇʀғᴜʟ, ᴇᴍᴘᴀᴛʜᴇᴛɪᴄ ᴘᴇʀsᴏɴ until she wasn't. She was famous for being just as mean as she was loving. Our whole marriage of the past 14 years was a radical emotional roller coaster ride. Still, she proved herself, over and over to be a great and capable partner. I'm certain that no one on this earth could have, or would have, hung on as long as she did. Every consideration, every move in our lives, was akin to hanging onto a tiger's tail. We couldn't hang on, and we couldn't let go.

I've pondered it all for years ad nauseum. The love we shared through thick and thin, was our glue. We were famously in love with each other. But sadly, change seemed inevitable; that final straw, the one that would break the camel's back, the knot at the end of the rope that would finally come undone… It was destined to fall apart.

* * *

It was March 18, 1994. Yousef Abboud's friend, Romero Gonzalez, called again to confirm that he'd be in Fort. Lauderdale in two days. He was in Miami partying hard with "friends." We set a time when we'd meet for drinks at Pier 66 on the 17th street causeway.

"Sweetheart," I said to Diana, "this guy Romero that Yousef has come up with, seems like a viable candidate. The problem is that I'll need to drive 200 kilos down to Ft. Lauderdale. He claims he can sell it to the Haitians west of Ft. Lauderdale. He's got some odd connection there."

"We've been paying to store that stuff for over a year. I don't think it is ever going to sell."

"But, if this guy wants it, I'll wish him all the luck in the world. In fact, if he hits me in the right frame of mind, I'll drag it all down there and give it to him, free of charge."

We had spoken of the value in just throwing it in the closest dumpster. That alternative was coming into our conversations more often these days. At some point the liability of just having it around could land us in a very serious predicament. The police would call it hashish. Even though we knew better, they wouldn't.

We agreed to put the last remaining 150 kilos of the dung, and 50 kilos of the kief in the trunk of a large rented Oldsmobile. We'd be left with 100 kilos of the tan and about 50 kilos of the green product. At long last, the black pucks of dung would be gone.

We planned to ride south on I -75, carefully adhering to the speed limits, just a young, conservative couple headed down to Florida for a vacation. Our room at the Marina Inn was a short walk to Pier 66 where I was to meet Romero in the afternoon.

The next morning Diana and I enjoyed breakfast in the hotel garden. I felt it prudent for Diana to return to Atlanta and leave me there alone. She would catch a late morning flight to Atlanta where she'd monitor my movements from home.

That morning there were four clown-like characters hanging over the railing and generally disturbing our breakfast with their revelry. They were enormously proud of their new point and shoot cameras and had a grand time posing for one another acting silly. I thought it seemed a bit early to be drunk. Probably been up all night. They were difficult not to notice, I worked hard to ignore them.

Diana railed at the thought of leaving me, but at my insistence she acquiesced. I took her to the Ft. Lauderdale airport to catch a noon flight home. Two o'clock arrived and I drove across 17th street to the Pier 66 parking lot. I strategically parked the car out of the way under cover of low shrubbery. I went up to the sundeck overlooking the inner coastal waterway and settled in to meet with Yousef Abboud's latest candidate, Romero.

Minutes later, a handsome young German introduced himself to me as Romero. He was accompanied by someone he introduced as an old friend. This "old friend" seemed incredibly nervous. They'd been partying all night with an endless supply of cocaine. Romero explained that his friend was the person responsible for making the sale happen.

We all sat on the sundeck and had a burger and a beer. They barely touched their food. The conversation was lean, and the feeling in the air was uncomfortable. Notably, our fellow patrons on the deck all seemed odd, though I couldn't put a finger on why. Everything seemed out of focus.

We paid our tab, and Romero with his "friend" followed me down to the rental car. I was glad I'd taken time to park in a shady, more secluded place. I raised the trunk and we all peered in at the pile of black hashish pucks. The heat in the trunk stimulated the full pungency of those "pieces of shit".

The friend quickly slammed the trunk lid and looked around.

Something just wasn't right. I sensed that these boys had been doing more than drinking beer that morning.

Then, sure enough, they offered me a "bump". Aha, cocaine…blasted cocaine. Any confidence in Romero or his buddy instantly evaporated. These guys were just another bunch of clowns held captive by a most heinous drug. How long, and how much of that trash, had they snorted? I considered running, canning the whole deal right then. Maybe just to put it off for another week, 'til things were more under control.

Things were not right.

A little while later after we'd parted company, at about 3 in the afternoon, Romero called me.

"They want the hash man. Now, you told me you'd take $800 per kilo and I told them $2,000 per kilo. You also told me there were 100 kilos in the trunk, but you could come up with another 150 quickly, and if they wanted, you could come up with another 1,000 kilos. So, they'll give me the $200k for this trunk full and I'll give you $80,000 and keep $120,000 for my troubles."

That really bugged me, but I needed to get over it now, in a hurry. Be happy man. Sometimes I amaze myself with stupidity.

"Oh, one more thing, they want you to bring it up to Jacksonville, where they will then pay me at the time of delivery. They don't want to drive for 5 hours with the money to Ft. Lauderdale, and then 5 hours back to Jacksonville with the product."

They agreed to fly Romero up, and we would all meet in the early afternoon at a Hotel bar by the river.

"Okay, okay, of course," at this point I'd do anything. I was so far out of my element that any comfort zone had vanished. Nothing was relative. I was pieced together.

"I'll meet you at the bar in Jax at one tomorrow."

I drove the car back over to my room at the Marina Inn and took a nap that lasted until 8 a.m. the next morning.

It had only been two days since my terrible phone conversation with Lupo. Bruno had disappeared after my blow up in the phone booth. I felt I needed to try to contact him one more time before heading to Jacksonville. I called his cell number on the trusty pay phone outside my room. To my amazement, he answered the phone. He didn't want to talk to me, but quickly said he had my money. I told him I'd be there in two days, and for him to expect my call. He abruptly hung up without a word.

I packed my bag and maxed out my last credit card at the motel desk. It took two calls to get the card company to accept the charge. As my paranoia grew, I noticed the desk clerk seemed ill at ease. He'd been very friendly when Diana and I had arrived. Now, he wouldn't even make eye contact, and mostly looked down at the floor. He pushed my receipt across the counter while staring pensively out the window.

"Thanks," I said, "see you next time."

Silence. I knew now that something was off. Maybe it was the absence of Diana that had disappointed him. Yep, no doubt that was it. Satisfied with my clear reasoning, I pulled out of Fort Lauderdale headed north for Jacksonville on I-95.

Nothing felt right, but my choices were nil. I had to play this to the finish, whatever that might be. Bypassing Jacksonville and heading to Atlanta was out of the question. I couldn't go home empty handed.

Hours later, I pulled off at the exit that led to the Hotel where we were to meet. I parked the car and walked into the bar where Romero introduced me to Captain Jack.

* * *

I liked Captain Jack right away. He was cool, easy going, and compared to Romero, who was wired to the gills, Jack was a haven of respite.

He was one big guy. Tall, over 6'4" and fit. His log red hair accompanied a bushy beard. He wore a loose Hawaiian shirt, baggy khakis, and old leather boat shoes. The coastal uniform. We drank a beer and talked nonstop about sailing. He was a likeable character. He handed me his business card. Fishing and Charters, it said. I put it in my pocket.

A quick hour went by. Romero was totally out of his mind. He was difficult to ignore. He would begin a thought, and then stop talking mid-sentence, his voice dwindling to a mumble. Then he'd nod, looking at Jack and me, waiting, nodding as if he expected a response. At worst, he needed another bump of cocaine before he went into withdrawals, likely heading that way from whatever drug he was taking to calm his cocaine jitters. One will make you larger, and one will make you smaller. The combination yielded a thick tongue, black dilated eyes, and nonsensical conversation. I would have thought his smell alone would have sobered him up. Anyone near him paid attention to this animal in our midst. All tried not to make eye contact.

Captain Jack looked him up and down stifling a smirk.

"We better get this over with. I don't know how much longer your partner can last."

"He's no partner of mine" I said. "I don't even know the guy. I just met him yesterday. He really is a mess." We were all relieved when Romero left to go to the restroom.

"Okay, c'mon, let's have a look at what you've got before that idiot comes back out here."

"Great, I'm so ready to be done with all this."

And I was. Nothing else mattered, I just wanted to be done, finally done, no matter what it took. So, in a way, I asked for it...and as usual, the gods gave it to me.

Jack and I talked as we walked out into the bright Florida sun. Romero was still lost in the restroom and hadn't yet made it out to the parking lot.

We got to my car, I opened the trunk, and showed him the product. Then, out of the corner of my eye the 9mm appeared from nowhere and came into sharp focus in the bright midday Florida sun.

My mind stopped...

My heart stopped...

"Jack," I croaked, "what's going on, what are you doing?"

Honestly, there was no doubt what it was, or where it was pointing, or what Jack was doing.

The only viable question was which side is he on?

The balance of my life was held by this stranger's index finger. Milliseconds later when I finally dared to open my eyes, they crossed at the proximity of the round barrel as it moved into position only inches from my nose. I could smell fresh gun oil and hot leather.

"Get down…goddammit, get down now… on the ground!"

These loud harsh words worked their way toward my brain. Everything warped into slow motion. In the heat, I was chilled. I was preoccupied with a demanding urge to pee in my pants, that ole uncontrollable, familiar reflex that most often accompanies abject fear. Had it finally happened, or could it be another one of those dreams?

Captain Jack, all 6'4" of blustering bear, holstered his Glock with a smooth familiar motion and a practiced slap. Having found what he was looking for, he slammed the trunk of the car hard, pulled me up from the ground, and with one hand tightly on the back of my head and neck, he pushed me roughly onto the hot trunk lid. Then in one fluid motion, his free hand adeptly handcuffed my wrists tightly behind my back.

And, I thought I liked the guy.

Several cars screeched in from nowhere, their occupants sprang into action, pistols flashed, all pointing in one direction. I could hear the pop of chopper blades low overhead. In seconds Captain Jack had all the assistance he needed. He had transformed before my eyes. I was caught. Really caught! He pulled me up from the trunk lid, and now, standing in front of me, feet apart, with a cold look in his green eyes, well-practiced to strike fear, he held his badge up to my eye level.

"My name is Burrous. I am an officer with the US Drug Enforcement Agency. You are being placed under arrest for conspiracy to distribute illegal contraband. Call your attorney if you've got one." I didn't.

Well, there you go. I knew which side he was on.

Without another word, he lowered me back down to the ground. Gravity pulled hard. He held me by my belt to lower me down, but let it go a little too soon. I couldn't tell if it was intentional or not. I'd hate to think it was. I turned my face just in the nick of time to prevent my nose from becoming one with the pavement. My move was rewarded with my cheek hammering down hard on the hot Florida asphalt. He spun around and walked away.

"Don't you make one move; not one move," he growled as he passed.

I felt the asphalt move under his weight as he walked by. It was high noon and the blazing sun knew no mercy. I remember feeling a small, stupid modicum of relief…well, it really is, all finally over. I was educated with 30 years of experiences and adventures. Surely, I should have known better than to end up in a mess like this. But somehow, I'd always known that one day I probably would. Desperation always takes its toll. The timing was just so damn inconvenient.

My vision began to focus as I laid there looking at eye level over all those hot little stones, then to the concrete curb beyond. I became aware that quite a crowd was gathering outside the bar where seconds ago, I'd left a cool Heineken dripping condensation onto its coaster. That unmistakable smell of hot, summer asphalt we all remember when we were kids, came back, and carried me away for just one peaceful moment. How did I get here?

Heads high around me bobbed, eager for a glimpse at what was going on. There were moms, dads, little kids, old people, young people all with one thing in common, an interest in me. Curious. Who is this guy? What's he done? Some whispered, they all pointed. They reveled in my plight, my sadness. Guns, strange contraband, police in uniforms, police in plain clothes, hot flashing blue strobes, traffic stopped, helicopters overhead; an electrified feeling of excitement filled the air.

I hoped no one recognized me.

Another official stepped up and took over the responsibility of insuring that I was compliant there on the ground with cuffs behind my back. I've always wondered what in the world they thought I might do. Try it sometime. Lay on the floor on your belly, hands behind your back. Imagine your wrists fastened together tightly with painful metal cuffs. I was most definitely compliant, willing to do what these showmen, these ringleaders, wanted. They were the center of attention. I was their prop. They loved it. They lived for this.

The last visit I had while I laid there on the ground, was from an officer everyone called JC. JC was an upper level US Customs agent sent to inspect their capture. Topsiders, khakis, golf shirt, badge, holster, Glock. A clean cut, fit man with a head of short cropped sandy curls, a kind face and a wide communicative smile. He'd arrived for the occasion via helicopter, and with badge and pistol by his side, he commanded respect.

"You okay?" he leaned over and asked quietly.

"As well as can be expected under the circumstances," I squeaked.

The overly abundant crew of law enforcement clearly hoped they had just taken down the new cartel kingpin. I hated to disappoint them, but I was just one more small-time smuggler trying to make a buck. Through my whole association with them, they never seemed to subscribe to this view. Having been captured by this group of heroes, I could never have been tagged less than important, less than very dangerous. I was the baddest of the bad, my product was the most potent ever, and it could never be any other way.

"Captured: Hundreds of kilos of highly potent Moroccan Hash," the local newspaper read.

Months later this branch of the DEA was still bragging about the superior quality of this hashish based on their "lab tests" prior to incineration. I, and everyone between Tangier, Atlanta, New York, and Montreal knew, oh so well, that this was just not true. This stuff had been junk, and its worthless nature was the predominant reason that I'd now landed in their hands.

Suddenly, after what couldn't have been more than thirty minutes, JC came straight over and hoisted me slowly and carefully, almost kindly, but not painlessly, from the hot road to my feet. Little asphalt pieces were burned into my face and with no way to wipe them away they remained there and burned deeper until they finally cooled off.

Then Captain Jack swaggered over, brandishing my little stainless Smith and Wesson .38 in the air. He'd been searching the rental car with the help of half dozen wannabes, all looking for anything of interest. They took the car apart right there on the spot and found the little pistol in its hiding place under the seat.

"You have just stepped into the big league," he said. As he unloaded the pistol on the roof of the car. "This just cost you seven more years."

Did I hear him say *seven MORE* years? I couldn't even think about what I'd just heard. I had no capacity to comprehend those words...*seven MORE* years. More. More than what!

Captain Jack was on the business card he'd handed me when I met him in the bar less than an hour earlier. He posed as the buyer for my hashish and gave an award-winning performance. I bought the ruse completely. Captain Jack was actually agent Jack Burrous, a character of intense presence.

On first seeing him, you'd never forget him. His long wild red hair with a matching beard encircled a round ruddy sun burned face. He gave a distinct impression of "don't fuck with me buddy". And if you were fool enough to do so, he was capable, willing, and ready to accommodate. He left no doubt that he could finish the job. Anyone would want Captain Jack on their team.

He came over and swept me aside, away from JC's ever watchful eyes. In that same motion, he whispered to me.

"You're a brother, a sailor. I want you to know I really do hate to do this to you."

No, I didn't misunderstand what he'd said. Nor did I understand it. There was no comforting effect on me other than it was just so out of place. Now, in retrospect, Captain Jack must have been employing the old "break down the barrier" process, to interrogate the catch more easily. But I always thought, and still think, that save for a compilation of words that define the law, Captain Jack could easily, at another time, be the same hero on the other team. My team. I'll never forget that moment.

Jack kept up our stride as he floated me toward the opened door of an unmarked car where I was pressed into the wire-caged back seat by a forceful hand on the back of my head. The door shut tight and it was cool and quiet.

In the relative calm of the caged back seat it all began to sink in, that yes… this is real. I shivered. There was no undoing, no turning back, no waking up from this nightmare. I had no option but to accept what happened, to work hard to gain control, and somehow pilot myself through this next part of life.

A very scary part.

CHAPTER THIRTY-SIX
Romero / Let Me Go!

JUST AS I was garnering what peace I could from the cool quiet in the caged back seat of the patrol car, the door on the other side flew open, and my solitude was abruptly interrupted. A loud, greasy, incorrigible, rude, smelly, strung out Romero, led by angry glazed eyes, was less than kindly thrown in the back seat with me.

He was incensed. He had a painfully strong, obnoxious smell, made stronger by the cramped back seat of the prowler.

"Man, you stink like a shit factory!" came from the front seat.

Nauseated, I asked Romero, "Man, really, did you shit in your pants, or just step in a pile?"

"I don't think I can stand this," the voice from the front seat said. "He's going to make me puke."

"Hey," I said, "you ought to be back here for a minute."

A real, no kidding heave, not wholly dry, intentionally erupted with a loud belch, and thickened the air in the front seat. The acrid aroma of pastrami and pickles revisited, along with the gaseous smell of the resident fecal blend, sent the driver tumbling out of the car vehemently staring back over his shoulder at us and his partner. He bent over and looked in the back seat shaking his head at Romero who was oblivious, turning more vicious by the minute.

242

I asked, "You're not including me with your source of misery I hope?". "You're going to have to let me out or you may arrive wherever we're going with a casualty on your hands."

I was half kidding.

"Okay, okay, I'll call another car for him. Quit complaining, you bunch of sissies. I'm agreeing with you, you're preaching to the choir."

"Hey, look here," I proposed, "why don't you guys just let me out up here at the next corner?"

"Hey, why don't you just shut the fuck up?" the voice shouted back at me, then continued on his radio. "Burrous, Jack Burrous, calling Jack Burrous."

"What do you want Mike?" I recognized Burrous's voice on the radio.

"You won't believe this, but I've got to get this stinking Mexican out of this car. We're all sick and getting sicker from his stench!"

"Tell me you're kidding, right?"

"C'mon Jack, I promise I'm not kidding."

Meanwhile Romero was loud, cuffed and belligerent. A dark-skinned, handsome man with black eyes, he was simply another of Yousef's desperate picks to help sell my useless contraband. I knew nothing about him. He seemed extraordinarily strung out on copious amounts of quality cocaine, no doubt provided by the informant "friend", who had led him to Captain Jack, and then led Captain Jack to me. Romero was on edge; Romero was on THE edge.

Unbeknownst to Romero, his "friend" was working for the DEA. In Miami, he'd kept Romero close, and fueled his endless supply of white powder. Romero had been talking. Way too much. While Captain Jack had been reeling me in out in the parking lot, Romero had finally been found in the restroom and apprehended, then kept at bay just outside the hotel bar.

In a short minute, another patrol car came from nowhere and slammed on brakes in the road cutting us off abruptly. Captain Jack and JC got out and walked back to our car. Mike hopped out.

"God damn man, "Captain Jack said. "You weren't kidding. That's awful."

The four agents had a meeting right there in the middle of the road. Mike's partner never said a word. He was off to the side, bent over, with his hands on his knees. Romero was using this time and situation to talk serious shit to the DEA. On and on, louder and louder. I hoped someone would finally blow up. Professionalism prevailed, and they swapped cars.

"Thanks Jack, I owe you."

Captain Jack and JC got into the front seat of the car now. They rolled all the windows down. The blistering hot Florida summer heat only added to the stench as they struck out with their catch; me and Romero.

I heard Jack say, "I wonder why those amateurs didn't roll the windows down?" Honestly, I had wondered the same thing.

Romero, already suffering the beginnings of withdrawal, got more disgusting in every way. He was out of his mind. They had handcuffed him to a steel bar in the back seat, but it was insufficient to corral his insanity. He kept on badgering the DEA about their intolerance to his rank odor.

"Shut the fuck up you son of a bitch," JC said. "You really don't want us to stop this car again."

I was thinking, come on Romero you idiot, keep it up.

Romero responded with a flurry of aggression in Spanish and German, and spit through the cage. A disgusting dollop of a lunger swung like a pendulum in between the steel bars of the cage. Romero began screaming in English, over and over.....

"Hashish is legal in my country; this is all legal in my country! Let me go! I want my attorney."

It was at this point that I lost it. Finally, the temper lying dormant in me came roaring out. A knee jerk reaction made me lunge at this idiot. I was quickly reminded that my hands were still in cuffs. They'd gotten so numb that I had lost all sense of their attachment to my body. Romero's lightning fast movement toward me was arrested only by the steel bar he was cuffed to. Romero's ferocity sobered me like water on a fire. He was dangerous to himself and to all around him.

I was quickly reminded that I still hadn't peed for a while.

I heard them whispering in the front seat.

"We've got to separate these guys." JC said.

I thought at first it was due to Romero's incessant fit, but I soon realized JC and captain Jack were simply cooking up a strategy for their next step. Keeping us together for too long raised the possibility that we might concoct a different truth, one that would interfere with their process of interrogating us separately.

Captain Jack mentioned quietly to JC that he needed to be careful with this bust. The day before, Jack had angered his superiors when he'd risked losing our bust completely by making an unauthorized change on his own and staging the bust in Jacksonville rather than Fort Lauderdale. Jack had intentionally disregarded the DEA's orders. The DEA had demanded that he not change the locale. Jack's orders were to assist the Southern District DEA with the bust which was to remain staged down in Fort Lauderdale. The DEA wanted to take no chances in scaring me away.

They had no idea how close I came to taking off. They still believed they had a big-time smuggler. Jack felt he'd done all the leg work, spent months with the huge Miami cocaine bust, and considered Romero's "friend" to be *his* informant. He considered bringing me to slaughter *his* deal and wanted all the credit for these captures. He had quit answering their phone calls, paid them no attention, and handled the case as he wanted.

The DEA called him down, and labeled his actions, frivolous and narcissistic, then nailed Jack personally for insubordination and acting unprofessionally for personal gain. Captain Jack laughed and agreed. He'd heard it all, and over the years he'd been defined in hundreds of ways, but inarguably his statistics put him miles in front of whoever was in second place.

He just laughed it all off as he carved one more notch in his pistol grip... me.

Thinking back, as I rode along in the patrol car, I recalled being connected to Romero through Yousef Abboud. I'd grown to trust Yousef since first meeting him in Tangier. Our "trust" wasn't a warm, brotherly trust born from a lifetime of experiences, but a trust born from necessity. I could not abandon our connection if I was to progress with my plan to get rid of this stuff. For me to sell it would have been an impossibility. My only hope was to finesse my relationship with Yousef in hopes he'd magically come up with a buyer. Hell, I'd had it in storage for months with zero success.

Therein lay my "Achilles heel". Yousef Abboud had been introducing me to people he felt could deliver. Months later, knowing I was still saddled with the bulk of a virtually worthless product, Yousef had tried again to help me. He had sought out riskier contacts. It wasn't his fault. He could not guarantee Romero's sobriety or his connections, nor could he vouch for Lupo's integrity.

He fairly warned me... "Pierce, be careful."

Bottom line...my desperation had made for sloppy thinking. This business punishes dearly for that.

Later I discovered that Romero's "friend", whom I'd met on the deck at Pier 66, had been involved with a large group of scammers, moving tons of cocaine into and out of South Florida. After several years of diligent work and careful planning, Captain Jack and the DEA set up a massive bust that yielded great success. RICO laws applied at that time, making the group scared and desperate. RICO nomenclature, originally started in 1970, now labeled the group as an ongoing criminal enterprise, which levied much heavier sentences. These guys were doing everything they could to save themselves from serious "time", some as harsh as life imprisonment. Romero's "friend" was saving himself at our expense. Who wouldn't?

Romero had flown from Munich to Miami not knowing that his South Florida group had fallen prey to the DEA three months earlier. When Romero approached his "friend" to help him find a venue to move my pile of shit, his "friend", a doomed "gang member- turned- informant", reeled ole Romero in along with me, for an easy catch.

* * *

Our patrol car came to an abrupt stop. I was pulled from the back seat. My wrists screamed with pain. I could hardly get out of the car and I stumbled when my feet hit the ground. My legs were numb. JC, the customs officer, saw my plight and came over.

"You're not gonna give us any problems like your buddy over here, are you?"

"Buddy, he's not my buddy! Hell I've never seen him in my life until five minutes ago!"

Something in the way I'd said that made JC stop for a moment and look directly into my eyes. He didn't say a word while he unlocked my cuffs. The relief I felt in my wrists gave me hope that things might be getting better already. At that point it didn't take much for me to feel better.

Romero was jerked from the car and fell to the ground, kicking and screaming. Two giant officers grabbed him by his arms, and dragged him away, sliding along the pavement on his heels. One of his shoes came off and bounced along the pavement. No one slowed down. I never saw Romero again. Rumor had it that he was extradited.

CHAPTER THIRTY-SEVEN
Breathe a Long Sigh for Plans Gone Awry / One Phone Call

I WAS UNCEREMONIOUSLY DEPOSITED into a 6x6 concrete block room that had a fresh coat of white paint and a stainless-steel toilet with no seat and no water, which took up most of the floor space. The fluorescent light recessed in the ceiling lent a ghastly hue to the cube.

That was it: me, the light, and the toilet. It was cool and quiet again. Really quiet. Too cool. I sat down on the edge of the toilet where the seat should have been with my face in my hands. Then and there, what was left of my world fell apart. A brand-new low was coming on. My personal barometer plummeted. Realities came charging at me from all sides. I was defenseless and in deep trouble.

I didn't cry, I wouldn't call it that. It wasn't the kind of place you'd cry. Tears just flowed like a river down my hands, past my wrists along my forearms, past my elbow, onto my knees and landed on the floor behind my heels. I don't know how long they flowed, but I do know I slipped in them when I finally stood up.

I stretched hard to the ceiling, and contemplated suicide. Each time I came up with a creative method, my dear old soul rejected the idea. After what I guess was about three hours of dreaming up and discarding alternative ways of killing myself, and after no more tears fell, I stood up, stretched again, popped my back and at that moment…yes, things took a slight turn towards getting better.

I berated myself. I knew that body *always* follows mind. My life was far from over, and who did I think I was to let such squirrelly destructive thoughts wander around in my head? I dug in. My mind spun around a sharp turn. It was time to gain control again.

* * *

In that cold holding cell, on that hot July day, I bounced off the bottom, a place I had never visited before, and a place I never want to revisit. It was no fun. But, the bounce back has been a gas. What a ride. What a story.

I began to conjure a plan. I needed to get in touch with Diana. All players needed an update. I had to be very careful now, careful how I communicated at this point. The walls had ears. These people were not my friends.

I'm not sure when they pulled me from the cube. I'm not at all sure of how long I was in there, but when I walked out, I was a different guy than the one who'd walked in. I sensed that it was most likely dark outside, and the faces I'd spent the afternoon with were long gone.

The Feds began the process of checking in their new catch. My hand, finger, and footprints were taken as I was moved through a maze of very unhappy people doing very unhappy jobs. There was no room for levity. It was as if these poor peons, sitting here, rolling my fingers in black ink, blamed me for their plight.

Hey, take it easy, I thought. Without me you would have no job. The jail housed hundreds of prisoners, but it seemed most of the employees tied behind their desks were more desperate that those behind the bars. One well-fed check-in clerk threw an orange suit at my chest, and soon the short-lived relief of wearing no handcuffs was replaced by fresh degradation. I was introduced to a new contraption, handcuffs attached to chains that led down to my ankles and then bound my legs to short steps with shackles. My recovering old wrist wounds burned sore again, and the leg cuffs rubbed my ankles raw in no time.

I was allowed the proverbial "one phone call." I chose my words with Diana carefully. I had to convince anyone eavesdropping of Diana's innocence. I told her the basics of where I was and what had happened. Her reaction was immediate hysteria. She knew something had happened when she hadn't heard from me.

As quickly as her sobbing would allow, I interrupted. I had to convey to her, without tipping my hand, what she must do, and do it fast. I sped up our conversation with careful phrases.

"Since you didn't know what was going on," and "I'm so sorry I didn't let you know what was happening," and "I felt it was best for you not to know what I was up to".

The illogical phrases rang true, and I knew Diana could tell what was going on as she responded in a conciliatory way.

"That's alright sweetheart, I wish I'd known. You have been acting oddly for a couple of weeks. We'll get you out of there as quickly as possible. I'll be in touch. I love you sweetheart."

The immediate problem at hand was a race, a race we must win, or we would have a whole new bar set for our predicament.

Diana and I had recently, just weeks earlier, moved the hashish to our basement from the storage warehouse where it had been for the past eleven months. Yousef had talked me into taking 200 kilos of the hashish from Atlanta to Fort Lauderdale for the rendezvous with Romero, leaving a balance of 150 kilos in our basement.

My history in Atlanta was based on the high-end design and build construction industry. Although we had no currently active project, I reminded her about a fictitious dumpster on a work site and how it must be removed quickly before the contents spoiled and angered the neighbors. She got it. I could tell she knew what needed to be done. I found out a worrisome week later that she immediately, single handedly in the dark of that very same night, fueled by fear and adrenalin, loaded our pickup with the remaining 150 kilos of hash, and drove in the dark to two random dumpsters where she deposited the sad remains, thus heralding the grand finale' of a very long journey.

"Breathe a long sigh for plans gone awry."

That remaining hash could easily have been a tremendous problem. Had it been found, Diana would have been implicated, and the criteria for my defense would be based on a substantially greater amount adding years to my sentence.

At that point, my story and my defense became forevermore based on a load of 250 kilos: the 200 in the trunk and the 50 that had gone to Bruno and Lupo.

On nights when I lay awake and my mind wanders, I think of the entire incredible effort. I think of how this well-traveled product was so unceremoniously thrown into a dumpster in the middle of the night and hauled away on the next morning's pull, taking with it all the dreams of financial reward and freedom. There would be no satisfaction of a venture well done, no excitement of sharing success, no celebrations, no peace of mind, and no funds for starting over.

Then I wonder what I would have changed. What could I have changed? Really, nothing. It all just had to be. Now it was time to begin repairs.

CHAPTER THIRTY-EIGHT
If you Can't Lose... What's the Point?

AFTER ALL THE PREP WORK, my wardrobe change, and a bout of minor superficial questioning, I was deposited in Jacksonville's Duval County Jail.

Captain Jack had the idea that I was running a well-honed, major drug operation, and with proper interrogation, he would undoubtedly uncover the balance of my empire. Much to his disappointment, he was to find out that it really was...only me.

I was escorted to one of many cells, stacked three high on top of each other, built to hold four inmates. My cell already housed four poor fellows. I made the fifth. One, a tall thin youngish guy, had veins that stood out on every part of his body. His head, his neck, his shoulders, his arms were all maps of thick veins, running around each other and leading nowhere. This dude was built totally outta muscle and blood. To cap his heinous appearance, two three-inch-tall Mohawks sprouted from above his eyes, each lacking an eyebrow, and ran to the back of his head, where a slight tint of purple shimmered in his bright blond hair.

Strangely, this cat had neither tattoos nor piercings. Two of the other three were laughing as he told them of his last Thanksgiving when he cooked a package of baloney on a garbage can lid for the big meal. The two laughing were college boys in polo shirts and khakis. They'd been pulled over for reckless driving, checked for drinking, and landed a DUI. They looked and acted like they were still under the influence. The cop who'd pulled them over made note that when he turned on his blue lights, they had pulled over, but kept on pulling over and over and over until they had landed in the deep concrete drain culvert beside the road.

The cops had towed the car out of the culvert. The driver burned up the Breathalyzer, while his partner tried to walk away, claiming he had been hitchhiking and didn't know the other guy at all and had nothing to do with it. He then started running. The arresting officer called another car, a K-9 patrol car, just for him. The preppies laughed at their own story. I was envious. Those guys would be out of here in a few hours.

Mr. Mohawk had beaten up his wife's boyfriend and would likely do a bit of time in the local lock up. He'd apparently made a habit of stalking this hapless suitor. He delivered his story embellishing it with his big, balled up fist that moved so fast it stirred the air in our crowded cage.

"My fist just kept on bouncing off that asshole's head. I was outta control and couldn't stop."

Since he'd been "out of control", he felt he was innocent. He felt he should be freed based on insanity. He'd seen too many movies.

Still laughing, the frat boys whole heartedly agreed with the wild man's logic.

The fourth cellmate was an older, smallish black man, with a dried, wrinkled, prune face. Saying nothing, he acted as if he hoped we wouldn't notice him. I found out later he'd been dragged from under a freeway bridge where he'd comfortably set up home after a grueling trip hiding in the belly of a small freighter from Jamaica. He would be released in the morning light, with his belly full of as much jailhouse breakfast as it could hold. Then off to look for the next suitable bridge for his next home. His routine appeared to be a way of life. Home is where the heart is.

I was quite different from the other four. Not one of them even looked my way, let alone spoke to me. When our cell door rumbled closed for the night, my four roommates lay down on the four bunks. I ventured to ask where my place was, hoping there might be an extra mattress. No response. I was in a primitive, political system where the scariest character assumed the role of President. Mr. Mohawk pointed at the floor, then reached around behind him and threw a blanket in my general direction. I was fairly sure he had a second green plastic mattress on his bunk, and even surer that's where it was going to stay. The two frat boys talked in soft tones all night, careful not to wake Godzilla.

In addition to my orange jumpsuit, my "welcome to jail" bundle included a blanket, a roll of toilet paper, a toothbrush, socks, and some rubber slip-ons. I shook out one blanket, laid down, and covered up with the one from Mr. Mohawk.

"Lights out," the speaker garbled, and it was instantly twilight in the cell block, but never totally dark.

I didn't realize my exhaustion until I fell into a sleep not unlike death on that cold concrete floor. I woke up in the middle of the night, cold, stiff, and sore. Really stiff. I lay for hours, staring into the twilight thinking, when suddenly, with a loud mechanical sound, the lights came back on and men began to rustle. Everything echoed. Every word, every movement. The cell doors clanged in harmony as their locks opened and released inmates to the main concrete floor of the jail house. Thinking a shower might improve my state of exhaustion, I crept down to the showers which were open to the whole cell block on one side.

I was alone, naked, with hot water running over my head and down my body, when the call for breakfast was announced. Everyone from that cell block suddenly came to life, joining a queue to pick up a tray of what could loosely be called breakfast. Their line filed right by the showers, putting me, naked, soapy and wet on stage.

The guys in the line had no trouble staring, pointing, and laughing with each other at my predicament. Choices were slim. I finished my shower, dressed, and barely made it to the tray line for a few cold, hard, scrambled eggs, burned bacon, a puck of grits, and funny tasting toast. I picked the biggest, baddest guy in the place and asked if he wanted my food. I figured, if I had to stay in the cell block for long, at some point it might be handy to have someone like him on my side. He looked me square in the eyes, then up and down, and finally at the tray. He reached out and took it out of my hand, turned away without a word, and began eating the meal with his big black, pink-scarred hand.

I returned to my cell. The frat boys were the only ones there. As the new day had dawned, they'd sobered up and were no longer the cavalier smartasses from the night before. When I walked into the cell, they turned and took a choreographed step backward, as if they thought I was there to kill them.

"Who are you"? they asked carefully, with fearful eyes.

Inebriation had evidently stolen their memory, or they had never noticed me the night before. I offered a short introduction, but their thoughts had no room for another jail bird. They wanted out. I could read their minds.

"Get us out of here and we'll be good for the rest of our lives."

Meantime, our wild man was animated, standing in the middle of the cell block where his white skin, blue hair, and tall double Mohawk set him apart from the sea of black. He presided over a constant rumble of conversation. The old Jamaican sat alone, quietly enjoying his breakfast and chancing a quick look to see if he could lobby for someone's leftovers. In our cell, sure enough, the wild man's bed did have an extra mattress. I sat down on the concrete floor, with my legs crossed on my blanket. I needed only a headdress and a peace pipe.

An hour or so later I thought I heard my name called over the barely intelligible intercom.

"Eberett, Mahvin Pears Eberett."

An inmate with tenure and some amount of authority, called my name again, louder. I jumped with my hand raised, thinking maybe it was possible that Diana had come to get me. Rolling his eyes with overt exasperation, he motioned me out of the cell block and to a chair in a long hallway. The hall was illuminated with tall, green tinted windows that sandwiched a layer of chicken wire between their glass panels.

"Mahvin… huh, I figgered you wuz a nigga." The "z" in "wuzzz, seemed to vibrate as it passed through the wide gap in his front teeth.

"Probably should have been." I quipped.

It was the first time I'd seen daylight since my fateful meeting with Romero and Captain Jack.

Less than 24 hours had passed.

Sunlight beamed through the wire-glass windows along the hallway where I had been parked. I'd forgotten just how great it felt to rest in a chair. Wonderful things, chairs.

In a few minutes, three other somber inmates, complete with chains and shackles came walking into the hallway from another cell block somewhere deep inside the jail. I was duly linked onto the end of this miserable train. The pains in my ankles and wrists immediately returned as the shackles were clamped over old wounds. None of us spoke as we shuffled, chains clanking, down the hall and outside to a waiting van. None of us knew where we were going. We rode along in silence, hardly looking at one another, for fear of seeing ourselves. We were immersed in our own private predicaments. One by one prisoners in the van were dropped off at different buildings and escorted away by waiting guards.

I was the last to be dropped off. A portly Latino fellow with a great, fuzzy black mustache, wearing grey trousers and a white Cuban shirt, was waiting for me when the door of the van opened. He was a jovial guy. Faux jovial. The worst kind. I got the feeling that my reputation as a "drug lord" had preceded me. Nodding toward me, he sized me up and down and asked the driver, "Any problems with him?"

The driver slowly shook his head side to side, "No Pancho, he been quiet de ho way." Because of the cumbersome chains, I was having difficulty maneuvering out of the van onto the ground. I slowly worked my way down off the seat, where I only managed to balance on the edge of the van's doorway, my chained feet dangling inches above the ground. Another face plant was in the making. He watched with great amusement as I lost my balance and almost fell forward out of the van. He unlocked the iron cuffs binding my ankles and threw them in the back of the van with a loud metal- chain crash.

Why hadn't he taken them off before I moved to get out of the van?

"Thanks man, those things were killing my ankles," I said, trying my best to quell the emerging sarcasm.

He turned away without speaking and walked at a practiced pace down the concrete sidewalk as it curved back and forth through a stand of shade trees.

"That's what they're supposed to do," he retorted over his shoulder.

He ignored me when I asked where we were going. We continued along in the early morning sun and entered a building that could have been the same building where I'd commiserated with my seat-less toilet the day before.

It seemed early in the day and more people were bustling in and out. Unlike the jail I'd just left, the people here were a smiling, pleasant group. I figured they were mostly DEA employees, and I was the only inmate in sight. I was self-conscious in my conspicuous orange jumpsuit. People seemed to stare at me as if they had never seen anyone in this get up before. They nodded pleasantly to me as they passed. The atmosphere was noticeably more at ease, almost friendly.

Poncho motioned to a chair along a corridor of doors. The smell that wafted through the air was that of ubiquitous, institutional, painted masonry. It reminded me of the hiding places I found while working as a teletype operator in the US Army. It reminded me of the first day of school each year. It reminded me of school hallways as a kid, where I sat on that red bench, waiting for Mrs. Harris the Principal.

A moment later, Pancho instructed me to follow him. My hands were still cuffed. He stopped abruptly, turned, and without expression motioned for me to hold my hands out. He unlocked the cuffs and took them from me. The relief was immeasurable. I felt that gravity had unleashed its hold as I floated down the long hallway.

At the end of the hallway beside a closed door, stood a shortish, sandy-haired, heavy set, serious young man. He wore a long-sleeved blue, button down collar, oxford shirt, tucked into pleated khakis, all pressed flat with heavy starch, and a polished badge mounted to his leather belt. His 9mm Glock rested in a holster at the small of his back. He and Pancho whispered a few words, nodded my way, and without adieu Pancho was outta there. My new escort looked at me without expression, turned, opened a heavy wooden door, and lightly pushed me to enter.

I was so surprised; I didn't know how to react. The room was crowded. It felt like a surprise party. I'd seen all these people before over the past week. I recognized one couple who had stood out to me on the deck at Pier 66 in Fort Lauderdale. They had looked like angels of doom. Maybe they were. Black everything--hair, beard, attitude. Easy to remember. Next, I recognized the four young men who had stood out to me at my last breakfast with Diana on the morning she'd left Fort Lauderdale. They almost smiled. I was astounded by this well-orchestrated surveillance, an incredible ruse.

Captain Jack stood in one corner in a fierce discussion with three other guys. They shared one common thread. Everyone sported a 9mm Glock strapped to their belts. Captain Jack came over and put his arm around my shoulders.

"Good morning Everett, I see you've met Griffin."

Captain Jack addressed the group.

"Yep, you all know Griffin here, he's a legend in his own mind."

They all smiled in agreement. Every move Griffin made was taken from a close study of Miami Vice. He brandished his 9 at every opportunity. As we spent more time together, I understood that Griffin was just "Gung Ho".

Everything seemed so surreal. I thought I knew what was happening, but the atmosphere was so affable, that I just wasn't sure. Captain Jack motioned for me to sit at the head of an exceptionally long table. The flurry of conversations ended, and everyone found a seat. They looked at me quietly, with most of their arms resting on the table.

"You're going to be asked a number of questions, "Captain Jack said politely, and we expect you to answer truthfully. If you are evasive, appropriate consequences would be forthcoming; including potential charges of perjury."

I wondered about the old line from the movies, "Get me an attorney!" At that moment, the door swung open, and JC, the customs officer, walked in. The time had come for me to do their bidding. Complete cooperation, as they say.

JC smiled at me, then pulled out a chair, sat down and cocked it back against the wall away from the organization of the table. With one-foot resting on the support between the front legs, he settled in to observe my proffer, and see what he was able glean from the questions and my answers.

A proffer is where a prisoner is prompted during an interrogation to provide information that might be useful to the government prior to formal negotiations.

Regretfully I had been captured during the era of "Mandatory Sentencing." This was a sad, ridiculous, heartless, thoughtless, process created to simplify sentencing predominantly directed at the illegal drug industry. It was an embarrassment for anyone who adhered to its brainless inception. There were thousands of prisoners in the system who should not have been incarcerated. Armed with a simple calculator that had a vertical list of illegitimate commodities and a horizontal list of weights, a person's sentence could be easily found by the number where the two lines intercept. The government proudly threatened that there was no possibility of deviation from this simple calculation. Officials in charge who had any judgement during this era quickly worked around the obvious and depending on the plaintiff and the charges there was still a small ray of hope running around in the grey areas that could be tapped.

It was candidly understood but rarely mentioned, that a valuable proffer could have positive impact on the balance of the proceedings. With a less helpful proffer, the opposite could follow.

CHAPTER THIRTY-NINE
My Proffer Begins / Get me an Attorney?

WHEN THE PROCESS BEGAN, the group became much more serious and somber.

One of the agents, a woman I didn't recognize, spoke first.

"First, Mr. Everett, you've adamantly claimed that your actions were sporadic, unplanned and borne from untenable financial stresses at home. I would like for you to tell our group what gave you the idea that you could even attempt to smuggle hashish into our country, and secondly, how were you able to pull such contacts together to make this attempt, as you say, sporadically without previous planning and no previous experience. We find these contacts, that you claim to so easily have found, are protective and difficult to corner or trust. Especially from our perspective."

A quiet laughter stirred in the room.

"These considerations lead us to look at you skeptically, with somewhat less trust in what you have to say. What's more, we all agree, it makes us wonder whether you are really the person you appear to be. You present a very different profile from the typical criminals we see passing through. Simply put, you don't fit the mold."

I took a chance. Spin was ultra-important.

"As you already know, I didn't *attempt* to smuggle the stuff into this country, I *did* smuggle whatever it was, into this country. When you guys came along, the dung had been in a storage warehouse for months. The reason for this remains…the contraband was totally worthless. This reality became apparent while in the middle of the Atlantic Ocean, I realized what I'd been given was, for the most part, not hashish. It was likely camel dung and wax."

I laughed at myself and shook my head.

"If you really believe that I'm the experienced career smuggler that you envision, just take a close look at the miserable product that I was sold. It was pure dung and worthless, certainly unacceptable and not up to the standards of a seasoned smuggler."

Thank goodness, a few souls acknowledged the humor with a soft laughter.

"Also, regarding the difficulty of making connections to find a seller in Tangier… come with me this minute, and we'll go to Tangier. With one question to anyone on the streets, we will be lined up with a dozen candidates ready to sell us hashish."

Captain Jack smiled, but then retook his stance regarding his opinion on the quality of the hash, and with a cold hard look, he dared me to refute him again.

"If the quality of my product had been what I'd thought it was going to be, I wouldn't be here right now. Not that your company isn't a total pleasure. But if I was anything other than a novice at this game, I most likely wouldn't have been in this unenviable situation, sailing around with a boat load of camel shit. Captain Jack… I am here with you now because the hashish you incinerated was literally, *SHIT*."

I'd gone on a bit too long and had dared again to challenge our differing opinions regarding the identity of the product that I had in the trunk of my car. Everyone at the table eyed Captain Jack nervously awaiting the inevitable explosion. The room was hushed. I heard JC's chair creak as he twisted in his seat against the wall.

I knew I needed to instantly quell any impression of me as a "smart ass", and hoped I wasn't too late. I reminded myself that these people were deadly serious about their jobs, and they didn't share my sense of humor...I needed *not* to get too comfortable in this situation.

Finally, the woman who'd started the proffer spoke up again.

"Mr. Everett," she persisted pleasantly, "we would like you to tell us about yourself. We all want to know your background and a little more about you. But, please remember this Mr. Everett, this is not a forum for you to exercise your talent as a comedian, or to rebuke us or our efforts. You are in the midst of your proffer, having been arrested and accused of committing a very serious federal crime. Years of your life are at stake here. It is here that our opinion of you, and the crime you've committed, is formed. It is here that the earliest attempts on your part to defend yourself are born. We are all intensely serious about our efforts to eliminate people like you who treat the laws of our country with frivolity. So, take heed of what I say. We are all here to put you away."

Those words hit hard, and I struggled to maintain a modicum of composure as the whole room stared at me in silence. The smart ass in me tucked its tail and crawled under the house. I squirmed in my seat.

"Understood and thank you for reminding me of the grave severity of my situation." I continued. "From my perspective, and I promise you that I couldn't possibly be more serious, this whole process at every turn, has been so ridiculous, so dangerous, so impossible, so daunting, and so skewed, that over the past two years, often the only things I've been able to do is laugh or cry. I've slowly and helplessly watched as the whole intent of my efforts crumbled before my eyes. I've been ripped off, cheated, misled, threatened, thrown on the ground, arrested with a gun to my head, accused, and tossed in jail. I've essentially lost everything and more. Again, please accept my apologies for my implying any frivolity on my part. I do know and understand that I'm in serious trouble. Believe me, I know."

After a sigh, I took a long deep breath.

"In response to your last question I'll share a brief description of my life if you feel that is in order and interrupt me if it's not what you're asking for, or if I'm not answering your question."

"From the beginning I had a great childhood with loving parents. Nothing about it was hard. I look at myself with confidence, as a good person. I'm a terrible liar. I care about people, and hold old friends close to my heart. My friends are each special and important people. They are in great part what makes me who I am. I hacked my way through high school and a bit of college. Finally, my indifference, as well as lack of prowess at regurgitating uninteresting curriculum, set me up as a perfect candidate for the US Army. I spent three years in the Army, narrowly avoiding Viet Nam. In the end, I was honorably discharged and returned to the world on my own two feet."

After leaving the army, I worked my way upward to a position of reasonable legitimate affluence in my hometown, Atlanta, Georgia. I had two construction crews working on properties that I would buy, renovate, or restore, and sell. They were in the affluent neighborhoods of North Atlanta, Ansley Park and Buckhead. I had also developed a machinery business where I would purchase large woodworking shops, rebuild the equipment, and resell it for profit. I had shops, trucks, forklifts, employees, and properties coming and going. Things were hopping. Times were lucrative, money was flying around, and days went by like minutes."

There must have been a dozen agents around the long table. I noticed that they all seemed to be interested in what I was saying and listened intently to every word. I felt no aggression or animosity from them or for them. Even the serious threat from the agent a few minutes before seemed to defuse and leave no cloud. I could tell she had other questions she wanted to ask, but she sat there with bated breath, listening, and taking notes. I appreciated them being so attentive and felt I should give them their money's worth. So, onward I wove the tale spinning a yarn that held everyone's attention.

"Then it all happened. In the late 80's and the early 90's, stock markets around the world crashed, the savings and loan crisis strained the housing market and the ensuing government bailout only added more pressure to our economy. Then Iraq invaded Kuwait, gas prices spiked, interest rates soared restricting credit, and unemployment continued its spiral upward. Money dried up, home sales plummeted, and the inflated value of real property halved. I found myself strung out overnight with four houses in Buckhead, all mid-project, and one in Ansley Park desperately for sale, without any prospective buyers on the horizon. My debt service on these properties alone was around $10k per month all underwritten by me personally. There was no walking away. I owed the bank well over a million dollars. There were many thousands of dollars past due to suppliers and sub-contractors. I was forced to sell off two of the main projects for half of what they were worth… a substantial loss. Things spun down the drain overnight. Bankruptcy loomed with both my businesses and me personally. Something I never dreamed I'd have to do."

"Our wonderful sailboat, now over in the Mediterranean was one of the last assets Diana and I had. We sadly set about making plans to bring *Whitetail* home. Neither Diana nor I wanted to sell her, but our options were nil."

Recalling this memory lured emotions out of hiding; they welled up in my chest. Those had been desperate times never to be forgotten, and at that moment, those memories froze me. I couldn't speak.

An odd comradery permeated the room. I seized this minute to take a short personal break. I just quietly sat there, head cocked to one side, watching the #2 yellow pencil held by two fingers, as it bounced, dancing on its red eraser. I gulped again and again quietly wishing for a place to hide. A few of the agents looked at each other raising their eyebrows, others just watched me as I pulled myself back together.

"Sorry…" that's all I could say, that's all I needed to say.

A full glass of water appeared by my side with the touch of a hand on my shoulder. This, and dogged determination helped me find the ability to carry on with the exploitation of my soul.

"So, we accepted the distasteful idea of sailing her home. For Diana and me it marked the end of an era.

Paralleling that plan, I began to formulate my own personal addition …the concept of loading *Whitetail* up with hashish. This new plan gained momentum as I realized that the profit from the hash might even negate the need to sell *Whitetail*. I would need to find a contact to enter that world. I would need this to be able to weigh the possibilities. Diana could not be a part of this new consideration.

I began contacting old sailing connections looking for a "key."

Suddenly one of the other women agents broke into the proffer for her first time.

"This 'key' you refer to, is this the person you needed for a contact in the Western Mediterranean, so you could find a safe seller where you would be able to procure the hashish that you wanted to bring back to the US?"

"Yes, without a trusted or well known "key" to open the door, these hooligans can, and will, easily take your money and leave you lost, broke, and lonely, or just plain dead."

"Tell me this then," she continued. "If you were so out of money, how were you going to finance this operation once you found your 'key'? For that matter, how were you intending to fund finding the 'key'? "

"I asked an old friend," I answered, "to loan me the money it would take to bring *Whitetail* home. He would be repaid the minute she sold. He had no knowledge of the hashish plan."

The proffer was getting tricky. I had to be oh so careful. Winging it was quickly becoming more difficult. I'd decided to try to weave a truth that would be acceptable, maybe even valuable to the DEA. But I wanted to avoid implicating friends.

Captain Jack saw through me; he knew exactly what I was up to. This wasn't his first rodeo. He'd seen and heard it all. He stood up from his place at the other end of the long table, kicked his chair back with the back of his knees and walked slowly around the table, holding a computer-generated document. he sat down in an empty chair next to me. He had the whole room's attention. His movements were wrought with intent, and I immediately began to feel distance.

Captain Jack theatrically ran a crooked trigger finger down a computer-generated list while he looked me straight in the eye. I flinched. No one said a word. I wasn't sure what to do. I did my best to bear up to his passive affront while he, still staring at me pointed to his list.

"Tell me all you know about this Lupo Rocco. He's here on my list time and again, and he's noted as being associated with a guy I've long wished to bring down, Yousef Abboud, your 'key'. The very one who has led you to your litany of bad news; Lupo, Bruno, Romero, and now to me. You made a dozen phone calls to those guys from that pay phone in Ft. Lauderdale, and Yousef Abboud's name came up in every one of them. We have tapes of these conversations, and I want to know everything about Yousef Abboud, but first I want to know everything you can tell me about Lupo Rocco. Everything."

Hard ball had begun. Chummy feelings were instantly dispatched, and I found myself stumbling over my thoughts for answers.

I was committed to keeping my plight to myself and preventing my bad luck from affecting people who I loved and cared about. It required an "off the cuff" process of rewriting the realities of the story to accommodate a script that left close friends out.

Lupo was the perfect, painless gift for the DEA. I had no loyalty for that criminal. He had twice seriously threatened my life. Even while I ground through the early afternoon round of my proffer, I was trying to figure a way to regain part of the 25 kilos he still had, or the $20k he owed me, hoping the product had sold. I hadn't heard Captain Jack's tapes, but I was sure I knew every recorded word.

I jumped back into my explanation.

"Much of that payphone time was spent trying to hound that shifty scoundrel into paying me the money he owed, $20k. Lupo and his goombah,

Bruno, were consistently, professionally evasive. I'm sure you picked up on my frustration from the tapes. The balance of these conversations would likely have been me trying to interpret a paranoid and incoherent Romero, trying to determine what progress he was making in marketing my trunk load of shit to you guys."

Captain Jack watched me closely, calculating my every reaction.

The biggest target for everyone was Yousef Abboud. He had been prolific at marketing hash on a large scale for years. When Captain Jack had heard Yousef mentioned on the tape, he immediately grabbed at a strong chance of reviving an old chase, with the possibility of cornering an old quarry. I had no option but to confirm that Yousef Abboud had, in fact, been my "key" in Morocco. Nabbing Yousef Abboud would be a first-place win for Captain Jack. Lupo was just a resource to be used for gaining money, other criminals, and Yousef Abboud.

* * *

We'd been going at it for about six hours. It must have been about two in the afternoon. After a 20-minute break to stand up and stretch, everyone wandered back into the room. I noticed during the break, that for the most part, I was ignored.

JC came over and handed me a bottle of water and asked if I was okay.

"I think so."

"Hang in there," he smiled. "You're doing really well."

There were some new faces. Four new agents had come in to listen. I wasn't sure why. The women had adjourned to the bathroom. Captain Jack was outside the door in the hall on an unpleasant phone call. Griffin was ever ready, hand on his pistol, watching everyone's moves.

I was somewhat relieved knowing that I really had nothing to hide from these agents that they didn't already know. I simply had to go with the flow, try to keep my nose above water, and spin a tale that would alleviate skepticism and, possibly, build a bond that might help me reduce my staggering projected sentence.

The first agent, who had been most interested in deciphering who I really was, immediately wanted to know more about Yousef Abboud. She was the only one taking notes.

"How did you actually meet this Yousef Abboud?"

I began again with what seemed to be their most interesting subject. It also kept questions about Diana at bay…

"I went to Tangier, and at a tea shop near the Kasbah, I asked about Yousef Abboud. A waiter who was serving me a cup of mint tea, leaned over and in good English quietly asked why I wanted to know about Yousef Abboud." I told him "A friend has recommended that I meet with him while I visited Tangier." Yousef Abboud was one of three brokers who'd been recommended to me from the sailing world. I'd called sailing friends in the Caribbean who confirmed that Yousef Abboud had a good reputation. It turned out he was well known, and after meeting with three candidates, I easily decided that Yousef Abboud lent me the most confidence. Also, he hadn't immediately wanted money. In fact, he had offered to supply the product for a 50% investment from me, as well as market it in Canada if I would bring it into the US for a set fee for smuggling, somewhere around $ 150,000. That was interesting to me as I was unsure of my abilities to get rid of the load after getting it into the country. After several meetings with Yousef Abboud I felt sure that he was to be my "key"."

The intently listening group of DEA agents all nodded.

"How much money are you talking about at 50%?" the agent persisted.

"Thirty thousand to Yousef Abboud."

"Where did you plan to come up with this cash?"

"The same friend in Atlanta, who'd lent me the initial money to get the boat ready to go, had at my request, offered to lend me additional funding as his last loan had quickly evaporated in the effort." Boats are expensive things to own and care for. Preparation for an Atlantic crossing requires a substantial amount of money.

"No, he wasn't aware of the real use for his loan."

"How were you planning to get the money to Tangier?"

"I flew from Atlanta to Madrid, caught a train to Algeciras, and ferried over to Tangier with the cash, shrink wrapped and stitched inside my blazer."

A couple of the new listeners leaned together to whisper behind open palms regarding what I'd just said. They never spoke but they listened intently.

One of the other agents whom I recognized as being one of the four watching us at the Marina Inn that morning at breakfast, spoke next.

"What part did Diana, your wife, play in your smuggling work?"

This was the question I was most dreading. I know my countenance changed as I answered, so I picked each word with care.

"First, it must be clear that I had no experience smuggling. It wasn't a familiar world for me. My decision to pick up a load of hash was truly impromptu. No, she knew nothing of the idea."

I worried... I'm a bad liar, but I carried on.

"Of course, she knew I was bringing our boat back to the United States after twelve years in Mallorca and Ibiza, but she wouldn't have approved of picking up a load of hashish."

One of the four young agents then said that they'd seen her with me at the Marina Inn at breakfast and wondered how she could have been there and not really have had any idea what was up.

"Yep I remember you guys taking photos of us from the second balcony while we ate breakfast outside in the courtyard".

Another agent quipped, "great undercover work men. Blend...remember, blend in, not stand out." Light laughter lifted some of the tension.

"I remembered seeing you guys, but I didn't think for a minute about why you were photographing us. Diana is an attractive woman, better said, she is beautiful, and she easily attracts attention, particularly from men. So, in answer, no, neither Diana nor I thought anything of these guys and their antics from the balcony."

This had been difficult, but I was fairly sure I had diminished their presumption that Diana must have been on board with the smuggling plans.

* * *

My proffer carried on. Another agent, a woman whom I didn't recognize, asked about my time on the payphone outside our hotel room door.

"I know this payphone in Fort Lauderdale was mentioned an hour ago," she said, "but it was a popular place for you that week."

"Your conversations there are a wealth of information for us."

This was a welcome subject change. It was the perfect time to further distract their interest from Diana's possible involvement.

It must have been close to four in the afternoon. The proffer continued. There were now 12 DEA agents in the room, some came and went. The three women hung in. One spoke up loudly amidst the questioning.

"I'm still not sure I understand the role that your wife played in your plan?"

Damn it! I worried that her raising the question once again was a sign that the group might not be sold on the idea that Diana was not involved.

"Diana had no idea what was going on," I repeated, "other than I was going to retrieve *Whitetail* with the intention of bringing her home to sell. She knew we were in terrible financial shape, and I was out to remedy the situation.

The agent adjusted her glasses and looked down at her notebook.

"Had Diana known about a parallel plan to load hashish into our boat on the way home, she would have disapproved adamantly, and likely she would have gone to great extremes to prevent it from happening."

I was getting tired. I thought they were intentionally doing this to wear me down to the point that I'd start making mistakes.

I waited a moment, then unsolicited, I carried on.

"I'd asked Diana to ride to Florida with me for a desperately needed break. I told her we were going to look at a boat for sale in Ft. Lauderdale that was an unusually good buy. I've always bought boats and restored them. This idea wasn't foreign to either of us over the years. In fact, I still do that. I explained that we would borrow against the upcoming sale of *Whitetail* to make the purchase before the bankruptcy court got wind of the purchase. I planned to resell the boat and apply that profit to further appease the court.

Then, on the way south to get a look at the boat, I told her it had already been sold, but suggested that we should carry on and enjoy a couple days off. When the connection with Romero regarding the hashish in the trunk was finally planned, I sent her home that morning after breakfast, with the idea I'd be home in a couple of days with the rental car, after I paid a visit to a friend who had a business in Fort Lauderdale selling expensive inflatable boats and dinghy's. He was always a great source for off market boats for sale. She knew I'd wanted to catch up with him and our "boat talk" bored her."

I had to wind this up.

"The first time she was privy to the hashish was when I called her from jail here in Jacksonville."

I paused. All of the quietly listening agents nodded with an air of understanding. I felt relieved. Maybe I'd just succeeded.

The DEA's tap on the phone booth outside at the hotel had yielded Yousef, Bruno, Lupo, Romero, and me. Romero was already a cooked goose from his association with the RICO group in Miami. He was "past tense." They knew more about him than I did. However, the fact that he had come to me from my association with Yousef was huge in Captain Jack's mind. Captain Jack had wanted Yousef Abboud for years. Morocco has no extradition agreement with the US, and Yousef had never moved from his safety in Tangier.

Finn and el Capitan' were also on Captain Jack's list. After a bit of thought, I felt safe saying I didn't know the other names on his list. I knew that Lupo would be valuable to them. I knew too that Lupo was immediately accessible for me to use in my defense. I had no problem letting them have him. The DEA also wanted money. They knew from their phone tap that Bruno worked for Lupo, and that Bruno had $20,000 he still owed me. The DEA wanted that cash, and any cash I may have left after my trip to NY to meet Lupo, incredibly less than a week ago.

Most seriously, they wanted Yousef Abboud.

Me…I was their pawn.

Their questions carried on through the afternoon and into early evening. As the day wore on, I began to feel more comfortable with my audience. We laughed at funny parts of my story and cringed at scary ones. My tale started with the hatching of the plan, followed by the procurement of the hash, the pickup of the hash in three phases, the glassing it into the hull at sea, the sailing it to Antigua, and then finally up to Thunderbolt, Georgia for landfall in the US. Then came the NY part of the story.

Each leg had its own life, a story that built to a phenomenal climax.

"You'd never have gotten away with that if you'd come in here with that contraband in your hull. We would have found you out the minute our dogs stepped on board."

"What kind of dogs do you have that you've trained to sniff camel's butts?"

I laughed. They didn't.

It was late in the afternoon, I was exhausted. We all stood up to stretch before I was to be shuttled back to my cell. JC, the customs agent, who'd been leaning against the wall not saying a word just about the whole day, came up and put his arm around my shoulders.

"Pierce, listen, you've got to write a book."

He wasn't smiling. I thought, *oh my friend…if only you knew.*

On the trip back to my cell, I went through the motions with Griffin. Captain Jack had given him the responsibility for my safe transport. He was proud to be my assigned escort for the journey.

First, he ordered me stand behind him as he pushed me tight against the wall. Then he held his Glock barrel pointing up while he slowly peered around the corner, went into a slight crouch and stepped out onto the walkway, quickly looking to the left, then to the right, ready for anything, and looking every minute, more and more like Inspector Clouseau.

I choked back a loud guffaw. This was pure comedy for sure.

When he was certain the coast was clear, he motioned for me to follow. He did this with such fervor that I began to wonder if he knew something I didn't. I started looking too. We came to a high-powered Mustang out in a parking lot and got in. I thought already my status has somehow changed. This was a far cry from the painful trip earlier that morning.

Griffin took off, pedal to the metal. "Gs" pushed me back in my seat as the horsepower laden mill pushed the car with absurd force. Griffin boasted how they let him use this car since he personally had captured the villain who used to own it.

When we arrived in front of the Duval County Jail, he pushed me back into the seat, and instructed that I wait until he came around to escort me into the cell block.

With his 9mm brandished, he pulled the passenger door open as he instructed me to climb out. With a hand on my shoulder, he guided me towards the waiting cell block. We entered the ominous grey concrete building, and he handed me off to one of the guards waiting there. He turned, without a word and was gone.

When I finally got back to my cell, I was pleased to see that I'd graduated to my own mattress on the floor of the cubical. I didn't know what time
of day it was, and I don't remember pulling the scratchy brown wool Army
surplus blanket over my shoulders before I fell into a comatose sleep.

* * *

When I awoke the next morning, I reflected on my exhausting intense
proffer. I felt I'd done well conveying my tale, closely reflecting on what had
happened, with few omissions. My adventure honestly had been a one man
show with the exception of Finn, a sailing acquaintance who had jumped at
the chance to crew on the sail to bring *Whitetail* home just for fun and
expenses. As the plan had morphed to include a load of hashish, he'd lit up
at the idea of an adventure.

Hell, I don't even know his last name.

I had answered hundreds of questions that told the DEA everything
they had wanted to know. At the end of the day, I felt as if I'd been successful
in creating an element of trust between us. I'd even begun to feel an odd
comradery with this group of agents. My proffer was over, and my next challenge was to get out of the Duval County Jail where I'd been a guest for two
days.

CHAPTER FORTY
Luís Esteban / No Public Defender

I NEEDED AN ATTORNEY. A good one. Unless it was absolutely necessary, I wanted to postpone the offer of a court ordered public defender. Why I ever thought I'd be able to find proper representation, I'll never know. What I did believe was, getting a public defender appointed by the court would likely yield a mildly disinterested, neophyte, dreaming of greater things. He or she would be largely focused on filling out legal forms, and working toward the most quickly acceptable plea bargain, which in my situation was based on a mandatory sentence of 12 years.

Diana dug in and began her search.

I had been in touch with Diana whenever the opportunity allowed. She had been in Jacksonville for the past three days searching diligently for legal counsel without much success. We were in a difficult fix. We had no money, and all our assets, had been seized by the DEA. At that moment, I was what make all attorneys run and hide. An indisputably, guilty client with no money, who needs help on a contingency basis, where there is no visible contingency.

* * *

Forty-two-year-old Jacksonville attorney, Luis Esteban had just finished with his last pro bono client. He and his wife had even gone out for a celebratory meal that evening. It was March 27th, 1994, and Luis was feeling happy about a plea bargain he'd wrangled for his criminal client that resulted in only 22 years in the slammer rather than the electric chair. He never took much pleasure in cases like these, but he wanted to further his lawyering skills in high risk, high stakes cases, as well as elevate his stature in the community, pro-bono cases were occasionally worth tackling. He viewed them as continuing education, and felt he'd finally graduated with this last case.

Luis was born in Cuba and practiced a serious Cuban work ethic. During his carefully calculated 15-year career, Luis had worked from many perspectives for plaintiffs as well as defendants. He had even worked for a brief time as prosecutor. Given his breadth of on-the-job experience coupled with book smarts, Luis Esteban was admired and well-liked by all. He was a kind, empathetic man, and for him, the law was there to help us all "just get along." He had just become the youngest partner of a well-known old Jacksonville firm located on the 23rd floor of an imposing edifice.

"Who gave you this number?" Luis kindly asked.

Diana wasn't sure. She'd contacted a dozen different law offices, in search of the impossible…a great attorney who would take on representing of a guilty drug smuggler who had no money. Most of the responses Diana had received would have sent a lesser person away in defeat. Her efforts had been stymied by protective assistants and secretaries, well trained in the art of evasion. Ever tough and insistent, Diana kept searching, undaunted. Finally, she found a chink in the armor. One call that almost ended with the usual canned dismissal yielded one more number. Rather than saying thanks and hanging up, Diana held onto the line creating a pregnant pause. To kindly get Diana off the line, the assistant offered, "Luis Esteban might be worth a call; here's his phone number." "Thanks." Diana immediately dialed, "Good morning, Schuller, Cannon, Wertz, and Esteban, how may I direct your call? Sure, I'll put you through to Susan, his assistant."

When Diana dialed Esteban's phone number, it could easily have been just one more hopeless call, except…the cosmos took over playing its miracle games.

Susan was running late for her lunch date, and in her hurry had pushed the wrong button on the phone, sending Diana straight through to Luis.

That morning, Mr. Luis Esteban, picked up his assistant's blinking line. Susan, seeing what had happened, reared back in her chair, jumped up and ran down the hall to his office throwing off one high heel as she made the cut into her boss's office.

Too late. "Good morning this is Luis Esteban, how can I help you?" He was in the clutches of one desperate Diana Everett. He never had a chance. Before he knew it, he'd agreed to meet her in the morning, amidst disclaimers, for "just one cup coffee".

Susan waited until the phone was solidly down on its cradle.

"Mr. Esteban, I am sooo sorry, I would never have put her through…"

"Don't worry, Susan, I'll just have a cup of coffee with Mrs. Everett in the morning and explain that my position has changed, and I am no longer taking on pro bono clients. Please look up that attorney…what's his name? …you remember the one we met at the hearing the other day? I think he is still taking on court assigned work. Get his number and I'll pass it along to Mrs. Everett in the morning."

"Right away Mr. Esteban, I'm so sorry."

At 8 a.m. the following morning, Diana met Luis Esteban at a popular local coffee shop.

She saw him first. Luis looked like someone you would know, a familiar face, a person you've met, though you can't remember where. His countenance portrayed a kind, easy going character, his heart attached to his brain. Diana began in earnest and told an abbreviated version of who I was, where I was and how I got there.

She was well prepared for Luis to turn her down with a conciliatory phone number for someone who may be able to help. But, in five minutes Luis was laughing and putting up both hands to protect himself from Diana's onslaught.

"You must help him!" she implored.

"No" was a word that rarely registered with Diana.

Coffee drinkers were staring over their bagels. One nearby attorney, mouth agog, buttered his shirt's cuff instead of the piece of wheat toast he held, while he stared, mesmerized by the confrontation.

"Mrs. Everett, I just don't do that anymore." he smiled. Diana knew then she had him.

Diana's bottom lip began to quiver, and tears quietly left little shining trails down her face. She began to sob at the table while Luis consoled her. Diana was about spent. Luis relented; he'd go by the jail to see this drug smuggler that afternoon. He'd at least make the gesture to calm Mrs. Everett. He figured he could surely escape someway after that.

* * *

The inmate who had more clout at the jail than the rest of us, told me to be up at the front desk at two thirty, I had a visitor scheduled. I was sure it would be Diana and braced myself, I hadn't seen her for a couple of weeks. I know I looked rugged.

At two fifteen, I waited at the desk, nervous as a cat. The inmate directed me down a dimly lit hallway that ended in a small, windowless concrete block room. On the right side were four chairs centered between dividers in front of a 1" thick piece of Plexiglas with a round metal-trimmed hole to speak through. Undoubtedly all conversations were monitored. The guard pointed.

"Sit here."

Precisely at two thirty the door on the other side of the glass panel opened, and to my utter surprise, it wasn't Diana who emerged. Instead, a most pleasant gentleman with kind eyes, a grey suit, and a blue tie took a seat across from me and acted as if he knew me. He pressed his hand on the thick glass that separated us. I reached up and pressed my hand against his through the glass. "I am Luis Esteban, an attorney sent by Diana Everett," he began with a warm smile. "You are Pierce, I presume?"

I was astounded. I choked back emotions that welled. Come on man, no time for this, pull yourself together, now. But, this small hint of kindness tipped me over the edge. My emotions, frayed to the breaking point since my arrest, erupted and I began to sob uncontrollably. I pulled myself together, apologized, and cried some more. Knowing I was wasting valuable time, I apologized again and straightened myself up.

"Mr. Everett, your wife Diana has shared your story with me."

"Yours is quite an extraordinary tale. Tell me…is it really true?"

"Yes, Mr. Esteban, it's all true."

"Pierce, we have a limited time here, but I want you to know that I will represent you pro bono, and we'll get you out of this place tomorrow morning."

Instantly and uncontrollably, Luis Esteban, the speaker, the glass, and everything around me blurred through tears. I needed to stop but I could not. I couldn't see him, nor could I speak. I managed to croak out something akin to "thanks." I hoped he'd heard me. When I could see again…he was gone. I wasn't sure it wasn't dream.

I slept well in my cage that night, knowing it could possibly be my last in this jail cell. When morning came, some facsimile of my name came over the loudspeaker, and I was ushered out the familiar long glass hallway where I stopped at a window to pick up my wallet and swap my orange jumpsuit for my blue jeans and t-shirt. I walked out the door into Diana's waiting arms, and a long hug. Clean air filled my lungs, a breeze caressed my face, and I was free once again.

* * *

I had been released to Diana's custody with a $50,000 bail. The bail bonding company wanted $5,000 of it to get me out. Diana had gone to the parents of her best friend to borrow $5,000. She had been instructed to stop by the DEA's offices to meet with Captain Jack and Griffin for a verbal shakedown.

We walked in the door and were met with huge smiles and pats on the back. Captain Jack took us back to a room with glass walls. We all sat down, and he shoved a piece of wrinkled copy paper toward Diana. There was something under it. She reached for the paper, and my little revolver almost slid off the table.

"Hey, be careful with that. Put it in your pocketbook. I unloaded it 'cause I need the ammo".

She quickly slid it into her purse. We looked at Captain Jack with obvious questions.

"Just keep that in your bag, and whatever you do, don't let him have it," he pointed at me with his thumb. Never say a word to anyone about this. Understand?"

We both nodded. We couldn't possibly have known then that Captain Jack had, in that moment, with that gesture, handed seven years of my life back to me. I wouldn't fully understand that for months to come.

We immediately hit I-10 and headed for home. It was a five-hour drive to Atlanta, not nearly enough time to cover all we had to go over.

I needed ten minutes of quiet to be thankful. Thankful for everything. My moment of peace came to an end when Diana swerved hard to miss a yellow cat that was booking it across the freeway. I was thankful he made it. I was thankful I'd made it. We talked nonstop the rest of the way home.

Diana told me that Luis Esteban, my new Cuban attorney had unexpectedly agreed to handle my case. He'd even surprised himself! Laughing, he admitted, in a weak moment, Diana had taken advantage of him. But to this day, I believe it showed real strength of character for him to have deviated from his professional plan and listen to his heart. We had an appointment with him in two days. It was time to rest and try to prepare for all that was about to befall.

Once home in Buckhead, we called friends who needed to know our plight and made lists of people we hoped to keep from ever knowing. Our situation was so involved, so twisty, so extraordinary, it was almost more than our minds could handle.

Diana told me in detail about the rainy night when she had managed to load the remaining hash into the truck, and how she'd gone to two dumpsters behind grocery stores and dumped the remains of my warped, crumbled, absurd adventure. We laughed at the irony… this last bit she had tossed was actually the best of the bunch.

We planned a quiet day at home for my re-entry. I had been gone for almost two weeks. When the cats first saw me, they took off running, looking over their shoulders at a person they didn't know. I looked at myself in the mirror and agreed with them.

I was 180 pounds when I'd struck out for South Florida. I now weighed a gaunt 160, and had dark circles under my eyes, and hollow cheeks. Friends said my head looked too big for my body.

Diana nor I had any idea of what I was up against. We speculated what Luis Esteban would tell us at our first meeting, but quickly stopped ourselves, as the possibilities seemed awfully dark. There was always the choice of changing our names and evaporating somewhere overseas. I'd heard of people who'd done that.

Money was laced into every conversation. We were still in a terrible plight and could see no relief. We needed to borrow from friends and family until we could sell our house and assets. We had no time to take a break. Everything was top priority, equally urgent, and needed to be addressed much sooner than later.

Sleeping in a bed was wonderful. Food began to be interesting again, especially sweets. I'd lost all interest in liquor and wine. I couldn't even consider smoking…anything. I felt I needed 110% of myself, prepped both physically and mentally, and I couldn't allow anything to threaten my sharpness of mind. We slept so hard that we woke up exhausted from sleeping.

* * *

On my second day out of jail, we struck out early in the morning for the five-hour drive to Jacksonville for our 10 a.m. meeting with Luis Esteban.

The first person we met was Esteban's assistant, Susan. Before we introduced ourselves, she knew who we were. She shared her story of the confused telephone pick up that led to Diana's introduction to Luis. We laughed and shared how much our new association with her boss meant to us.

Susan directed us to the office of Mr. Luis Esteban. He stood up, shook my hand, and gave Diana a hug. This was the first time we'd met since the jail just two short days' earlier. His manner was calm and confident. We knew we were in good hands. His jacket was hanging on the back of his chair, and his tie hung loose in his collar. He had boxes all around the floor, and paintings leaned randomly against the walls. He was in the process of moving into his new-partner position. He laughed and said he was intimidated by his much larger office.

"I'll have to find more things to hang on these big walls," he joked.

We were high up in the building, and Luis' new office commanded a grand view of Jacksonville's skyline. We sat down at his beckoning in two chairs that floated amidst the confusion. I pulled them to his desk. He opened a file, his brow furrowed as he rubbed his forehead with two fingers. Excusing himself, he pushed a button on his intercom and asked Susan to bring him all the paperwork pertaining to my case.

Diana and I had a long list of questions. Luis knowledgably and professionally addressed each one. After an hour's discussion, the bottom line was, yes, I would likely have to do time in prison. The mandatory sentencing topped out at twelve years.

Good God! 12 years!

In my mind, "running" quickly became the preferred option.

Luis read my stunned expression

"These sentences are considered indelible," he explained, "but there may be a way we can put a spin on your situation."

He suggested we pursue a defense that revolved around my dire financial straits, employing the theory that I was insane with panic regarding my plight. I had been tempted with an offer to bring a load of hashish home with me, and while my logic was skewed, a load would offer me instant financial relief. This potential relief blinded me from the fact that I would be committing a serious felony. So, when I was at my weakest, at the end of my monetary and mental rope, I made a grave mistake.

His argument seemed a good foundation for my defense, in hopes of gleaning some modicum of understanding from the court. I didn't realize that it seemed so right and logical, because, for the most part, it *was* the truth.

I asked Luis about the fact that the hash was mostly camel dung, and very little THC remained in the product that I'd smuggled into the US. He said that while that possibility could be argued, it would most likely put Jack and his agents on the defensive, and that was the last thing we needed to risk right now. Furthermore, the DEA was in possession of a report regarding the nature of my product. The report stated they had incinerated very high-quality hashish. My claim would challenge and offend the authorities who would already deem it a waste of time.

I was so frustrated. Again, I thought, had it been high quality I wouldn't be here right now. But, no one cared, about the quality… that wasn't the point. The point was, it was all dressed up like hashish, but it wasn't, and the proof of that is gone, incinerated. Luis leaned over and said, "Also, another real complication is that Pierce, you must remember you told a CI, Romero, and Jack, of all people Jack, that what you had was high quality hashish. We definitely don't want any of these people at your proffer to know you're changing your mind about what you were selling. You understand the problem with that, can't you."

"Listen Pierce," Luis wrapped it up, "your fate depends totally on the DEA, and our prosecutor Gerhardt Besler, who is a tough cookie, and what deals they may be willing to work with us. You need to understand how valuable it is that the DEA has shown open signs of a willingness to work with you. This character Yousef Abboud is your most valuable asset, and we must keep it working to our advantage."

It was hard to project the bottom-line results. Both Diana and I were totally disheartened by the harsh reality of my plight.

* * *

Luis had arranged two meetings for us that day. He explained our schedule. The first was a 1 p.m. appointment with Jack Burris (Captain Jack) at his office in the DEA building.

Luis wanted to discuss an idea he'd concocted while reading the transcription of my proffer. He had already spoken with Jack about his level of interest in two of the names that had popped up frequently during my proffer; Lupo Rocco, and Yousef Abboud. After our talk with Jack, we had a 3 p.m. appointment with the fearsome prosecutor, Gerhardt Besler at his office, to weigh possibilities.

At a restaurant where everyone knew Luis, we had a quick lunch. He was making copious notes the whole time. There was a maze of circles and arrows. After a quick lunch we took off to see Jack at his office in the DEA building. "I hope Jack has made enough time to accompany us to see Besler."

Jack rose from his desk chair. Towering high, he motioned for Luis and me to have a seat while he grabbed a wooden folding chair for Diana. He held it for her as she took a seat. I didn't remember him being so tall. Jack smiled as we shook hands. It was good to see him again.

"Luis, where'd you run into these criminals?" nodding at Diana and me.

"They slipped in the back door when Susan wasn't looking. I tried all my tricks, and even offered to give them the name of someone I could recommend."

Luis then leaned forward, rested one forearm on the desk, and with a "raised brow-faux serious" look, he said, "Jack, have you ever tried to say 'no' to Mrs. Everett?"

I smiled at Diana and reached for her hand. She wasn't looking so tough at the moment. Her eyes welled up, fighting tears. She gathered herself to return the smile and apologized. We were both on thin ice emotionally.

Jack and Luis were obviously old acquaintances, maybe even friends. I'm sure they'd worked hundreds of cases together.

"Okay Mr. Esteban…what's on your mind today?"

Luis opened the file he was carrying and pulled the paper he wanted from a stack. He showed it to Captain Jack.

"I mentioned to you the other day regarding these two men that you might be interested in catching up with. They both appeared many times in Mr. Everett's proffer."

"Yep, Lupo Rocco and Yousef Abboud."

I watched Jack as he leaned way back in his office chair that groaned under his stature. He had both hands behind his head as he looked straight at me.

"You'd mentioned that asshole, Lupo, has money that's owed to you. The DEA wants that money. It sounded like it was around $20k. I might want to work with you to retrieve that money for us if you're interested." Something in my heart lifted. I saw what was happening here. There may be a chance after all.

There was no love lost between Lupo and me. In the short time I'd known him, he'd twice threatened my life, and tried to rip me off for $40k. I'd already entertained the idea that he might be a ticket for less prison time. The $20,000 just sweetened the pot for everyone.

Now, Yousef Abboud was a different situation. I really liked Yousef Abboud. Best I could tell, he was a good person, and I'd had enough dealings with him to have established an odd affection. I really didn't want to pull him out of Morocco, even if I could. Yousef was consistently a step ahead of anyone's attempts to lure him from Morocco. He had been entrenched in Tangier for many years, safe and happy with no threat of extradition. I wanted to protect him, and yet I couldn't' afford to put Jack's interest in Yousef Abboud on the shelf.

"Sure," I responded. "I'd be interested in helping with anything that might reduce my sentence."

"Good," Jack slapped his desk with two big hands and stood.

Diana jumped at the boom. We all stood.

Luis asked, "How's your schedule this afternoon, Jack? I'd like for all of us to visit Besler together if that's possible. We have a three o'clock meeting with him today".

"Only for you Esteban, only you. Let's go."

Gerhardt Besler had worked as the District Attorney for Dade County for several years. He was good at his job and considered a hard nut with little empathy for anyone who tampered with the law…his law. He was lobbying hard to become a judge soon.

When we were invited back to his office, it was evident that he was not to be coerced, and Luis had better have a good proposal, or it wasn't going to be worth even one minute of his time.

Besler was tall, thin, and gaunt. His gray suit emphasized his countenance and his complexion. This guy was no one's friend, yet Luis and Jack were clearly comfortable, even laughing, in his presence. It felt to me that Gerhardt Besler might even have been a little bit happy to see them. It was a tight community here in the North Florida district. Jack walked into the office first, pulled up the nearest chair and plopped down with his head cocked to one side as he tested Beseler's general disposition that afternoon.

Luis, Diana and I stood until Gerhardt motioned for us to have a seat.

"OK, what's on your mind?"

"This is Pierce Everett."

I stood up and extended a hand. No one else made a move, including Besler. I was the enemy. I sat back down. He seemed condescending and rude, but Mr. Gerhardt Besler was the boss. His job and intent were to make me pay. I didn't like him very much. Why would I? Who cared? Certainly not Mr. Besler.

"Mr. Everett is my client," Luis continued. "I've taken on his case and want to speak further with you regarding my idea concerning his sentencing and his potentially helping Jack acquire money and people."

"Tell me who and how much," Besler responded.

Luis cut to the chase and quickly described what he'd cooked up with Jack.

"Can you keep this guy busy?" Besler asked.

"I expect he could bring $20,000 cash to the table as early as the following week," Jack replied.

"What are the chances of him running off?" Besler asked, never looking at me.

"He knows better than to try that."

"Okay, I've got to get going. I don't see a problem with any of this, but let me tell both of you guys, for sure, this isn't the Wild West. I'm not going to have any more of your ridiculous antics in my district. You both know what I'm talking about. Mr. Esteban, I need all the usual paperwork from you before anything gets started, and Mr. Burris try to keep all this a manageable effort. We are not extending this opportunity to this plaintiff for any reason other than the government's gain. I'm in no way suggesting that this decision, or his actions, will have any bearing on the outcome at his sentencing. I'll leave it up to the two of you to keep me in the loop and let me know when it's time for us to move towards sentencing and buttoning up this case."

* * *

I didn't feel that great leaving Besler's office. Jack and Luis talked to each other intently as we drove back to the DEA building. Diana and I sat quietly in the back seat. Words like "jerk," and "asshole" were frequently used in the front seat. Diana's silence reinforced my disappointment.

When we arrived back at Jack's office, he invited us in to sign papers, releases, disclaimers, and to tell me that I could get going on our arrangement whenever I wanted. The sooner the better. He said the simplest way to work my expenses was to keep a detailed tally.

"When it reaches $1,000 you can submit for reimbursement," Jack told me. "I want to hear from you the first part of next week about your plans to get that money from Lupo's henchman. Here are all my contacts. Keep me informed of your every move. Every move. I want hotels, flight numbers, and a schedule that includes the time and date of every move you're going to make, and every move you've already made. Is this clear?" He handed me a couple of business cards. One said Captain Jack.

CHAPTER FORTY-ONE
The Oldest Trick in the Book / Oh, My God, You Idiot!

DURING THIS PERIOD, Diana and I had to look long and hard to find much positive. We seemed to be in a deep valley surrounded by tall treacherous mountains. It was damn hard.

In those days, there were several books on the process of "disappearing". We bought them all. We figured that if it looked like I was going to end up with more than two or three years in prison, I'd split. More time than that was incomprehensible.

Every time I moved the fingers on my right hand, I was reminded of Bruno. When I had last spoken with him, a long ten days ago, he'd indicated that he had my money. I could only hope that he still did.

I went to my favorite payphone and pushed in quarters. Unreal, he answered.

"I told you I had the money, where ya been?"

"Family emergency. I'll be up tomorrow morning.

He told me to meet him at the Harley Café on the south side of the park at 11 a.m. I was there the next morning, waiting at the bar. I felt different. I couldn't be busted, because I already had been busted. I'd checked in with Jack about my schedule and plan. He told me to bring the twenty thousand directly from NYC to him.

"Do not go to Atlanta" he ordered.

"No problem," I agreed.

"Call with a flight number. Griffin will pick you up. And look here, you remember, I've heard it all. I don't want no 'cock and bull' story about how you lost ten grand. Don't even try it."

I was beginning to get an inkling of just how many DEA agents could be set in motion during one of these escapades. I looked around the crowded restaurant to see if I could pick anyone out of the crowd. Half a dozen people might have been DEA, but I couldn't tell for sure. They all looked just like you and me. In fact, they looked more like you and me than you and me.

Bruno walked in with another guy who I didn't recognize. He then looked straight at me with no sign of recognition. I wasn't sure if it was just his MO when engaged in this sort of activity, or if he really didn't recognize me. After all, he'd only seen me a couple of times before.

He came over to the bar and stood beside me.

"How's everything?" I said.

"Let's get a table."

"Fine with me." The three of us sat down at a table in the middle of the restaurant. We hadn't been seated for two minutes when this guy with Bruno began pulling rolls of bills from his overcoat, tossing them on the table.

Oh my god, you idiot! I thought.

I started grabbing the cash to get it out of sight. Too late. Most of the people near our table were staring and whispering. I doubt many of them had ever even seen $20,000 in cash, not to mention seeing it thrown out on a table in a crowded restaurant.

Bruno looked at the idiot.

"Hold on, hold it, what the fuck ya think ya doing?"

I sat with my lap full of hundred-dollar bills, simultaneously trying to make sure none hit the floor and trying to cover the left-over pile on the table with napkins. I dared not look up at anyone. What would I say?

Bruno flagged our waitress down and asked for a couple of takeout boxes and several bags. She laughed and looked down at the pile of bills.

"You haven't even ordered anything yet," she said in that special NY way.

"Fuck…bring me a cuppa coffee," he responded in his special Italian way. "Now bring me some fuckin' bags and boxes over here in a hurry."

She huffed away having been "out-ruded" Italian style. When she got back with the containers, we were able to corral most of the bills. The waitress started to try and help with the process, but suddenly thought better of it and decided she should just leave us alone with our mess.

I looked up at her at the same moment she opted not to help. She seemed beautiful, through and through. I empathized with her dilemma, not knowing what to do. Hell, *I didn't know what to do.*

"Sorry for this mess," I sputtered. "This really wasn't supposed to go like this…" I reached into my lap and handed her three of the bills. She hesitated, shaking her head. Suddenly, her face broke into a most brilliant smile. Her green eyes danced. I grabbed her wrist and pushed the bills into her hand.

"Take it…just take it please. You've earned it."

She took the money and left.

"Look here Bruno, send this lunatic up the street to buy a nice large leather briefcase for me. Here's $200, that should cover it."

I reached into a pile still in my lap and threw $200 at this goombah. He sulked out the door, into the early afternoon light. I wondered again how many DEA agents were sitting around the restaurant. I wondered what they were thinking. What was the beautiful waitress thinking?

I laughed to myself, imagining the story Captain Jack would surely hear before I was back in Jacksonville.

When the assistant came back with the briefcase, I pulled the tags off the handles and filled it with "C" notes. There was no way to count the money, and most likely some lucky patron nearby had the fortune of cornering a wayward bill or two to take home as a souvenir. Bruno brashly ordered two Reubens and a couple of beers from the waitress. I noticed thankfully only two were ordered, a sign that I should split. All I wanted to do was run. I worried that NY, notorious for curbside criminals, might have produced one who had seen what had happened. He could possibly be lying in wait for my departure. Then it occurred to me that I hoped there were some DEA agents in there. In a worst-case scenario, they may be helpful. An odd change of heart.

I asked our waitress, "Would you please call a cab to get me out of here as quickly as possible?"

I left the café without saying goodbye to Bruno, leaving him and his buddy choking down their Reubens as every eye in the place watched me walk out the door and get into the cab. In the taxi, with my new briefcase and all my bags, I looked as if I'd had just endured a dose of retail therapy.

"LaGuardia," I said.

* * *

I landed in Jacksonville around 6 p.m. During the wait at the airport in NY, I used the time in a bathroom stall to get the bunches and bundles of bills more in control. I felt like 'Pigpen', surrounded by a dervish of hundred-dollar bills, swirling around me.

"Hey big spender, I can't wait to hear your side of this story. I hear you were giving my money away. You owe me $500. Griffin will pick you up at the airport and bring you back to the office. Have you even counted that money yet?" Incredible, did he really just ask me that? When and where could I possibly have counted the money?

$500? Really?

When I got to his office. Jack and I organized and counted the bundles of dirty bills of every denomination. After two counts and some serious organization the total came to $17,800. I was pretty sure the whole episode was a set up to clip me one more time for an extra two grand. Jack was sure it was.

"It's not uncommon for these kinds of guys to show up with less cash than they're supposed to have, then bumble around and drop the cash, or kick it, or just throw the bundle of bills on the floor, and make it look like an accident, then claim that bystanders were grabbing up the bills and that's why the payment is short.

Crafty, really crafty. Nevertheless, Jack said according to his reports, I had done very well, and I'd handled a difficult situation perfectly.

"I hate that that asshole clipped us for $2,000 with the oldest trick in the book, but I'll get that back and more before long."

I didn't even ask Jack what he meant. I didn't want to know.

* * *

I caught a late flight to Atlanta. Diana picked me up at the airport. I'd come up with a pretty good idea during all my time alone on those flights. A close longtime friend was involved with the installed sales for Building Depot. He'd contacted me about starting a company that would handle all the installations of all the cabinets that Building Depot sold in its new installed sales program. At first, I discarded the idea as my personal situation was so complicated.

But now that my sentencing was on hold, I reconsidered. Maybe I could get a new business up and going before I got locked up. I had no idea how much time there was, but I was confident that if I could get the business organized and staffed properly, it might possibly provide Diana with an income while I was gone. If we worked it right, maybe Diana could even run it until I came home.

We named it, "Dynasaw", developed a logo, and ran ads for carpenters, cabinet builders, foremen, and CAD literate people. We began interviewing and prepping to plug into the BDS system. Things were beginning to come together. In the back of my mind, I thought just maybe showing up at sentencing having started a new business could bode well for me.

The next morning, I was conducting interviews. We had already hired five carpenters when the phone rang,

"Be in Jacksonville at 2 p.m."

"I can come tomorrow but today is impossible, I have to..."

"Be in Jacksonville at two."

The phone was silent.

CHAPTER FORTY-TWO
A Nice Person and a Competent Seaman/OK

WHAT CHOICE DID I HAVE? It felt like that question had become an "all too common" refrain in my life.

Diana said she'd cover Dynasaw that day, so I hopped a plane to Jacksonville per Jack's instruction. Griffin was there in the high-powered Mustang waiting for me.

"Man," he said brow furrowed, in his very serious way, "if Big Jack wants you for something, you just need to drop everything and c'mon. He really blew up after he got off the phone with you yesterday. You better get ready for him this morning."

I could not afford for Jack to get frustrated with me. I started to explain to Griffin but thought better of it. I was the lowest man on the totem pole, and I had to work this opportunity, as much to my advantage as possible. It was, once again, my only chance.

We drove up to the DEA offices. I walked into the lobby. Jack was there waiting. He didn't say a word, but turned as I entered, clearly expecting me to follow, which I did. In his office, he sat down in his well-worn chair and spun it around to face me. He did not ask for me to sit.

"Do you know what the fuck is going on here?" He glared.

"I think I do," I said.

"Do I need to explain it to you, or are you going to take working for me seriously? I stuck my neck out to get you to a place where Luis could put something together for you on your "judgment day." You did well with the money situation in NY, but when I need you, I need you. When I plug you into a situation that will benefit me, as well as benefit you, you hop, and ask only "How high?" When that jerk Besler, finally calls to show you what an ass he is, and to sentence you, you will need to have hopped often and high."

"Yes, I understand," I replied.

"This afternoon we have a suspect who's coming up to meet us at four. I need help moving our boat around to where we're to rendezvous.

Our boat? I wondered.

"The idea is that you and I drive up with the boat, then tie it up at the dock by the restaurant. We get off and go inside to meet this clown. He's a big hotel guy in the Dominican Republic and he's looking to invest about 500 large in a deal. We want to help him find his deal and take his money. You know the ins and outs of smuggling hashish from Tangier." I laughed inside to myself. "This scheme is unusual, and I think its uniqueness may interest him. I need for you to sit down with us and tell him what it's going to take, time and money, to get a load of hashish from Tangier to Canada. You don't know it, but I happen to be a specialist on hashish in Canada. Between the two of us I hope to talk this guy into laying his money down. Understand?"

Jack and I went out to the canals and picked up a pretty Bertram 42' which had been confiscated in a scam years earlier. We drove it in the Florida sun for about an hour, until we came to a dock connected to a restaurant. We got out, and I tossed the dock lines around the cleats and turned to go.

"Wait, wait, wait," Jack said. "You gotta to do it this way if you and I are gonna to get along."

He reached down and carefully turned each line into a neat coil beside the dock cleat. I've done it the same way since, and I think of him every time.

"Listen, Everett," Jack told me when we'd finished tying the boat. "After we've been in there for about two hours, say that you have a taxi coming, then walk out. Griffin will be waiting for you."

"Got it."

We walked into the cool restaurant. There must have been a dozen agents there, all fitting into the scene. I remember several of them from my proffer. It was like a movie set. I walked with Jack to the table where a couple of businessmen were deep in conversation. He introduced me as Bill.

"Bill has experience smuggling hashish from Morocco."

They asked good, sensible, interesting questions, and I answered them with long descriptions and stories. There was no doubt that I knew what I was talking about. I left the "camel turd" part out.

We carried on for about two hours. The tables with the other agents would empty, and a new batch would sit down. I stood up. "Good luck, gentlemen," I said. "I have a taxi waiting for me."

When I stepped into the bright sunlight, Griffin was there in his Mustang. He motioned for me to get in quickly. I did, and that was the last I ever saw or heard anything about those businessmen. Again, I didn't want to know. Ignorance was safer. Griffin took me to the airport where I waited for the next plane to Atlanta.

* * *

Early the next morning, my eyes popped open, and I had to lie there for a minute to understand where I was, who I was, and how I got there. Incredible, simply incredible. Was it true? It was dark, 5 a.m., and the new carpenters for Dynasaw were to show up in two hours. I had a lot to do to get prepped for them. They had to fill out tax papers, insurance papers, employment contracts and more.

Diana was already up and, in the kitchen having a cup of coffee. There was a cup on the table waiting for me. Steam from the hot coffee swirled up into the kitchen lights. It was still dark outside. Diana didn't turn around when she started to speak.

"Sweetie, I hate to tell you, but Jack called late last night. He left a message for you to be in Jacksonville this afternoon at two."

I retraced yesterday's footsteps through the all too familiar gates in the Atlanta airport, then the gates in Jacksonville, and into the Hot Rod where Griffin bade me good morning.

"Good morning Griffin."

Another hair-raising ride with Griffin, trying his best to rival Steve McQueen at the wheel in "Bullet." Then into the offices where Jack met us, pointing his finger back out of the doorway we had just entered.

"Back in the car." Grumpy

The three of us rode the familiar route to the courthouse, and I soon figured we were heading to the DA's office, home of the fearsome Gerhardt Besler. Jack motioned with a flat hand for Griffin to wait in the car, and struck out, again correctly assuming I'd follow.

We entered the DA's office. Gerhardt Besler didn't look up. Big Jack loudly plopped into one of two chairs and motioned for me to do the same. An instant later Luis Esteban came into the office and smiled at Jack and me. I offered my seat, but he quietly insisted no. On his entry, I felt an incredible relief. My team had arrived. Gerhardt looked up at the three of us for the first time. Without expression, he nodded at Luis and Jack. I remained nonexistent. What a jerk this guy was. A rare jerk.

He spoke directly to Jack.

"I want this guy Yousef Abboud. I also want this other guy Lupo Rocco. I want them both very badly. They've been making a fool of me for too long."

Jack then looked at me and asked, "You up for making ole Gerhardt's dream come true?"

"Yes," I said, "of course". This whole process didn't exactly sit well with me, but hey man, I had been in survival mode long enough to know that I was the only one who could save me. Glass houses can be built with little effort; it's the maintenance that gets tricky.

My intention had always been to remove Lupo from the equation. After all, I figured that if I ever ran into him again, heaven forbid, he'd likely try to make good on all his threats. Yousef Abboud was a totally different problem. I bore him no ill feelings and really didn't want to put him in harm's way. Despite the sad outcome of the whole smuggling affair, I never blamed him; and in fact, I felt he did just about all he could to try and remedy a very bad situation.

"Find out where Lupo is," Jack said, "and let the DEA know as quickly as possible."

"The last I'd heard from Lupo's aunt, was that he had moved to Amsterdam," I replied, "But I'll try to come up with another tack."

Jack reached into his jacket pocket and pulled out an undecipherable jumble of wires.

"Contact Abboud and try to cook up a new plan for another load, this time more substantial…say 2,000 kilos. We want to lure him out of Morocco, so the DEA can get their hands on him."

Jack showed me how the jumble of wires would be connected to a tiny microphone that would fit in my ear and record my conversations with Yousef Abboud. The recordings were for measuring my performance and potential success.

"Okay Sherlock, you got the plan?"

Once every couple of weeks I was to bring those recordings to Jacksonville and leave them with Jack as well as update him with any intelligence I'd garnered. I was also to bring expense receipts for reimbursement.

"No problem," I said.

Jack looked at Luis for approval. He nodded. They took it for granted I'd agree. They were right.

Luis had prepared the paperwork for my involvement in the plan, so the next three minutes were filled with the sound of shuffling papers and hieroglyphic signatures. No one spoke. Gerhardt maintained an air of irritation, as if he was being inconvenienced by the whole affair.

"What an asshole," Jack said when we walked out.

I couldn't have agreed more.

*　*　*

It had only been about a month since my arrest, but it seemed like a year since my life took that spin. I set about with a grand scheme to try and solve everyone's problems including my own.

I conjured up an impossible plan to wave in front of Yousef Abboud. He was endlessly patient. Every time we spoke, he politely carried on as if my scheme were totally plausible. From the start, I sensed he knew what was going on as he listened and agreed with every part of the plan. I recorded every conversation faithfully, and every two or three weeks I'd take a bundle of mini cassette tapes down to Jack to have a listen and field questions.

I had located a yacht rental company in Marbella, Spain, just inside the strait of Gibraltar, that had a 60' sailboat available, perfect for hauling 2,000 kilos of hashish. Jack offered to get a helicopter that was stationed up in Cadiz, to sweep down at the right moment to Capture Yousef Abboud and transport him to Spain. Just the thought made me very sad. I could never do that. But how long could I carry on? Long enough for Luis to gather enough ammo to use in his effort to lower my sentence.

Luis had instructed Diana and me to get all our close friends in high places (and we had a few) to write notes of credibility and character references. Long-time friends, friends of family and friends of friends all came through in spades. Every letter had impact and was most certainly an asset for me on my day in court. Of course, DA Gerhardt was making plans on his end as well.

Luis had cornered a psychiatrist that he had worked with in the past. His idea, which I still think held water, was to get this doctor to say that I was out of my mind under the duress of my ever-failing financial state, and my normal decision-making process was seriously compromised. I was unable to make rational decisions.

Following through with Luis' plan, I met the psychiatrist for his assessment.

Below is the diagnosis he gave Luis after my complete evaluation. Quoted verbatim:

Mr. Esteban,

You questioned me in your letter, and in person whether or not I could identify any feature in Mr. Everett which might reflect favorably in your efforts to seek a reduced sentence on his behalf. Generally, the events of the last part of the decade of the 1960's seemed to affect him greatly as, indeed, it did many. From our discussion, the day of the examination, it appears that his election to smuggle contraband was at least in part determined by his 1960's background and orientation for even now, I am not sure he is committed to the notion that hash and indeed, marijuana are drugs and worthy of sanctions. There seems no question that he was very disheartened by the financial events descending upon him, but at no time does he appear to have reached a point where he was manifestly depressed from a clinical standpoint.

In gist, the economic factor may have diminished his capacity somewhat and this coupled with his 1960's background make it perhaps easier for him to undergo this moral lapse. I regret that there is little that I can say aside from the fact that he seems to be a nice person and a competent seaman. Thank you for the privilege of serving as consultant. Please let me know if there are any further questions on the matter sincerely

Edward Reynolds, M.D."

"Undergo this moral lapse!" This idiot had to be kidding.

My head spun. I wanted to scream that my morality was and still is in perfect order, seemingly more so than most, and that it remains well intact and unscathed by my association with marijuana. But who'd listen?

CHAPTER FORTY-THREE

The Snake in the Sharkskin Suit / Mr. Bad News

WHAT HAPPENED NEXT requires a little flashback to June of 1992.

Palmer and Johnson had just opened their Savannah location in Thunderbolt, Georgia. After our long sail from Antigua, I'd unloaded *Whitetail* on Memorial Day, and then motored her over to their new boat yard. I was their very first client.

I frequently checked on her progress. During these visits I stoked my relationship with P.J. as they began to check off projects from the long list I'd left before returning to Atlanta.

Then I went off to sell the hash. I'd figured after I repaid El Capitan and paid Finn, I would at least squeeze $100,000 out of it to cover the cost of repairs to *Whitetail.* This was based on selling the hashish quickly at giveaway prices.

One morning I was observing the progress on *Whitetail* while three workers made repairs to her heat exchanger.

"Good morning gentlemen. How's it going with the new marina?"

I noticed they were particularly ill equipped with tools as simple as vise grips, screwdrivers, and a drill. The lead guy continuously went to pick up more tools or simple parts like screws or WD40, leaving his two charges twiddling their thumbs until he returned. I had to say something.

"Do you guys know that you're costing me ninety bucks and hour for each of you?"

"Hey man, we don't see any of it. We get a very small part of that hourly figure. You need to talk to the manager about it."

On one of these occasions it was clear that a supply run had included a stop at the coffee maker. I noticed the lead man stumbling back over the gravel on his long walk back from the shop to *Whitetail*. He had three cups of hot coffee in his hands and the tools in a canvas bag over his shoulder.

All these hours, including coffee breaks, were turned in at the end of the day at $90 per hour for a grand total for the three of them being $270 per hour. I watched the gross inefficiency and became distraught at the alarming sums it was costing to get *Whitetail* back in reasonable condition after her long hard voyage.

"Hey Joe," I said. Joe Owens was a very pleasant man in charge of managing the expansive exclusive yard. "I need to have a word with you. These guys you've got working on my boat are being billed out to me at almost double their efficiency!"

"Pierce, I know, I see it every day. It's just the rigors of building an efficient crew in a totally brand-new operation. It takes time and we know that." He reassured me, "Don't worry, the billing will be adjusted to reflect their down time."

In the months that followed, I quickly got distracted dealing with the hashish in Atlanta, making trips to Fort Lauderdale, trips to NY, and finally getting busted by the DEA. It was then, about halfway through her repairs, that the DEA seized *Whitetail*. What next!

Over the next ten months I would scrape up just enough money to periodically send P.J. and keep them from putting a lien on her.

One day I confided in Joe Owens that I'd been captured by the DEA. This turned out to be a big mistake. He immediately, without my knowledge, carelessly moved her to the back of the yard where she was left open and unattended. Meanwhile, my insufficient payments didn't make a dent on the already bulging invoices.

I'd been keeping records of all the charges and highlighting the questionable ones. Then one day in the mail came a very thick envelope from the boat yard. It contained a detailed accounting and invoice for my present balance of $56,344. I sat down hard in my desk chair and immediately began reviewing the statement. Many of the itemized charges were ridiculously high. After pouring over the invoices for hours I came up with a legitimate figure of $22,600.

I called Joe who immediately turned from the nice communicable fellow I'd been dealing with, into a raging jerk. He told me that he had moved *Whitetail* to the rear of the yard, until we could sort out this discrepancy.

"All work on your boat has ceased," he added with a threatening tone.

A month later, Joe contacted me to say they'd reviewed my challenges to the statement and were happy to report I owed them $38,000 rather than the $56,344. Payment in full was due in one week.

* * *

The first thing I needed to do was to schedule a meeting with Mr. Bad News, Gerhardt Besler. I dreaded it, but I had to be sure I could eventually get my boat back from the DEA. If not, all the Palmer and Johnson disputes would be the Fed's problem.

I needed to go in with a solid argument. I calculated that *Whitetail* was good for only

$ 50,000 in a quick sale. Currently she was encumbered with the debt to P. J. to the tune of

$56,334, which meant her real true value was negative $ 6,334. Not only that, since her rebuild had been terminated mid-stream, she was in pieces and showing the wear and tear of being left in the yard open to the weather.

I approached Gerhardt like a water moccasin with Luis by my side. Neither of us were confident about our odds. All I knew is that I had to try.

Luis and I watched while Gerhardt pondered the idea of returning the boat to me, given the hassle of the DEA's potential involvement getting involved in the Palmer and Johnson dispute. Gerhardt focused on me for the first time in three months and spoke to me more sincerely than I thought him capable.

"Mr. Everett, *why* do you want this boat under the circumstances? Do you plan to go out and sell her as quickly as you get her?"

"Mr. Besler," I replied earnestly, "I've had that boat for 16 years now, and I've traveled thousands of miles with her. I guess my main reason for wanting her is an emotional attachment. We've been through so much together. The love of a boat is totally irrational and could never be related to monetary value. It's difficult to understand for those who've never felt it. I know you're out to guarantee that I spend time in prison, but one day I'll be free, and I want to have *Whitetail* waiting for me to help me keep my head together while I endure this impending experience."

He seemed to be turning over options in his head while he stared expressionlessly at the stacks of paper on his desk. It was quiet for what seemed like a long moment. Finally, without looking at me.

"Okay, Mr. Everett, you keep your boat. Luis, draw up some paperwork pertinent to our agreement."

I couldn't believe my ears.

"Thanks," I said.

I wanted to say more, but Gerhardt Besler didn't want to hear any more. Make no mistake…he wasn't my friend. When we got out of the building and entered the bright afternoon, I gave Luis an unexpected hug. We laughed.

Emboldened by my success with the DEA, I went to the next step… settling the Palmer and Johnson invoice discrepancy.

* * *

With the help of Ned Daniels, an Atlanta attorney who'd been recommended to us I threatened to sue Palmer and Johnson. Ned notified them of our pending suit and expressed our desire to settle the discrepancy out of court if they were willing. We needed to establish a fair cost for their completed repairs, less the cost of repairs for the new damage she'd incurred while in the care of Palmer Johnson. This would allow me to come to Savannah and collect my sailboat. A date was set for a hearing in the Judge's chambers with Palmer and Johnson who was represented by a "Snake in a Sharkskin Suit". This guy looked like a TV mattress salesman. To me, it seemed obvious that he wanted *Whitetail* for his own. He was out to get her from Palmer and Johnson for a salvage song.

The day before the hearing, I received a call from Captain Jack.

"Be here at two tomorrow afternoon."

I couldn't believe my ears. I dreaded calling Captain Jack to explain. Unbelievably, Jack understood, and told me to call him tomorrow and let him know how it all went. I took a deep breath and exhaled with a long sigh.

The next morning, I picked Ned Daniels up at four, and struck out on the five-hour drive to Savannah. Meanwhile, Diana would keep Dynasaw cooking through the day with the help of our newly hired foreman.

Everyone was on time. We all sat down in the judge's chambers. There was me, Ned my attorney, Joe Owens, PJ's manager, and PJ's attorney, a most hateful smirky kinda guy.

The judge cleared his throat.

"Mr. Everett, please be so kind if you will, and explain your side of the story."

I shared my perspective in detail. He seemed almost disinterested, just waiting for me to finish, so he could deliver his predetermined judgment. I had the feeling he and the "Sharkskin Suit" had breakfast together and discussed the outcome of my visit. Probably planned to repair over a round of golf that afternoon.

"Now Mr. Everett," he asked. "I understand you've been found guilty of smuggling illegal contraband into the country, and you're going to have to spend some time in prison, Is this correct?"

"Yes, your honor, but I haven't been charged or sentenced yet. We're still working on my case."

The air in the room thickened, borne from an instant mutual dislike on opposing sides of the desk.

"Well, it seems to me that you would likely have difficulty paying your debt to Palmer and Johnson if you're locked away in prison."

"Yes, Your Honor," I agree, "It would seem that way, but I haven't been sentenced yet, nor have I gone to court to address my case, so we don't know how long I'll be locked away, if at all; and you, sir, have no idea of my financial status. Also, we are presently in the process of building a new business in Atlanta, which should soon begin to throw off substantial income. It is designed to cover my debts should any of your thoughtless presumptions come to pass."

I paused, then continued.

"I'd like to keep the dispute at hand in focus. The only questions here are the unreasonable invoice amounts for work done to my boat, as well as the cost of repairs to damage she incurred while in the care of Palmer and Johnson. When my objection to the unfair yard bill is fairly resolved, and I'm paid for the damages due to carelessness by Palmer Johnson, I plan to pay the invoice and bring my boat home."

The snake spoke.

"Your honor, the invoice from Palmer and Johnson is not in question here. Mr. Everett's ability to pay the bill is the question. Mr. Everett is already sufficiently in arears with his payments, to the point that I would recommend a labor lien be put on the vessel immediately to protect Palmer and Johnson's interest in the matter. I don't see how he will be able to pay the bill or remove the boat from the Palmer and Johnson yard if he's locked away in prison."

Didn't this sub-human hear me? It seemed that nothing I'd just said was heard or given any credibility.

Ned put his hand on my shoulder.

"Let me handle this," he said quietly.

As expected, the Judge quickly came to his forgone conclusion.

"Gentlemen, under the circumstances, I can see no reason that Palmer and Johnson shouldn't be allowed to proceed with the seizure of Mr. Everett's boat, in lieu of the outstanding balance due them from work performed almost a year ago,"

Wham, his gavel came down and we all stood up. All but me. What had just happened made no sense. Ned kindly thanked the judge, ignored the Snake whose smirk had turned into a sneer, and prodded me to get up and shake it off. "I've got it covered Pierce. Come on quickly."

The three of us walked out together and into the same elevator. I briefly considered taking the chance to pummel this stuffed shirt but abstained.

Ned was instantly on a phone call, talking numbers and names with his secretary.

"Good, then it's all completed," he said.

The elevator reached bottom and we all stepped out. Ned turned, smiled, and addressed the Snake.

"You should know that Mr. Everett has just now officially filed for bankruptcy. All his assets are frozen as he seeks shelter under the Chapter 13 bankruptcy laws. The sailing vessel *Whitetail* represents a good portion of his assets at this point, and her fate will be dealt with by the bankruptcy courts, unless of course," he turned to The Snake, "we can do what we came here to do…work out a fair figure to pay Palmer and Johnson to release all liens on this boat. Otherwise it may be years before anything will be determined."

The look on that cocky bastard's face said it all.

Ahh, the last laugh.

* * *

It was early Tuesday morning, exactly a week after our coup with Palmer and Johnson. Dynasaw was preparing for another busy day. Diana and I were to meet the truck driver on Wednesday morning at the Palmer and Johnson yard in Thunderbolt. We'd load Whitetail and bring her to Lake Lanier, just north of Atlanta. There we planned to leave her out of the water, under a plastic cover, where she'd be safe until I finished my time of incarceration…should it happen.

I had asked our longtime friends, Britt and Shannon, for a $25K loan for up to 4 years at 10% interest. They had agreed, knowing they were helping Diana and me in a time of real need.

Palmer and Johnson had exercised good sense and decided a bird-in-hand was better than trying to wring any more money from a 40' sloop tied up in a bankruptcy with the stigma of being a smuggler's boat seized by the DEA. They had agreed I could retrieve "that damn boat" from their yard if I would cover $22k of the yard bill, the exact payment I had earlier concluded would be fair.

How miniscule was the ten-thousand-dollar discrepancy on my bill compared to Palmer and Johnson's behemoth of a business? I imagine it was hardly noticed. Once, when I was visiting *Whitetail,* I was talking with a worker as we looked up at a 100'aluminum cruiser, built by Palmer and Johnson's Wisconsin facility. She was mid project, housed in one of many huge buildings on their Thunderbolt yard. Palmer and Johnson was building a new aluminum swim platform on the stern of the boat.

"How much do you think that swim platform is costing to build?" The worker asked me. I speculated a fat guess.

"$100,000?"

"How 'bout $250k dude."

* * *

It was pouring rain when Diana and I drove from Atlanta to Savannah to retrieve *Whitetail*. It was raining so hard it was making for tough driving. We pulled into Savannah after dark, and stopped at a small, old style motel. I could hear the torrent banging on the car's roof not far from my head. About four in the morning I woke up to go for a pee. When my feet hit the floor, I realized the water was over my ankles. The place was flooding.

I splashed to the window. The scene outside was surreal. There was water standing two feet deep everywhere. I woke Diana and we rushed to our truck. I judged where the motel drive was by following along the front of the rooms in a gently curving row. We found our way to the highway, and then to a Waffle House on higher ground. The place was packed, and the air inside felt tense, like that found in the midst of disasters. It was still dark and pouring rain. Word was that the storm would soon move over.

After a hearty breakfast, the rain let up, and we changed our wet boots for dry socks and shoes and worked our way over to the Thunderbolt yard. We began the process of getting *Whitetail* towed from the rear of the yard to the front where we waited for the semi who'd called to say he was about an hour away. By then, the yard workers were our friends. I felt like some kind of folk hero to them. Any chance they got to talk with me, they'd start with endless questions about my adventures that they'd heard through the grapevine.

We had quite a different dynamic with Joe Owens and the Palmer and Johnson office management.

I was public enemy number one. It made me feel good.

"*Whitetail's*" parts had been scattered around the huge yard. It took most of the morning to find the mast, the boom, the gooseneck, all the lifelines and stanchions, the running rigging, the standing rigging, millions of bolts, screws, and miscellaneous parts galore.

A real cowboy was at the wheel of the semi. He sauntered up, stuck out his hand, and with a broad grin.

"They call me "Memphis."

Memphis was undaunted by difficulties and worked alongside us to help get all the parts for *Whitetail* onto his trailer.

It took all morning and into the early afternoon, but we finally got her loaded onto the flatbed trailer specifically rigged for moving sailboats. The rain had let up, and a thin beam of sun fired through the wet air.

When ole Memphis got going, it was hard to keep up with him. He hit Hyw-16 headed west at 70 mph. I thought, man, *Whitetail* has never gone this fast in her life.

Six hours later, as we neared Lake Lanier, the sun finally came out of its hiding place about 5 p.m., as it was on its way down. The resulting bright red sky was a proper welcome. The yard there had a "travel lift" substantial enough to easily lift *"Whitetail's"* twenty thousand pounds. Stormy, the yard supervisor, had kindly waited for our arrival to get her unloaded and resting on a cradle, towards rear of the yard where the owners, the Adams brothers, had indicated she could stay for several years if necessary.

I knew that may be necessary. *Whitetail* would have to wait for me. I also knew I'd be back for her. I had her shrink-wrapped to help weather any storms in my absence. She seemed to understand. I left her there with a promise from my dear, old friend Bill, that he'd come by and say hello every once in a while.

* * *

Jack's call from the previous day, had been to tell me that my sentencing date now was set to be December 16, 1993.

"Gerhardt Besler," Jack said, "has become convinced that you're not going to help him capture Yousef Abboud. He's pissed and thinks you're running him around, and you never intended to help. What do you say?"

"Jack, it'll take another year to set up what I think will work. If he's not willing to work on building this case with us, then I've got no choice but to give up and take it on the chin. I've got no control over his lack of patience."

"Well get yourself together and come down on Tuesday, next week, for a pre-sentencing debriefing with me and George. You better make sure Luis will be with you. Besler won't be there. He's setting it all up to pound you at your sentencing."

* * *

Two weeks later I would appear in court with suit and tie, where Gerhardt Besler would be the really bad guy. Luis and I were to be the good guys.

CHAPTER FORTY-FOUR
Sentencing / The Good Guys and the Bad Guys

DECEMBER 16, 1993 came all too quickly. Diana and I rented a room at a hotel near the Jacksonville courthouse. I had my dark blue Hickey -Freeman suit, freshly cleaned, in a bag on the hanger. When morning came, my belly was a hollow. I wanted no coffee, no breakfast, nothing. My sentencing was at 10 a.m.

I sat in a chair in the corner of the hotel room looking out an aluminum window over the crowded parking lot and felt bad. We were to meet Luis in the lobby of the courthouse at 9:30 a.m. We had spoken with him the night before and he had assured me that I was going to prison. I had taken it hard. My heart moved into my stomach. I'm not sure what I'd expected. In my clouded mind, I'd thought there just might be the chance I'd get off with probation.

The time came, and I donned my suit. White shirt, conservative tie. It wasn't the occasion for my Jerry Garcia tie. Diana was the best. She knew not to over console me, yet she was empathetic and protective of my wandering emotions. Again, running crossed my mind. What would be a good time to run? Would they want me to go straight from the courtroom to a cell? My chest was heavy. I thought about six years from now when I'd be 50, and all this would be behind me.

We walked out into the bright morning sun. Diana held my hand on the drive in the car and as we walked up wide, granite steps and into the courthouse lobby via the swinging door.

Luis was waiting. I was glad I had my sunglasses on. I began to lose it at the sight of his kind face. I excused myself, went to the restroom and washed the first tears of many from my face. I was alone and looking in the mirror.

I growled at myself. "Get your shit together idiot." Back into the lobby.

Luis said we may as well go on into the court room and have a seat. The heavy oak door moved with ease as Luis held it open for Diana, then me, as he followed. He motioned for us to go right on down to the front row. We found seats, and I looked around at a dozen people I'd never seen before. Jack was not there. Somehow, I'd hoped he wouldn't be. Besler shuffled through files on the other side of the front row.

He didn't look our way, nor did he say anything to us. Luis walked over to him, and they shook hands. They spoke low, in low serious voices and nodded toward the front of the courtroom. They both walked up around and behind the Judge's big chair and through an open door behind his seat. They were gone for about 15 minutes…a very long 15 minutes. When they returned, Luis had a look on his face I'd never seen before. A grave look.

"Will the Court rise? The honorable Judge Clifton Harper presiding."

I didn't look at Luis again. It scared me too much.

The next few minutes seemed to go by without me. I'd separated from myself; I was terrified and out of control. I heard "Plaintiff", I heard "Council", I heard "Please step forward Mr. Everett." Diana could tell I was out of my mind. She squeezed my hand so hard it hurt, and said, "Baby they want to you take the stand on the left side. It's all going to be OK. Don't worry."

I think it was me who walked up to that stand, but I can't swear to it. The judge said he understood that I was pleading guilty and asked that I make a statement. A statement regarding my plea of guilty. I didn't know what to say.

"My name is Pierce Everett," I started. "I plead guilty to bringing 200 kilos of hashish into the country...*I thought to myself, hell you know it wasn't hashish...*"

Right there in front of God and the world, I felt a real breakdown coming on. I tried to speak. I tried to explain to these people in front of me in the court room, people who had never laid eyes on me, people who didn't know me and would never know me. I told these people who really didn't care, how sorry I am to have broken the law. These are the same people who'd crowd around a Guillotine. They just sat there staring at me, as I crumbled for their entertainment, enduring the inevitable.

"No, your honor, there is no doubt that I am guilty." I tried to carry on, "I hate that I put my wife and family through all of this, and..." my voice dried up. No sound would come out.

The judge told me to take a seat. I couldn't speak, I couldn't look at anyone but Diana, and all I could do was shake my head. The court had heard the word guilty and that was all they wanted. Gerhardt declined to question me, as did Luis. No one doubted that I'd done what they claimed. I'd just confessed it.

After an eternal 2 minutes, Judge Harper stood.

"Mr. Everett has pled guilty to the charges brought here against him. It is obvious that he is deeply regretful." He then turned and addressed me. Mr. Everett, both the work you've done with the DEA as detailed by officer Jack Burris, and your good standing in your community, as witnessed by the surprising number of letters we've received from character witnesses on your behalf, all bode well for you. With everything dutifully considered and based on the level of the crime you've committed, Mr. Everett, you are hereby sentenced to a total of eight years' restitution. Your sentence will be served as follows; you will spend 36 months incarcerated at the Federal Prison Camp in Atlanta, Georgia. After serving three years of incarceration, you'll be released to Federal Probation Services, where you will be monitored closely for five years of strict supervision.

The Defendant will self-surrender to the Federal Prison Camp in Atlanta, Georgia on January 17, 1994 at 11 a.m.

A brief pause and, "Wham!" I jumped when his gavel fell loud and hard.

Gerhardt Besler went berserk. He was outraged. He banged on his desk with his fist, glaring at the Judge. He was yelling, "…not right!" "More culpable than…!" The court room was emptying, but at Gerhardt's outburst, everyone stopped to see what the commotion was all about. The Judge half rising from his seat glared at Besler this time his gavel rang harder and louder.

"Court is adjourned!"

Besler just started shaking his head in surrender and throwing papers into file folders. I didn't have a second to ponder my sentence or even look at Diana or Luis. I stole a glance his way, fearful of my own emotions. Then I stole a glance their way. Diana was crying and holding onto Luis. He must be wanting for air. Luis wore a smile that spread wide across his face. He even chanced a wink at me.

They both came over to collect what was left of me. We all three hugged hard, I asked through tears, "Luis, how did we do?"

"Pierce, we couldn't have done better. Let's talk after we get out of here." Diana was animated in her excitement. Tears flowed…happy tears for a change.

"How about lunch before you hit the road?" Suddenly, I realized I was ravenous. Lunch sounded good to me.

Gerhardt Besler had disappeared.

* * *

Our lunch was a celebration. I don't remember ever feeling such a heavy load lifted from my soul. Luis told us he felt Judge Harper had had a moment of compassion for Pierce Everett, the person, rather than the drug smuggler, and handed down a sentence that technically complied with the

DA's demands, while at the same time commuted so much of the sentence the DA had expected me to receive. Judge Harper had turned it into a true gift.

My sentence was so close to the limit of the three years that Diana and I had previously agreed would lead to our running. We confirmed with each other that was not going to be necessary. We were grateful not be running.

We would remain Pierce and Diana Everett.

Suddenly my thoughts got clearer, my brain started working again, and my life and outlook greatly improved. The huge feeling of limbo vanished, and Diana and I could make pertinent plans for our future. Then January 17th began to loom. We had about six weeks to put a world together that would support my absence and leave Diana an income while I spent 36 months in a Federal Prison Camp. "Dynasaw" seemed the answer. We set about tuning it, prepping our new foreman, Rick, to work with Diana. It all seemed perfectly plausible.

When January 16th dawned, I was confident we were ready for what we both hoped would be a short three years. Still, I didn't sleep that night and I feared the coming of the dawn. I got out of bed in the early morning and set about double-checking all I could. Eleven a.m. just kept on coming. Running continued to cross my mind.

"No way man, you're off on another adventure," I told myself. *"It's time to begin getting all you can out of this next journey."*

CHAPTER FORTY-FIVE
The Slammer / Club Fed

Aᴛ 9 ᴀ.ᴍ., Diana and I slowly worked our way through morning traffic to the fearsome edifice of the Atlanta Federal Prison.

The prison was notorious for housing violent inmates. Fortunately, the Judge had decided that I was a candidate for the Federal Prison Camp next door. We drove down the long hill that terminated in front of the prison camp office. I walked in…

"My name is Pierce Everett and I'm self-surrendering."

Diana held my hand hard as we stood in front of the desk.

"Take that watch off,"

"It's really a very cheap watch," I said.

"They don't know that in there." He nodded toward a heavy closed steel door. I tried to turn my imagination off as my mind went wild with ideas of what was on the other side. I turned to Diana and tears flowed again. I felt like I'd cried enough for the rest of my life. I hugged and kissed her goodbye. I was ushered through that fearsome door, by a most unfriendly character.

* * *

My time in the prison camp is riddled with stories. Some funny, some very sad, some violent and some magical.

I did my best to make the most of it. I immersed myself in the study of religions and spirituality. I spent time meditating, and working with this rare opportunity, to turn it all into a positive part of the ongoing adventure of this life. I was pretty sure this would be the last time for me to be plucked from life and frozen in time. I had no bills to pay, no promises to keep, no phones to answer, and no one calling with lists and demands.

It was oddly a time of peace. I found all the hiding places. I learned how I could exist and eat relatively healthfully, by smuggling vegetables out of the mess hall in my socks and cooking with the microwave with a limited supply of spices Diana would sneak in on visiting days. Smuggling again…?

I learned all that can be done with a razor knife blade. I learned how to avoid razor knife blades. I read more books than I'd read in my life, prior to and after incarceration. I ran around, and around, and around the track outside. Worked out with weights like a demon. I learned to steer clear of the violence, the overbearing guards, and the ever-threatening racial disturbances. Being in the 20% minority brought out the diplomat in me.

I was threatened that while I slept, a very sharp pencil would find its way into my eye. I slipped around and hid from a boisterous celebration that sent the whole black population into a furious native rave, when OJ was acquitted.

The guards were doubled, and unusually intense during this OJ wildness. I escaped, unscathed, from a storm trooper disciplinary lockdown that made the Atlanta news, after a demonstration by a few idiots burning library books. No one even knew what they were demonstrating about. I endured a battle with folding metal chairs in the TV room, that escalated over a discrepancy about the next show to watch. I couldn't get out of the door, so I lay down on the floor in the dark at the rear of the room, with my hands over my head. One chair hit me on the back, but its force was diminished when it hit the wall behind me first.

I escaped the arrival of a group of rabid guards by slipping out a half-closed door on the floor, and standing up, then turning around to join the crowd outside the door watching in at the action. Most of the inmates in that room were hauled away, and I never saw them again. The guards in the hallway were banging on the walls with Billy-sticks and screaming at us in the hallway to get back to our cells. I did as I was told.

It was all just one day after another. On and on. My first assigned job was Cell Block Orderly. I hosed the showers and the toilets down daily and swept the floors. Gross beyond belief. Human beings are hard to believe. For me, a new bar was set. The advantage of the orderly job was that no one wanted it, and if I kept everything pretty clean, they would leave me alone, and I could spend my days in the "Art Room" working on one painting after another.

Most of the inmates had government jobs they went to every day. They were paid an incredibly low weekly salary and kept busy by their daily routine. Then one day a job opening for a chapel statistician came available and I took it. My job then was to count the number of each religious sect that attended, or made use, of the Chapel for their services. I also had to water the ferns hanging in there. I was able to hang out in the chapel pretty much unnoticed.

A friend was going to be released in a couple of weeks and offered me his easel in the art room. That was the best thing that happened to me while I was incarcerated. I worked on my painting's day and night. I'd never had so much undisturbed time to concentrate and lose myself in practice. I was even able to ship out five of the paintings, to people who had indicated interest in purchasing them. Diana picked them up and delivered them to the new owners and collected the desperately needed money. It was there that I resolved to go back to painting full time on my release.

I'd gotten my world in the slammer to work with me to make personal progress while I counted off the days, one by one.

CHAPTER FORTY-SIX
It Was There I Started Over

DIANA WAS AN EXEMPLARY PARTNER throughout our marriage and during my incarceration. No one could have done more. No one could have done better. I was the benefactor of her great love for me, and my love for her grew and grew in my absence from her. I believed we were invincible.

Valentine's Day, 1997, was just six months before my release to the halfway house. Tim had been my cell mate for the past two years. We'd become very close, even considering business ideas we might implement when we'd finally be free. He was released six months earlier. I asked Diana to help him find clothes and a truck and help him get going.

That Valentine's Day I called Diana to let her know how much I loved her and how excited I was to be headed home in a few months.

"Happy Valentine's Day Sweetheart."

Quiet.

"Baby are you there?"

I could hear her crying.

"Diana, tell me what's wrong."

"Baby, I'm so sorry to hurt you like this," her little voice on the other end quivered.

"What do you mean, sweetheart. What's wrong?"

"Pierce, I'm going to move to Andersen, South Carolina with Tim. He and I have fallen in love."

What in the world was she talking about?!

The hallway where I stood in the phone line began to spin. My chest tightened. Surely, I had heard this all wrong.

"What did you just say?"

"Baby, I've fallen in love with Tim," she repeated, "and I'm going to live with him."

"What? When? How?... Sweetheart, please just wait a few months, until I am released. We're so close, let's wait and talk it out. Let's get counseling. Why do you want to throw away 15 years of our lives and our love?"

"I'm sorry baby, I'm sorry."

The line went quiet...then dead.

I put my head between the pay phones. I had never been so floored. Although I'd experienced pain, fear, and anguish, none had ever compared to that moment. I was cut to the bone.

I found my way to my cell and lay down with my arm over my face. No one could see me in this shape. If for any reason, they felt something this severe had happened, they wouldn't let me out. I had to keep it a secret from everyone. I had no one to talk to. I couldn't eat, I couldn't sleep. All the available sadness and anger passed through me day after day. I felt vengeful, disbelief, and betrayal all at once. I was surely out to hurt him, and her...this was incomprehensible. Over the next few days I just lay on the bunk in my cell.

One day, Joe, a long tall "drink of water" who'd been incarcerated for a long time, stepped into my cell and spread his long arms out wide.

"I don't know what has happened to you but let me tell you that you've got to get up and move, you've got to eat, you've got to get over it. You have no choice here. You are only making things worse. The guards are talking about you in ways you don't want. Make your life what you will, but right now get your shit together to get outta here...and I mean right now."

Before he walked out of my cell I put both feet on the ground.

"Thanks Joe."

I went outside, stared up at the bright sun, walked around the track one loop, then another, then another. I ran, hard, huffing and puffing, and sweating. That was when I began to pull myself up by my bootstraps, to look to the future. I was certainly poised to start anew in every way. The sadness and anger were slow to depart. Even today, over 24 years later, those scars remain. They just don't hurt so much anymore.

* * *

It was Saturday. My last day for visitors in the slammer. For nearly three years, Diana had come to visit every Saturday and every federal holiday. This Saturday she wasn't there. She wasn't coming.

My dear brother came instantly when he got the news. My best friend, Bryan, came immediately when he heard. And Diana finally did come in the afternoon. I almost didn't answer the call when the speaker said "Everett, you have a visitor." I went slowly, with apprehension, knowing it was her.

"You look too thin, Pierce. You must take care of yourself."

I shook my head. I'd lost 20 pounds over the past two weeks. I implored Diana to acquiesce, to our seeing a counselor, to at least make some attempt to work things out after all we'd been through. I realized during her visit, that all my pleading was to no avail. Her decision had been indelibly made that Valentine's Day, and she was not going to stray from it. All my groveling was not becoming.

When it came time for my release from prison to the half-way house, I could only be released to a family member. Diana agreed, of course she'd pick me up at the same fearsome door where she'd left me three years earlier. Even then, in the back of my mind, was the hope that I'd have one more chance to convince her to stay with me. I can be pretty bull headed sometimes.

When that day arrived, my divergent emotions reaped havoc with my soul. In one way, it was one of the happiest days of my life, while at the same time it was one of the saddest. On our drive, mile after mile, I slowly came to terms with my new reality. I had finished my much-dreaded time of incarceration and finished my time with Diana.

Despite my efforts, I realized on my ride to the halfway house that I had lost Diana. She would not entertain even the slightest thought of reconciliation. I gave up, and in silence. She let me out and I walked through those doors alone.

The next 6 months passed quickly, and with the help of friends and family, I was soon "integrated" back into real life. Diana was to come get me one last time. I was to be released only to her custody. We rode along solemnly with little said. She pulled into our little garage apartment on Peachtree Ave., the place where we'd first met. The place where we had returned, adventure after adventure. The place where we had spent so many extraordinary times.

Diana and I had purchased the house from our friend, Susan Bennett, about four years ago and we owned the property together. Diana had rented out the main house to improve her income in my absence. Now she was going home to Tim, and I was moving into the Carriage House, in back. As soon as I was somewhat stable we planned sell the property and *Whitetail* to pay off so many insurmountable debts. Susan had financed the property to us when she purchased a farm up in Richmond, Virginia. A five-year balloon note to Susan would be coming due soon.

I walked into the little cottage alone. Diana drove away. Memories rushed back. I laid down on the floor of my studio amongst my canvases. The smell of turpentine filled the air. I jumped when something softly brushed my hand. The cats, Fischer and his buddy Max, quietly circled me. I was glad to see their fuzzy faces. They were glad to see me. I sat up on the studio floor and they both climbed into my lap and purred loudly, "Welcome home, Pop." We stayed like that for hours. We remembered old times together.

My welcoming committee. I was happy to see them.

It was there that I started over…

EPILOGUE

THESE EVENTS all seem as if they happened only a moment ago. They are a marker for me regarding the speed and value of passing time.

I insist that my life remains adventurous. Every day is a thrill. I am blessed with wonderful old fast friends who can cook up an exciting exploit as quickly as a great meal or spin a tale at the drop of a hat. Oh man… the stories we can tell.

I look back at all the characters. Over half of them have passed on, into the great unknown. I won't bore you with the who or how.

Me, I'm still loving it all. I'm lucky and I know it. I'm banking on enough time to wring out all the good this gift of life has to offer. There's so much to share.

I've always said, "Whenever I'm tapped, it will be too soon."

But now, the circumstances from a world lost, and a world regained, prepared me to meet the most wonderful woman. I think it was when I said I could cook, that our relationship took a magical turn.

Life has not been the same since. Bebe and I are married now. With her, life is magical. She is extraordinarily beautiful through and through. My feelings for her are impossible to articulate. Talk about fortune, magic, and luck. I most certainly would never have met her had this hurricane not ransacked my life. Knowing this result, I'd happily endure it all over again. Happiness has set a new bar bringing to mind the intervention of my gods. I tell you, for sure, seek out your own personal gods and hang on tight. Let them work with you; let them work against you.

Believe in them. Hold faith close.

* * *

In conclusion I could say: I'm wiser…I'm not. I could say I've learned my lesson…I have not. I could say my tolerances have narrowed…they have not. I could say I'm happy and in love…I am…beyond comprehension. Success is measured in so many ways.

"Three Strike Runner" is a true story

BIO / ABOUT THE AUTHOR

Pɪᴇʀᴄᴇ ᴇᴠᴇʀᴇᴛᴛ is creative in every sense of the word. He has produced art all his life via a wide spectrum of mediums. In 1983, at the Atlanta College of Art he fueled his talent and furthered his earlier studies auditing programs and classes that would specifically lead him toward his passion, painting with oils.

Pierce then studied with well- known artist and professor, Doctor Joseph Perrin. He fondly remembers Joe; "Any time Pierce would run into Joe at a gallery opening or a show, he would always ask with sincere interest, one hand on his shoulder and the other in a firm handshake; Everett, where're ya hangin'?" An old friend and inspiration, renowned artist Henry Barnes, once succinctly labeled Pierce's work as "thematic surrealism."

Sailing for the past fifty years has given him access to colorful people, countless places, and adventures, not attainable in any other way. "Three Strike Runner," Pierce's debut novel shares here with the reader, one of his extraordinary tales.

During one of his travels, the sirens cast their magic, and lured him to the island of Mallorca, about 100 miles east of Barcelona, Spain. He settled into the north part of Mallorca in the small port town of Puerto Pollensa. It was there he had the fortune of studying and painting with Antonio Cabanellas and Sebastian Ensenat'. Pierce fell in love with Mallorca's magic, and treasures extraordinary times spent there as well adventures on the other islands of the Balearic archipelago, Ibiza, and Menorca. Many of his favorite paintings stem from this era, and these islands. Several are still offered as Giclee' prints.

While sailing in the western Mediterranean, Morocco captivated his curiosity. He traveled extensively in the Riff Mountains just south of Tangier, all the while acquiring memories and experiences to fuel his passion for writing and painting.

When Pierce returned to the U.S. after years of travel and study, he settled briefly in his hometown of Atlanta, Georgia. During that time, he served as art director for the international environmental education program, "Visions United".

* * *

Pierce is now intrigued with newfound magic in Tennessee. He works from his studio in Chattanooga, writing and exploring endless possibilities with his favorite medium.

These days he can be found hiking the endless trails of the Tennessee mountains, writing stories of his adventures, and painting his own brand of surrealism. He and Bebe work happily on their 140-year-old house in Chattanooga. Lookout Mountain stands guard.

"*Tiger*," his beautiful old Chris Craft express cruiser has twin 327's. Pierce brought her from Chicago down to Chattanooga.

Now, "*Tiger*" is tied up not far away. A perpetual project, always ready to slip up the river and catch a sunset or play with the millions of stars Pierce has befriended.

A short walk down to the bottom of the hill, his street ends at the scenic and powerful Tennessee River. Pierce's wanderlust is satiated for the moment with the knowledge that from this vantage point he can set sail to any destination in the world. All he needs is a sturdy, blue-water sailboat to take him there.

One day Pierce may just disappear into his dreams that pleasantly haunt him from the places he loves most. Some will know where to find him.